The
Spirit of Man
An Anthology in English & French
from the Philosophers & Poets
made in 1915 by
Robert Bridges, O.M.
Poet Laureate
& dedicated by gracious permission
to His Majesty
King George V

Longmans Green & Co. Ltd. London
New York, Toronto, Calcutta, Bombay & Madras

LONGMANS, GREEN AND CO. LTD.
OF PATERNOSTER ROW

43 ALBERT DRIVE, LONDON, S.W. 19
17 CHITTARANJAN AVENUE, CALCUTTA
NICOL ROAD, BOMBAY
36A MOUNT ROAD, MADRAS

LONGMANS, GREEN AND CO.

55 FIFTH AVENUE, NEW YORK
221 EAST 20TH STREET, CHICAGO

LONGMANS, GREEN AND CO.

215 VICTORIA STREET, TORONTO

BIBLIOGRAPHICAL NOTE

First Edition with *India Paper*, January 1916

New Impressions :

  Ordinary Edition: February 1916, March 1916, August
    1916, January 1917, March 1918, January 1919,
    July 1919, March 1923, February 1925, June
    1927, May 1929, March 1930, February 1934,
    November 1934, January 1937, July 1939,
    November 1939, January 1940, August 1940,
    February 1941, August 1941 and February 1942

  India Paper Edition: February 1916, January 1917,
    March 1918, January 1919, July 1919, September
    1921, June 1927, March 1930, November 1934
    and January 1937.

CODE NUMBER : 182024

Printed in Great Britain at THE BALLANTYNE PRESS
SPOTTISWOODE, BALLANTYNE & CO. LTD.
Colchester, London & Eton

PREFACE

THIS book was compiled with a special purpose, and if it should not satisfy those for whom it was intended, no preface can save it; but that does not forbid some words of explanation.

First then, the reader is invited to bathe rather than to fish in these waters: that is to say, the several pieces are to be read in context; and it is for this reason that no titles nor names of authors are inserted in the text, because they would distract the attention and lead away the thought and even overrule consideration. Yet, although there is a sequence of context, there is no logical argument: the demonstration is of various moods of mind, which are allowed free play, a sufficient guide to them being provided in the page-headings. As for the sequence chosen, that might no doubt have been other than it is without damage and perhaps with advantage; but, as will readily be perceived, the main implication is essential, namely that spirituality is the basis and foundation of human life—in so far as our life is a worthy subject for ideal philosophy and pure aesthetic—rather than the apex or final attainment of it. It must underlie everything. To put it briefly, man is a spiritual being, and the proper work of his mind is to interpret the world according to his higher nature, and to conquer the material aspects of the world so as to bring them into subjection to the spirit.

Explanation of lesser matters is given in the preface to the Index at the end of the book : but it may be well to warn the reader at the outset against one possible misunderstanding ; it should not be thought that there is any pretence of having collected together all the best illustrations that literature can provide.   The compiler might perhaps congratulate himself if the high standard that he has tried to maintain should provoke such a mis-conception, but he is well aware that the collection might have been much better.   As it is, whatever merit or attractive quality it may have, will lie in its being the work of one mind at one time ; and its being such implies the presence of the peculiarities and blemishes that mark any personality and any time : these he has not sought to avoid.

The progress of mankind on the path of liberty and humanity has been suddenly arrested and its promise discredited by the apostasy of a great people, who, cast-ing off as a disguise their professions of Honour, now openly avow that the ultimate faith of their hearts is in material force.

In the darkness and stress of the storm the signs of

the time cannot all be distinctly seen, nor can we read them dispassionately ; but two things stand out clearly, and they are above question or debate. The first is that Prussia's scheme for the destruction of her neighbours was long-laid, and scientifically elaborated to the smallest detail : the second is that she will shrink from no crime that may further its execution.

How far the various Teutonic states that have been subjugated by Prussia are infected or morally enslaved by the machinery that overlords them, how far they are deluded or tempted by a vision of world-empire, how far their intellectual teachers willingly connive at the contradictory falsehoods officially imposed upon their assent, and what their social awakening will be, we can only surmise. We had accounted our cousins as honest and virtuous folk ; some of us have well-loved friends among them whom we have heard earnestly and bitterly deplore the evil spirit that was dominating their country : but we now see them all united in a wild enthusiasm for the great scheme of tyranny, as unscrupulous in their means as in their motives, and obedient to military regulations for cruelty, terrorism, and devastation.

From the consequent miseries, the insensate and interminable slaughter, the hate and filth, we can turn to seek comfort only in the quiet confidence of our souls ; and we look instinctively to the seers and poets of mankind, whose sayings are the oracles and prophecies of loveliness and lovingkindness. Common diversions divert us no longer; our habits and thoughts are searched by the glare of the conviction that man's life is not the ease that a peace-loving generation has found it or thought to make it, but the awful conflict with evil which philosophers and saints have depicted; and it is in their abundant testimony to the good and beautiful that we find support for our faith, and distraction from a grief that is intolerable constantly to face, nay impossible to face without that trust in God which makes all things possible.

We may see that our national follies and sins have deserved punishment; and if in this revelation of rottenness we cannot ourselves appear wholly sound, we are still free and true at heart, and can take hope in contrition, and in the brave endurance of sufferings that should chasten our intention and conduct; we can even be grateful for the discipline: but beyond this it is offered us to take joy in the thought that our country is called of God to stand for the truth of man's hope, and that it has not shrunk from the call. Here we stand upright, and above reproach: and to show ourselves worthy will be more than consolation; for truly it is the hope of man's great desire, the desire for brotherhood and universal peace to men of good-will, that is at stake in this struggle.

Britons have ever fought well for their country, and

their country's Cause is the high Cause of Freedom and Honour. That fairest earthly fame, the fame of Freedom, is inseparable from the names of Albion, Britain, England: it has gone out to America and the Antipodes, hallowing the names of Canada, Australia, and New Zealand; it has found a new home in Africa: and this heritage is our glory and happiness. We can therefore be happy in our sorrows, happy even in the death of our beloved who fall in the fight; for they die nobly, as heroes and saints die, with hearts and hands unstained by hatred or wrong.

CONTENTS

They walk in the city
that they have builded,
The city of God
from evil shielded

THE
SPIRIT OF MAN

Book 1

AFTER experience had taught me that the common occurrences of ordinary life are vain and futile, and I saw that all the objects of my desire and fear were in themselves nothing good nor bad, save in so far as the mind was affected by them; I at length determined to search out whether there were not something truly good and communicable to man, by which his spirit might be affected to the exclusion of all other things: yea, whether there were anything, through the discovery and acquisition of which I might enjoy continuous and perfect gladness for ever. I say that *I at length determined*, because at first sight it seemed ill-advised to renounce things, in the possession of which I was assured, for the sake of what was yet uncertain. . . . I therefore turned over in my mind whether it might be possible to come at this new way, or at least to the certitude of its existence, without changing my usual way of life, [a compromise] which I had often attempted

Spinoza is telling of himself.

B

before, but in vain. For the things that commonly happen in life and are esteemed among men as the highest good (as is witnessed by their works) can be reduced to these three, Riches, Fame, and Lust; and by these the mind is so distracted that it can scarcely think of any other good. With regard to Lust, the mind is as much absorbed thereby as if it had attained rest in some good: and this hinders it from thinking of anything else. But after fruition a great sadness follows, which, if it do not absorb the mind, will yet disturb and blunt it. . . . But love directed towards the eternal and infinite feeds the mind with pure joy, and is free from all sadness. Wherefore it is greatly to be desired, and to be sought after with our whole might . . . [and] although I could perceive this quite clearly in my mind, I could not at once lay aside all greed and lust and honour. . . . One thing I could see, and that was that so long as the mind was turned upon this new way, it was deflected, and seriously engaged therein; which was a great comfort to me; for I saw that those evils were not such as would not yield to remedies: and though at first these intervals were rare and lasted but a short while, yet afterwards the true good became more and more evident to me, and these intervals more frequent and of longer duration.

2

La belle
dame sans
merci.

O WHAT can ail thee, Knight-at-arms,
    Alone and palely loitering?
The sedge has wither'd from the lake,
    And no birds sing.

Sadness

O what can ail thee, Knight-at-arms,
  So haggard and so woe-begone?
The squirrel's granary is full,
  And the harvest's done.

I see a lily on thy brow
  With anguish moist and fever dew;
And on thy cheeks a fading rose
  Fast withereth too.

I met a Lady in the meads,
  Full beautiful, a faery's child;—
Her hair was long, her foot was light,
  And her eyes were wild.

I made a garland for her head,
  And bracelets too, and fragrant zone;
She look'd at me as she did love,
  And made sweet moan.

I set her on my pacing steed,
  And nothing else saw all day long;
For sidelong would she bend, and sing
  A faery's song.

She found me roots of relish sweet,
  And honey wild, and manna dew;
And sure in language strange she said—
  'I love thee true!'

She took me to her elfin grot,
  And there she wept and sigh'd full sore,
And there I shut her wild, wild eyes
  With kisses four.

And there she lulled me asleep,
  And there I dream'd—Ah! woe betide!
The latest dream I ever dream'd
  On the cold hill-side.

I saw pale Kings and Princes too,
　　Pale warriors, death-pale were they all;
They cried—' La Belle Dame sans Merci
　　Hath thee in thrall ! '

I saw their starv'd lips in the gloam,
　　With horrid warning gaped wide,
And I awoke, and found me here
　　On the cold hill-side.

And this is why I sojourn here
　　Alone and palely loitering,
Though the sedge is wither'd from the Lake,
　　And no birds sing.

3

Shakespeare
bids adieu
to the stage.

YOU do look, my son, in a movèd sort,
As if you were dismay'd; be cheerful, sir:
Our revels now are ended: these our actors,
As I foretold you, were all spirits, and
Are melted into air, into thin air:
And, like the baseless fabric of this vision,
The cloudcapp'd towers, the gorgeous palaces,
The solemn temples, the great globe itself,
Yea all which it inherit, shall dissolve;
And, like this insubstantial pageant faded,
Leave not a rack behind.　We are such stuff
As dreams are made on, and our little life
Is rounded with a sleep.—Sir, I am vexed;
Bear with my weakness; my old brain is troubled:
Be not disturbed with my infirmity.
If you be pleased, retire into my cell
And there repose: a turn or two I'll walk
To still my beating mind.

Weariness

4

AH Sunflower weary of time,
Who countest the steps of the Sun ;
Seeking after that sweet golden clime
Where the traveller's journey is done :

Where the Youth pined away with desire
And the pale Virgin shrouded in snow
Arise from their graves, and aspire
Where my Sunflower wishes to go !

5

It irked him* to be here, he could not rest.   * The poet
He loved each simple joy the country yields,   Arthur
He loved his mates ; but yet he could not keep   Hugh
(For that a shadow loured on the fields)   Clough.
Here with the shepherds and the silly sheep.
Some life of men unblest
He knew, which made him droop, and filled his head.
He went ; his piping took a troubled sound
Of storms that rage outside our happy ground ;
He could not wait their passing, he is dead. . .

Too quick despairer, wherefore wilt thou go ?
Soon will the high midsummer pomps come on ;
Soon will the musk carnations break and swell,
Soon shall we have gold-dusted snapdragon,
Sweet-William with his homely cottage smell,
And stocks in fragrant blow ;
Roses that down the alleys shine afar,
And open jasmine-muffled lattices,
And groups under the dreaming garden-trees,
And the full moon and the white evening star. . .

6

.. I see the Deep's untrampled floor
With green and purple seaweeds strown;
I see the waves upon the shore,
Like light dissolved in star-showers, thrown:
I sit upon the sands alone,—
The lightning of the noontide ocean
Is flashing round me, and a tone
Arises from its measured motion. ..

Alas! I have nor hope nor health,
Nor peace within nor calm around,
Nor that content surpassing wealth
The sage in meditation found,
And walked with inward glory crowned ..

Yet now despair itself is mild
Ev'n as the winds and waters are;
I could lie down like a tired child,
And weep away the life of care. ..

7

.. Hard is the way and shut the gate,
And life is in a narrow strait.
Once only did my soul aspire
To scale the Orient dropping fire;
Once only floated in the ways
Of heaven apart from earthly haze:
And then it was a foolish soul,
And knew not how the heavens do roll.

8

OISIVE jeunesse
A tout asservie,
Par délicatesse
J'ai perdu ma vie.

Ah que le temps vienne
Où les cœurs s'éprennent. . .

J'ai tant fait patience
Qu'à jamais j'oublie.
Craintes et souffrances
Aux cieux sont parties.

Et la soif malsaine
Obscurcit mes veines. . .

Qu'il vienne, qu'il vienne,
Le temps dont on s'éprenne.

9

MARGARET, are you grieving
Over Goldengrove unleafing ? . .
Ah ! as the heart grows older
It will come to such sights colder
By and by, nor spare a sigh
Tho' world of wanwood leafmeal lie ;
And yet you will weep and know why.
Now no matter, child, the name :
Sorrow's springs are the same.
Nor mouth had, no, nor mind express'd,
What heart heard of, ghost guess'd :
It is the blight man was born for,
It is Margaret you mourn for.

10

 . . Behold the white clouds roll along the blue,
    And like the clouds do flocks o'erspread the plain;
And like them winds the forest out of view;
    Shall not Joy's chariot come with splendid train,
And he descend and walk the living air,
    With Melody and Peace, and Happy Love,
Wing-footed, rosy-limbed, with myrtle rare
    And olive crowned from old Eleusis' grove?
Ah, no, the fury Night will soon be here;
    She comes with storms that drive the flocks away,
And takes the large free clouds to make her bier,
    And rends the leaves; no longer youth can stay
            Nor joy appear.

11

        SWIFTLY walk over the western wave,
                Spirit of Night!
        Out of the misty eastern cave,
        Where all the long and lone daylight
        Thou wovest dreams of joy and fear,
        Which make thee terrible and dear,—
                Swift be thy flight!

        Wrap thy form in a mantle gray,
                Star-inwrought!
        Blind with thine hair the eyes of Day;
        Kiss her until she be wearied out,
        Then wander o'er city, and sea, and land,
        Touching all with thine opiate wand—
                Come, long sought!

Night

When I arose and saw the dawn,
        I sighed for thee;
When light rode high, and the dew was gone,
And noon lay heavy on flower and tree,
And the weary Day turned to his rest,
Lingering like an unloved guest,
        I sighed for thee.

Thy brother Death came, and cried,
        Wouldst thou me?
Thy sweet child Sleep, the filmy-eyed,
Murmured like a noontide bee,
Shall I nestle near thy side?
Wouldst thou me?—And I replied,
        No, not thee!

Death will come when thou art dead,
        Soon, too soon—
Sleep will come when thou art fled;
Of neither would I ask the boon
I ask of thee, belovèd Night—
Swift be thine approaching flight,
        Come soon, soon!

12

POURQUOI la lumière est-elle donnée au malheureux,
Et la vie à ceux dont l'âme est pleine d'amertume,
Qui attendent la mort, sans que la mort vienne,
Qui la cherchent plus ardemment qu'un trésor,
Qui sont heureux jusqu'à en tressaillir,
Et se réjouissent, quand ils ont trouvé le tombeau;
A l'homme dont la route est couverte de ténèbres,
Et que Dieu a entouré d'un cercle fatal?

Adversity

Mes soupirs sont devenus comme mon pain,
Et mes gémissements se répandent comme l'eau ;

A peine conçois-je une crainte qu'elle se réalise ;
Tous les malheurs que je redoute fondent sur moi.

Plus de sécurité, plus de repos, plus de paix !
Sans cesse de nouveaux tourments !

13

K. Henry
VI at the
battle of
Wakefield.

THIS battle fares like to the morning's war,
When dying clouds contend with growing light ;
What time the shepherd, blowing of his nails,
Can neither call it perfect day nor night.
Now sways it this way, like a mighty sea,
Forced by the tide to combat with the wind :
Now sways it that way, like the selfsame sea
Forced to retire by fury of the wind.
Sometime the flood prevails, and then the wind ;
Now one the better, then another best :
Both tugging to be victors, breast to breast,
Yet neither conqueror nor conquerèd :
So is the equal poise of this fell war.
    Here on this molehill will I sit me down.
To whom God will, there be the victory !
For Margaret my queen and Clifford too
Have chid me from the battle, swearing both
They prosper best of all when I am thence.
Would I were dead !—if God's good will were so ;
For what is in this world but grief and woe ?
    O God ! methinks it were a happy life
To be no better than a homely swain :
To sit upon a hill, as I do now,
To carve out dials quaintly, point by point,
Thereby to see the minutes, how they run :

Failure

How many make the hour full complete,
How many hours bring about the day,
How many days will finish up the year,
How many years a mortal man may live.—
When this is known, then to divide the times:
So many hours must I tend my flock;
So many hours must I take my rest;
So many hours must I contemplate;
So many hours must I sport myself;
So many days my ewes have been with young;
So many weeks ere the poor fools will yean;
So many years ere I shall shear the fleece:
So minutes, hours, days,—months and years,
Pass'd over to the end they were created,
Would bring white hairs unto a quiet grave.
Ah! what a life were this! how sweet! how lovely!
Gives not the hawthorn bush a sweeter shade
To shepherds, looking on their silly sheep,
Than doth a rich embroider'd canopy
To kings, that fear their subjects' treachery?
O yes it doth; a thousand-fold it doth.
And to conclude,—the shepherd's homely curds,
His cold thin drink out of his leather bottle,
His wonted sleep under a fresh tree's shade,
All which secure and sweetly he enjoys,
Is far beyond a prince's delicates,
His viands sparkling in a golden cup,
His body couchèd in a curious bed,
When care, mistrust, and treason wait on him.

14

Observe, however, that of man's whole terrestrial
possessions and attainments, unspeakably the noblest are

his Symbols, divine or divine-seeming; under which he marches and fights, with victorious assurance, in this life-battle: what we can call his Realised Ideals. Of which realised Ideals, omitting the rest, consider only these two: his Church, or spiritual Guidance; his Kingship, or temporal one. The Church: what a word was there; richer than Golconda and the treasures of the world! In the heart of the remotest mountains rises the little Kirk; the Dead all slumbering round it, under their white memorial-stones, 'in hope of a happy resurrection': Dull wert thou, . . if never in any hour . . it spoke to thee things unspeakable, that went to thy soul's soul. Strong was he that had a Church,—what we can call a Church: he stood thereby, though 'in the center of Immensities in the conflux of Eternities', yet manlike towards God and man; the vague shoreless Universe had become a firm city for him, a dwelling which he knew. Such virtue was in Belief; in these words well spoken: *I believe.* Well might men prize their *Credo*, and raise stateliest Temples for it, and reverend Hierarchies, and give it the tithe of their substance; it was worth living for and dying for . . .

But of those decadent ages in which no Ideal either grows or blossoms? when Belief and Loyalty have passed away, and only the cant and false echo of them remains; and all Solemnity has become Pageantry; and the Creed of persons in authority, . . . an Imbecility or a Machiavelism? Alas, of these ages World-history can take no notice; they have to be compressed more and more, and finally suppressed in the Annals of Mankind; blotted out as spurious,—which indeed they are. Hapless ages: wherein, if ever in any, it is an

unhappiness to be born.   To be born, and to learn only,
by every tradition and example, that God's Universe is
Belial's and a Lie; and 'the Supreme Quack' the
hierarch of men!   In which mournfullest faith, nevertheless, do we not see whole generations . . live, what
they call living; and vanish? . . .

15

VANITY of Vanities, saith the Preacher,
   Vanity of Vanities, all is Vanity.
What profit hath a man of all his labour
   wherein he laboureth under the sun?
Generation passeth away, and generation cometh,
   and the earth abideth for ever.
The sun ariseth and the sun goeth down,
   and hasteth to the place where he ariseth.
The wind goeth toward the south,
   and turneth round unto the north;
   Around and around goeth the wind,
   and on its rounds the wind returneth.
All the rivers run into the sea,
   yet the sea is not full;
   Unto the place whence the rivers come,
   thither they return again.
All things are full of weariness;
   man cannot utter it.
   The eye is not satisfied with seeing,
   nor the ear filled with hearing.
The thing that hath been is that which shall be,
   and that which is done is that which shall be done:
   and there is nothing new under the sun.
Is there anything whereof it may be said, See, this is new?
   it hath already been in the ages that were before us.

There is no remembrance with us of former days,
  neither of the days that shall be will there be any re-
    membrance among them that shall come after.

I, the Preacher, was king over Israel in Jerusalem,
and I applied my heart to seek and to search out by
wisdom concerning all that is done under heaven : this
sore travail hath God given to the sons of men to be
exercised withal.   I have seen all the works that are
done under the sun ; and, behold, all is vanity and vexation of spirit.

  The crooked cannot be made straight
    and that which is wanting cannot be number'd.

I communed with mine own heart, saying, Lo, I have
gotten me great wisdom above all that were before me
in Jerusalem : yea my heart had great experience of
wisdom and knowledge.   And I gave my heart to
know wisdom, and to know madness and folly.   I perceived that this also is vexation of spirit, for

  In much wisdom is much grief,
    and he that increaseth knowledge increaseth sorrow.

16

  . . Have we not then found . . a narrow path [of
thought] which promises to lead us and our argument
to the conclusion that while we are in the body, and
while the soul is contaminated with its evils, our desire
will never be thoroughly satisfied : and our desire, we
say, is of the Truth.   For thousand-fold are the troubles
that the body gives us. . . .   It fills us full of loves, and
lusts and fears, with all kinds of delusions and rank nonsense ; and in very truth, as men say, it so disposes us

that we cannot think wisely at all, never a whit. Nay, all wars, factions, and fighting have no other origin than this same body and its lusts. . . We must set the soul free of it, we must behold things as they are, and then, belike, we shall attain the wisdom that we desire, and of which we say we are lovers: not while we live but after death, as the argument shows; . . For then and not till then will the soul be parted from the body, and exist in herself alone. . . And thus having got rid of the foolishness of the body we shall, it would seem, be pure and hold converse with the pure, and shall in our own selves have complete knowledge of the Incorruptible, which is, I take it, no other than the very Truth.

17

O FRIEND, hope in Him while thou livest,
    know Him while thou livest,
  For in life is thy release.

If thy bonds be not broken while thou livest,
    What hope of deliverance in death?

It is but an empty dream that the soul must pass into
    union with Him,
  Because it hath passed from the body.

If He is found now, He is found then:
  If not, we go but to dwell in the city of Death.

If thou hast union now, thou shalt have it hereafter.

Bathe in the Truth: know the true Master:
  Have faith in the true Name.

Kabir saith: It is the spirit of the quest that helpeth.
  I am the slave of the spirit of the quest.

MY home
The shimmery-bounded glare,
The gazing fire-hung dome
Of scorching air.

My rest
To wander trembling-weak,
On vague hunger-quest
New hope to seek.

For friend
The dazzling breathing dream,
The strength at last to find
Of Glory Supreme.

BENEATH the canopy of the skies roam I night and day:
My home is in the desert by night and day.
No sickness troubleth me nor silent pain tormenteth;
One thing I know, that I sorrow night and day.

Homeless am I, O Lord: whither shall I turn?
A wanderer in the desert, whither shall I turn?
I come to Thee at last, driven from every threshold;
And if Thy door be closèd, whither shall I turn?

Blessèd are they who live in sight of Thee,
Who speak with Thee, O Lord, and dwell with Thee.
Faint are my limbs, and my heart is fearful;
Humbly I sit with those who are dear to Thee.

Drunk tho' we be with pleasure, Thou art our Faith;
Helpless, without hand or foot, Thou art our Faith;
Whether we be Nazarenes, Mussalmans or Gebres,
Whatsoe'er our creed, Thou art our Faith.

BEING upon a certain day overburdened with the trouble of worldly business, in which men are oftentimes enforced to do more than of very duty they are bound, I retired to a solitary place congenial to grief, where whatever it was in my affairs that was giving me discontent might plainly reveal itself, and all the things that were wont to inflict me with sorrow might come together and freely present themselves to my sight : And in that place, after that I had sat a long while in silence and great affliction, my very dear son Peter the deacon joined me, who since the flower of his early youth had been attached to me by close friendship and companionship in the study of the sacred books. He, when he saw me overwhelmed in heaviness and languor of heart, questioned me, saying : 'What is the matter ? or what bad news have you heard ? for some unusual grief plainly possesses you.' To whom I answered : 'O Peter, the grief that I daily endure is with me both old and new : old through long use, and new by continual increase. And truth it is that my unhappy soul, wounded with worldly business, is now calling to mind in what state it once was when I dwelt in my monastery ; how then it was superior to all transitory matters, and how it would soar far above things corruptible : How it was accustomed to think only of heavenly things, and tho' enclosed in mortal body would yet by contemplation pass beyond its fleshly bars : while as for death, which is to almost all men a punishment, that did it love, and would consider as the entrance to life, and the reward of its toil. But now by reason of my

Pope Gregory the Great regrets his monastic life.

pastoral charge my poor soul must engage in the businesses of worldly men ; and after so fair a promise of rest it is defiled in the dust of earthly occupations : and when through much ministering to others it spendeth itself on outward distractions, it cannot but return impaired unto those inward and spiritual things for which it longeth. Now therefore I am meditating on what I suffer ; I weigh what I have lost : and when I think of that loss my condition is the more intolerable. For do but look how the ship of my mind is tossed by the waves and tempest, and how I am battered in the storm. Nay, when I recollect my former life, I sigh as one who turneth back his eyes to a forsaken shore. And what grieveth me yet more is that as I am borne ever onward by the disturbance of these endless billows, I almost lose sight of the port which I left. For thus it is that the mind lapseth : first it is faithless to the good which it held, tho' it may still remember that it hath forsaken it : then when it hath further strayed, it even forgetteth that good : until it cometh at length to such a pass that it cannot so much as behold in memory what before it had actively practised : All behaveth according to my picture : we are carried so far out to sea that we lose sight of the quiet haven whence we set forth. And not seldom is the measure of my sorrow increased by remembrance of the lives of some who with their whole heart relinquished this present world. Whose high perfection when I behold, I recognise how low I lie fallen : for many of them did in a very retired life please their Maker, and lest by contact with human affairs they should decay from their freshness, almighty God allowed not that they should be harassed by the labours of this world.'

21

A LITTLE onward lend thy guiding hand
To these dark steps, a little further on;
For yonder bank hath choice of Sun or shade;
There I am wont to sit, when any chance
Relieves me from my task of servile toyl,
Daily in the common Prison else enjoyn'd me,
Where I, a Prisoner chain'd, scarce freely draw
The air imprison'd also, close and damp,
Unwholsom draught: but here I feel amends,
The breath of Heav'n fresh-blowing, pure and sweet,
With day-spring born; here leave me to respire. . .

22

I HEARD a thousand blended notes,
While in a grove I sate reclined,
In that sweet mood when pleasant thoughts
Bring sad thoughts to the mind.

To her fair works did Nature link
The human soul that through me ran;
And much it grieved my heart to think
What man has made of man.

Through primrose tufts, in that green bower,
The periwinkle trailed its wreaths;
And 'tis my faith that every flower
Enjoys the air it breathes.

The birds around me hopped and played,
Their thoughts I cannot measure:—
But the least motion which they made,
It seemed a thrill of pleasure.

The budding twigs spread out their fan,
To catch the breezy air;
And I must think, do all I can,
That there was pleasure there.

If this belief from heaven be sent,
If such be Nature's holy plan,
Have I not reason to lament
What man has made of man?

23

. . And this was on the sixtë morwe of May,
Which May had peinted with his softë shoures,
This gardin ful of levës and of floures :—
And craft of mannes hand so curiously
Arrayed had this gardin trewely,
That never was ther gardin of swich prys
But-if it were the veray Paradys.
The odour of flourës and the freshë sight
Wold han maad any hertë for to light
That ever was born, but-if to gret siknesse
Or to gret sorwë held it in distresse,
So ful it was of beauty with plesance . . .

24

. . We wandered to the Pine Forest
      That skirts the Ocean's foam,
The lightest wind was in its nest,
      The tempest in its home.
The whispering waves were half asleep,
      The clouds were gone to play,
And on the bosom of the deep
      The smile of Heaven lay;

Autumn Quiet

It seemed as if the hour were one
  Sent from beyond the skies,
Which scattered from above the sun
  A light of Paradise.

We paused amid the pines that stood
  The giants of the waste,
Tortured by storms to shapes as rude
  As serpents interlaced,
And soothed by every azure breath,
  That under heaven is blown,
To harmonies and hues beneath,
  As tender as its own;
Now all the tree-tops lay asleep,
  Like green waves on the sea,
As still as in the silent deep
  The ocean woods may be. . .

SEASON of mists and mellow fruitfulness!
  Close bosom-friend of the maturing sun;
Conspiring with him how to load and bless
  With fruit the vines that round the thatch-eaves run;
To bend with apples the moss'd cottage-trees,
  And fill all fruit with ripeness to the core;
    To swell the gourd, and plump the hazel shells
  With a sweet kernel; to set budding more,
And still more, later flowers for the bees,
Until they think warm days will never cease,
    For Summer has o'er-brimm'd their clammy cells.

Who hath not seen thee oft amid thy store?
  Sometimes whoever seeks abroad may find
Thee sitting careless on a granary floor,
  Thy hair soft-lifted by the winnowing wind;

Or on a half-reap'd furrow sound asleep,
    Drowsed with the fumes of poppies, while thy hook
      Spares the next swath and all its twined flowers ;
And sometime like a gleaner thou dost keep
    Steady thy laden head across a brook ;
    Or by a cider-press, with patient look,
      Thou watchest the last oozings, hours by hours.

Where are the songs of Spring ? Ay, where are they ?
    Think not of them, thou hast thy music too,
      While barrèd clouds bloom the soft-dying day,
And touch the stubble-plains with rosy hue ;
    Then in a wailful choir, the small gnats mourn
    Among the river sallows, borne aloft
      Or sinking as the light wind lives or dies ;
And full-grown lambs loud bleat from hilly bourn ;
    Hedge-crickets sing ; and now with treble soft
    The redbreast whistles from a garden-croft,
      And gathering swallows twitter in the skies.

26

I WILL arise and go now, and go to Innisfree,
And a small cabin build there, of clay and wattles made ;
Nine bean-rows will I have there, a hive for the honey-bee,
    And live alone in the bee-loud glade.

And I shall have some peace there, for peace comes dropping slow,
Dropping from the veils of the morning to where the cricket sings ;
There midnight 's all a glimmer, and noon a purple glow,
    And evening full of the linnet's wings.

I will arise and go now, for always night and day
I hear lake-water lapping with low sounds by the shore ;
While I stand on the roadway, or on the pavements gray,
    I hear it in the deep heart's core.

27

WHEN winds that move not its calm surface sweep
The azure sea, I love the land no more;
The smiles of the serene and tranquil deep
Tempt my unquiet mind.—But when the roar
Of Ocean's gray abyss resounds, and foam
Gathers upon the sea, and vast waves burst,
I turn from the drear aspect to the home
Of earth and its deep woods, where interspersed,
When winds blow loud, pines make sweet melody.
    Whose house is some lone bark, whose toil the sea,
Whose prey the wandering fish, an evil lot
Has chosen.—But I my languid limbs will fling
Beneath the plane, where the brook's murmuring
Moves the calm spirit, but disturbs it not.

28

COME sit aneath this pinetree, whose lofty tressèd crown
    Sighs, as her tufty sprays stir to the west wind's kiss:
And with the babbling waters my flute thy care shall drown,
    And lull thy dreamy eyelids to sweet forgetful bliss.

29

    .. Men seek out retreats for themselves, cottages in the
country, lonely seashores and mountains. Thou too *The*
art disposed to hanker greatly after such things: and *emperor*
yet all this is the very commonest stupidity; for it is *Marcus*
in thy power, whenever thou wilt, to retire into thy- *Aurelius is*
self: and nowhere is there any place whereto a man *reproaching*
may retire quieter and more free from politics than his *himself.*

own soul; above all if he have within him thoughts
such as he need only regard attentively to be at perfect
ease : and that ease is nothing else than a well-ordered
mind.   Constantly then use this retreat, and renew thyself therein : and be thy principles brief and elementary,
which, as soon as ever thou recur to them, will suffice
to wash thy soul entirely clean, and send thee back
without vexation to whatsoe'er awaiteth thee.

30

    But when the soul giveth heed with her proper faculty,
she is at once away and off into that other world of
Purity, Eternity, Immortality and things unchanging ;
and finding there her kindred, she leagueth herself with
them (so long at least as she is true to herself and
possesseth herself), when she wandereth no more, but
ever in that way and with regard to those things, she
remaineth constant, since such they are that she has laid
hold of.   And this state of the soul is called Understanding.

31

BEFORE the starry threshold of *Joves* court
My mansion is, where those immortal shapes
Of bright aëreal Spirits live insphear'd
In Regions mild of calm and sérene Ayr,
Above the smoak and stirr of this dim spot
Which men call Earth, and with low-thoughted care
Confin'd, and pester'd in this pin-fold here,
Strive to keep up a frail and Feaverish being

Spiritual Desire

Unmindful of the crown that Vertue gives,
After this mortal change, to her true Servants
Amongst the énthron'd gods on Sainted seats.
Yet som there be that by due steps aspire
To lay their just hands on that Golden Key
That opes the Palace of Eternity :
To such my errand is, and but for such,
I would not soil these pure Ambrosial weeds
With the rank vapours of this Sin-worn mould. . .

32

The day now approaching when she was to depart S. Augus-
tine and
S. Monniea.
this life,—which day Thou knewest but we not,—it
came to pass, thyself, as I believe, by thy secret ways
so ordering it, that she and I stood alone, leaning in
a certain window which looked on the garden of the
house wherein we lodged at Ostia ; for there before
our voyage we were resting in quiet from the fatigues
of a long journey.   Discoursing then together alone
very sweetly, and forgetful of the past, and reaching
forth unto those things which are before, we were
enquiring between ourselves in the presence of the
truth, which Thou art, of what sort the eternal life of
the saints may be, which eye hath not seen, nor ear
heard, nor hath it entered into the heart of man.   And
all the while did our hearts within us gasp after the
heavenly streams of thy fountain, the well of Life, which
is in Thee, that being sprinkled thence according to our
measure, we might in some sort meditate on so high
a mystery.

And as our talk was leading us thither where we

would be, so that no delight of the senses whatsoever, in any brightness possible to them, seemed in respect of the joy of that life worthy of mention, far less of comparison, we upraising ourselves with intenser desire unto that Self-same, went on to explore in turn all things material, even the very heaven, whence sun and moon and stars give light upon the earth : and thus ascending by meditation and speech and admiration of thy works, we were drawing yet nearer, and had come to our own minds, and left them behind, that we might arrive at the country of unfailing plenty, where Thou feedest thy people for ever in pastures of truth ; there where life is the WISDOM by which all those thy works are made, that have been or that shall be ; Wisdom uncreate, the same now as it ever was, and the same to be for evermore. Nay rather to have been and hereafter to be cannot be spoken of it, but only to be, since it is eternal. . . . Of that heavenly Wisdom as then we talked and hunger'd after it, lo, with the whole effort of our heart we apprehended somewhat thereof : and we sighed, and abandoning on that far shore those firstfruits of the spirit, we fell back to the sound of our own voices, and the determinate words of human discourse. . . . .

And we began to say, If to any the tumult of the flesh were hushed ; hushed the images of earth, of waters and of air ; hushed also the poles of heaven ; yea, were the very soul to be hushed to herself, and by not thinking on self to surmount self ; hushed all dreams and imaginary revelations, every tongue and every sign ; if all transitory things were hushed utterly,—for to him that heareth they do all speak, saying ' we made not ourselves, but He made us, who abideth for ever '— ; if,

when their speech had gone out they should suddenly
hold their peace, and to the ear which they had aroused
to their Maker, He himself should speak, alone, not by
them, but by himself, so that we should hear his word,
not through any tongue of flesh, nor Angel's voice, nor
echo of thunder, nor in the dark riddle of a similitude,
but might hear indeed Him, whom in these things we
love, himself without these,—as we but now with effort
and in swift thought touched on that eternal Wisdom,
which abideth over all—; could this be continued, and
all disturbing visions of whatever else be withdrawn, and
this one ravish and absorb, and wrap up its beholder amid
these inward joys, so that life might ever be like that
one moment of understanding, which but now we sighed
after; were not this ENTER THOU INTO THE JOY OF
THY LORD?

33

Scanty the hour, and few the steps, beyond the bourn of care !
Beyond the sweet and bitter world,—beyond it unaware !
Scanty the hour, and few the steps ; because a longer stay
Would bar return and make a man forget his mortal way ! . .

34

THE path thro' which that lovely twain
Have past, by cedar, pine, and yew,
And each dark tree that ever grew,
Is curtained out from Heaven's wide blue ;
Nor sun, nor moon, nor wind, nor rain,
Can pierce its interwoven bowers,

*The path
of spiritual
desire
described,
thro' divine
glooms.*

Nor aught, save where some cloud of dew,
Drifted along the earth-creeping breeze,
Between the trunks of the hoar trees,
Hangs each a pearl in the pale flowers
Of the green laurel, blown anew; . . .
Or when some star of many a one
That climbs and wanders thro' steep night,
Has found the cleft thro' which alone
Beams fall from high those depths upon
Ere it is borne away, away,
By the swift Heavens that cannot stay,
It scatters drops of golden light,
Like lines of rain that ne'er unite:
And the gloom divine is all around,
And underneath is the mossy ground. . .

There those enchanted eddies play
Of echoes, music-tongued, which draw,
By Demogorgon's mighty law,
With melting rapture, or sweet awe,
All spirits on that secret way;
As inland boats are driven to Ocean
Down streams made strong with mountain-thaw:
And first there comes a gentle sound
To those in talk or slumber bound,
And wakes the destined. Soft emotion
Attracts, impels them: those who saw
Say from the breathing earth behind
There steams a plume-uplifting wind
Which drives them on their path, while they
Believe their own swift wings and feet
The sweet desires within obey:
And so they float upon their way,
Until, still sweet, but loud and strong,
The storm of sound is driven along,

Sucked up and hurrying : as they fleet
Behind, its gathering billows meet
And to the fatal mountain bear
Like clouds amid the yielding air.

First Faun.
Canst thou imagine where those spirits live
Which make such delicate music in the woods ?
We haunt within the least frequented caves
And closest coverts, and we know these wilds,
Yet never meet them, tho' we hear them oft :
Where may they hide themselves ?
 Second Faun.   'Tis hard to tell :
I have heard those more skilled in spirits say,
The bubbles, which the enchantment of the sun
Sucks from the pale faint water-flowers that pave
The oozy bottom of clear lakes and pools,
Are the pavilions where such dwell and float
Under the green and golden atmosphere
Which noontide kindles thro' the woven leaves ;
And when these burst, and the thin fiery air,
The which they breathed within those lucent domes,
Ascends to flow like meteors thro' the night,
They ride on them, and rein their headlong speed,
And bow their burning crests, and glide in fire
Under the waters of the earth again.
 1st F.   If such live thus, have others other lives,
Under pink blossoms or within the bells
Of meadow flowers, or folded violets deep,
Or on their dying odours, when they die,
Or in the sunlight of the spherèd dew ?
 2nd F.   Ay, many more which we may well divine.
But, should we stay to speak, noontide would come,
And thwart Silenus find his goats undrawn,
And grudge to sing those wise and lovely songs

Of Fate, and Chance, and God, and Chaos old,
And Love, and the chained Titan's woeful doom,
And how he shall be loosed, and make the earth
One brotherhood : delightful strains which cheer
Our solitary twilights, and which charm
To silence the unenvying nightingales.

35

. . What might this be ?   A thousand fantasies
Begin to throng into my memory,
Of calling shapes, and beckning shadows dire,
And airy tongues that syllable mens names
On Sands and Shoars and desert Wildernesses. . .

36

. . Spirit of BEAUTY, that dost consecrate
    With thine own hues all thou dost shine upon
    Of human thought or form,—where art thou gone ?
Why dost thou pass away and leave our state,
This dim vast vale of tears, vacant and desolate ?
        Ask why the sunlight not for ever
        Weaves rainbows o'er yon mountain river,
Why aught should fail and fade that once is shown,
        Why fear and dream and death and birth
        Cast on the daylight of this earth
        Such gloom,—why man has such a scope
For love and hate, despondency and hope ?

No voice from some sublimer world hath ever
    To sage or poet these responses given—
    Therefore the names of Demon, Ghost, and Heaven,
Remain the records of their vain endeavour,

Intellectual Beauty

Frail spells—whose uttered charm might not avail to sever,
    From all we hear and all we see,
    Doubt, chance, and mutability.
Thy light alone—like mist o'er mountains driven, . . .
    Or moonlight on a midnight stream,
Gives grace and truth to life's unquiet dream.

Love, Hope, and Self-esteem, like clouds depart
    And come, for some uncertain moments lent :
    Man were immortal, and omnipotent,
Didst thou, unknown and awful as thou art,
Keep with thy glorious train firm state within his heart. . .

While yet a boy I sought for ghosts, and sped
    Thro' many a listening chamber, cave and ruin,
    And starlight wood, with fearful steps pursuing
Hopes of high talk with the departed dead.
I called on poisonous names with which our youth is fed ;
    I was not heard—I saw them not—
    When musing deeply on the lot
Of life, at the sweet time when winds are wooing
    All vital things that wake to bring
    News of birds and blossoming,—
    Sudden, thy shadow fell on me ;
I shrieked, and clasped my hands in ecstasy !

I vowed that I would dedicate my powers
    To thee and thine—have I not kept the vow ?
    With beating heart and streaming eyes, even now
I call the phantoms of a thousand hours
Each from his voiceless grave : they have in vision'd bow'rs
    Of studious zeal or love's delight
    Outwatched with me the envious night—
They know that never joy illumed my brow
    Unlinked with hope that thou wouldst free
    This world from its dark slavery. . .

He who has been instructed thus far in the science of Love, and has been led to see beautiful things in their due order and rank, when he comes toward the end of his discipline, will suddenly catch sight of a wondrous thing, beautiful with the absolute Beauty;—and this, Socrates, is the aim and end of all those earlier labours:— he will see a Beauty eternal, not growing or decaying, not waxing or waning; nor will it be fair here and foul there, nor depending on time or circumstance or place, as if fair to some, and foul to others: nor shall Beauty appear to him in the likeness of a face or hand, nor embodied in any sort of form whatever, . . . whether of heaven or of earth; but Beauty absolute, separate, simple, and everlasting; which lending of its virtue to all beautiful things that we see born to decay, itself suffers neither increase nor diminution, nor any other change.

When a man proceeding onwards from terrestrial things by the right way of loving, once comes to sight of that Beauty, he is not far from his goal. And this is the right way wherein he should go or be guided in his love: he should begin by loving earthly things for the sake of the absolute loveliness, ascending to that as it were by degrees or steps, from the first to the second, and thence to all fair forms; and from fair forms to fair conduct, and from fair conduct to fair principles, until from fair principles he finally arrive at the ultimate principle of all, and learn what absolute beauty is.

This life, my dear Socrates, said Diotima, if any life at all is worth living, is the life that a man should live,

in the contemplation of absolute Beauty: the which,
when once you beheld it, would not appear to you to
be after the manner of gold and garments or beautiful
persons, whose sight now so ravishes you, that you and
many others consorting with your lovers forget even to
eat and drink, if only you may look at them and live
near them.   But what if a man's eyes were awake to
the sight of the true Beauty, the divine Beauty, pure,
clear and unalloyed, not clogged with the pollutions of
mortality, and the many colours and varieties of human
life?   What if he should hold converse with the true
Beauty, simple and divine?

O think you, she said, that it would be an ignoble
life for a man to be ever looking thither and with his
proper faculty contemplating the absolute Beauty, and
to be living in its presence?   Are you not rather convinced that he who thus sees Beauty as only it can be
seen, will be specially fortuned? and that, since he is
in contact not with images but with realities, he will
give birth not to images, but to very Truth itself?   And
being thus the parent and nurse of true virtue it will be
his lot to become a friend of God, and, so far as any
man can be, immortal and absolute?

38

THOU art the sky and Thou art also the nest.
O Thou Beautiful! how in the nest thy love embraceth
    the soul with sweet sounds and colour and fragrant
    odours!
Morning cometh there, bearing in her golden basket the
    wreath of beauty, silently to crown the earth.

c

And there cometh Evening, o'er lonely meadows de-
    serted of the herds, by trackless ways, carrying in
    her golden pitcher cool draughts of peace from
    the ocean-calms of the west.
But where thine infinite sky spreadeth for the soul to
    take her flight, a stainless white radiance reigneth;
    wherein is neither day nor night, nor form nor
    colour, nor ever any word.

39

Aristotle.
See note.

There is then something which is always moved with
an unceasing motion: and that motion is in a circle:
and this is plain not by reasoning only but in fact: so
that the first heaven must be eternal. There is then
something [also] which moves it. But since †a mover
which is moved is an intermediate, there must be also
some mover which is unmoved ⌊by another⌋', eternal,
existing as substance and actuality (or energy). Now
the object whether of thought or desire causes movement in this way; it causes movement without being
itself moved. And the primary objects of thought and
desire are the same; for while the object of appetite is
the apparently good, the primary object of rational desire
is the really good, and our desire is consequent on our
opinion, rather than our opinion on our desire: for the
first cause is the thinking. And the Reason (or intellect)
is moved by the object of its thought: and *in the classifica-
tion of objects of thought* substance (or Being) is primary,
and of substance that which is absolute and in energy
(or actuality) . . . . But moreover also the good and

the absolutely desirable are in the same class; and that is best, always or proportionally, which is primary.

But that the Final Cause is among things unmoved is shown by logical distinction, since it is [an object which exists] for the sake of something (which desires it): and of these [two terms] the one (the object) is unmoved, while the other (which desires it) is not. The Final Cause then causes movement as beloved, and something moved by it moves all other things.

Now if something is moved it is capable of being otherwise than it is. Therefore if the first †turning of the heaven be an energy (or actuality) and is so by virtue of its being set in motion [by another agency than its own]†, it might be otherwise, in place if not in substance. But since, on the other hand, there is some mover, itself unmoved, existing in energy, this may not be otherwise in any way. For locomotion is the primary change, and of locomotion that which is circular: and this circular motion is that which this unmoved mover causes.

Of necessity then it is Being, and so far as of necessity, excellently, and so a Principle (or first Cause) . . . . . . From such a first cause then are suspended the Heaven and Nature. And the occupation (or living work) of this Principle is such as is the best, during a little while indeed for us, but itself is ever in this state,— which we cannot be—since its energy is also its pleasure.—And therefore it is that our waking and sensation and thinking are pleasantest to us, while hopes and memories are pleasant indirectly thro' these activities.— And thought, in itself, deals with the object which is best in itself, and the supreme with the supreme. Now it is itself that thought (or intellect) thinks, on account of its participation in the object of thought: for it becomes its own object in the act of apprehending and thinking its objects: so that thought (intellect) and the object of thought are one and the same thing. For that which is receptive of the object of thought and can apprehend substance, is thought (or intellect). But it is in energy by possessing its object, so that this (final energy of possession) rather than that (initial receptivity) is what thought seems to have *divine*: and the energy of intellectual speculation is what is pleasantest and best.

If then in this good estate, as we are sometimes, God is always, it is wonderful, and if more so, then still more wonderful. But God is so, and life indeed belongs to God. For the energy of thought is life, and that is God's energy. We say then that God is a living being, eternal, best: so that life and an age continuous and eternal belong to God, for this is God.

40

. . Then Socrates said: I must tell you, Kĕbes, that when I was young I had a marvellous appetite for that branch of philosophy which they call Natural Science; for I thought it must be splendid to know the causes of things, what it is that makes each thing come into being, exist, and perish: and I was always rushing into opposite extremes of opinion in speculating on such questions as these, Is the growth of animals the result of a corruption which the hot and cold principle contracts, as some have said? Is it by virtue of the blood that we think? or is it the air, or fire? or perhaps

nothing of this sort ? . . . . And then I went on
to examine the decay of things, and the changes
which the heavens and earth undergo; until at last I
came to see that I was by nature utterly incompetent
for such enquiries, as I can easily convince you was the
case, for under the influence of these speculations I grew
wholly blind to matters which hitherto, so far at least
as I could judge of myself or others of me, I had understood quite well. . . . . Then I heard someone reading
out of a book of ANAXAGORAS, as he told us, and saying
that Mind was the disposer and cause of all : and I
was delighted with this notion of the (first) cause,—
indeed it gave me a sort of comfort to think that Mind
was the cause of all things, and I said to myself, If
this be so,—if Mind is the orderer, it will have all
in order, and put every single thing in the place that is
best for it. And arguing thus I rejoiced to think that,
with respect to causation, I had found in Anaxagoras
a teacher after my own heart . . . . .

Ah my friend, how speedily was my glorious hope
dashed, as I went on to read, and found my philosopher
making no use whatever of Mind, nor of any other valid
principle for the ordering of Nature, but alleging Air and
Ether and Water, and many other like absurdities. He
seemed to me to have fallen exactly into the predicament
of a man who, maintaining generally that Mind is the
cause of the actions of Socrates, should then, when
he undertook to explain my conduct in detail, go on to
show that I sit here because my body is made up of
bones and muscles ; and the bones, as he would say,
are hard and have joints which divide them, and the
muscles are elastic, and so on . . . . That is what he

would say; and he would have a similar explanation
of my talking to you, which he would attribute to sound,
and air, and hearing; and he would assign ten thousand
other causes of the same sort, neglecting to mention the
true cause, which is that the Athenians have thought
fit to condemn me, and accordingly I have thought it better
and more right to remain here and undergo my sentence.
—for, by the dog, I think that these muscles and bones
of mine [if they had had any say in the matter] would
have consulted their own interest and gone off long ago to
Megara or Bœotia, if I had not thought it better and
nobler not to play truant and run away, but rather to
remain here and undergo whatever punishment the state
may inflict. To call such things as these causes is quite
absurd. If any one should care to say that unless I
had bones and muscles and the other parts of the body,
I could not do what I would, that is well enough: but
to say that I act as I do because of them, and that this
is the way in which my mind acts, and not from choice
of the best, why, that is a very careless and idle way
of speaking.

41

DOTH not Wisdom cry,
   and Understanding put forth her voice? . .

The Lord possessed me in the beginning of his Way,
   before his works of old.
I was set up from everlasting, from the beginning,
   or ever the earth was.
When no depths were, I was brought forth:
   when there were no fountains abounding with water.

Logos

Before the mountains were settled,
  before the hills was I brought forth:
While as yet he had not made the earth nor the fields,
  nor the first dust of the world.
When he prepared the heavens, I was there:
  when he set a compass upon the face of the deep:
In his empowering of the clouds above:
  in the strong gathering of the fountains of the deep:
When he gave to the sea its boundary
  that the waters should not pass his commandment:
  when he determined the foundations of the earth:
Then was I by him as a master-workman:
  and I was daily his delight, rejoicing always before him;
Rejoicing in his habitable earth:
  and my delight was with the sons of men . . .

Blessed is the man that heareth me,
  watching daily at my gates,
  waiting at the posts of my doors;
For whoso findeth me findeth life . . .
  but he that misseth me wrongeth his own soul.
    All they that hate me love death.

IN the beginning was MIND*,
  and that Mind was with God,
  and the Mind was God.
The same was in the beginning with God.
All things were made by it:
  and without it was not anything made that was made.
In it was life,
  and the life was the light of men.
And the light shineth in the darkness,
  and the darkness overpowered it not . . .

* i. e. the mind of God, and its expression. See note.

43

O HOW may I ever express that secret word?
O how can I say, He is unlike this, He is like that?
If I should say, He is within me, the universe were shamed.
If I say, He is without me, it is false.
He maketh the inner & the outer worlds to be indivisibly one.
The conscious and the unconscious, both are his footstools.
He is neither manifest nor hidden:
He is neither revealed nor unrevealed:
There are no words to tell what He is.

44

O LORD, Thou hast searchèd me out and known me,
   Thou knowest my downsitting and mine uprising,
   Thou understandest my thoughts afar.
Thou discernest my path and my bed,
   and art acquainted with all my ways.
For lo! ere the word is on my tongue,
   Thou, O Lord, knowest it altogether.
Thou dost compass me behind and before,
   and over me Thou hast laid thine hand.
Such knowledge is too wonderful for me;
   it is high, I cannot attain unto it.

Whither shall I go then from thy spirit,
   or whither shall I flee then from thy face?
If I climb up into heaven, Thou art there:
   if I lay me down in hell, Thou art there also.
If I take the wings of the morning, and remain in the
     uttermost parts of the sea,
   even there also should thy hand lead me, and thy
     right hand hold me.

Omnipresence

If I say, Peradventure the darkness may whelm me;
   let my day be turnèd into night,—
The darkness is no darkness with Thee,
   the night is as clear as the day,
   darkness and light to Thee are both alike.

The stirrings of my heart were of Thee;
   Thou didst knit me together in my mothers womb.
I will give thanks unto Thee in my fear and wonder:
   Marvellous are Thy works, and that my soul knoweth
      right well.
My frame was not hid from Thee,
   when I was made secretly and richly wrought in the
      deep of the earth.
Thine eyes did see my substance yet being imperfect:
   And in thy book they were all written,
The days that were outshapen for me,
   when as yet there was none of them.

How dear are thy thoughts unto me, O God;
   O how great is the sum of them!
Should I tell them, they are more in number than the sand.
   My spirit awaketh, and still I am with Thee. . .

Try me, O God, and seek the ground of my heart;
   prove me and examine my thoughts.
Look well if there be any way of sorrow in me,
   and lead me in the way everlasting.

45

THE everlasting universe of things
Flows thro' the mind, and rolls its rapid waves,
Now dark, now glittering, now reflecting gloom,
Now lending splendour, where from secret springs

The Universe

The source of human thought its tribute brings
Of waters, with a sound but half its own . . .

* The
Ravine of
the Arve.
See note.

Thou art the path of that unresting sound,
Dizzy Ravine!* and when I gaze on thee
I seem as in a trance sublime and strange
To muse on my own separate phantasy,
My own, my human mind, which passively
Now renders and receives fast influencings,
Holding an unremitting interchange
With the clear universe of things around ;
One legion of wild thoughts, whose wandering wings
Now float above thy darkness, and now rest
Where that or thou art no unbidden guest,
In the still cave of the witch Poesy,
Seeking among the shadows that pass by,
Ghosts of all things that are, some shade of thee,
Some phantom, some faint image ; till the breast
From which they fled recalls them, thou art there !

Some say that gleams of a remoter world
Visit the soul in sleep,—that death is slumber,
And that its shapes the busy thoughts outnumber
Of those who wake and live.   I look on high ;
Has some unknown omnipotence unfurled
The veil of life and death ? or do I lie
In dream, and does the mightier world of sleep
Spread far around and inaccessibly
Its circles ?   For the very spirit fails,
Driven like a homeless cloud from steep to steep
That vanishes among the viewless gales !
Far, far above, piercing the infinite sky,
Mont Blanc appears, -- still, snowy, and serene :
Its subject mountains their unearthly forms
Pile around it, ice and rock . . .

Power

Is this the scene
Where the old Earthquake-dæmon taught her young
Ruin? Were these their toys? or did a sea
Of fire envelope once this silent snow?
None can reply: all seems eternal now.
The wilderness has a mysterious tongue
Which teaches awful doubt, or faith so mild,
So solemn, so serene, that man may be
But for such faith with nature reconciled.
Thou hast a voice, great Mountain, to repeal
Large codes of fraud and woe; not understood
By all, but which the wise, and great, and good
Interpret, or make felt, or deeply feel.

The fields, the lakes, the forests, and the streams,
Ocean, and all the living things that dwell
Within the dædal earth; lightning, and rain,
Earthquake, and fiery flood, and hurricane;
The torpor of the year when feeble dreams
Visit the hidden buds, or dreamless sleep
Holds every future leaf and flower; the bound
With which from that detested trance they leap;
The works and ways of man, their death and birth,
And that of him, and all that his may be;—
All things that move and breathe with toil and sound
Are born and die; revolve, subside, and swell.
Power dwells apart in its tranquillity,
Remote, serene, and inaccessible . . .

. . And whence are we? Of thy divine love-store,
Loving, hast Thou our slender love-life made,
That unafraid
We may thy dazzling love see and adore.

47

GRASP the Skirt of his Grace, for on a sudden He will
    flee away:
But draw Him not impatiently to thee, lest He fly as
    an arrow from the bow.
What shape will He not assume? What shifts He
    employeth!
If He be apprehended in Form, He will flee by way of
    the Spirit:
If thou seek Him in the sky, He will gleam in the water
    like the moon:
If thou go into the water, He fleeth to the sky:
If thou seek Him in the spaceless, He beckoneth to
    Space:
When thou seekest Him in Space, He fleeth to the
    spaceless . . . .
His Name will flee, the while thou mouldest thy lips for
    speech:
Thou may'st not even say, Such an one will flee:
He will flee from thee, so that if thou paint his picture,
The picture will flee from the tablet, and his features from
    thy soul.

48

What then? Do they not remember that they have
seen God? Or rather do they not always see Him,
and while they see Him, it is not possible for them to
say that they have seen Him; for that would be the
state of those who had ceased to see.

Faith

49

SINCE I believe in God the Father Almighty,
Man's Maker and Judge, Overruler of Fortune,
T'were strange sh^d I praise anything & refuse Him praise,
Shou'd love the creature forgetting the Creator,
Nor unto Him in suff'ring and sorrow turn me:
Nay how coud I withdraw me from His embracing?

But since that I have seen not, and cannot know Him,
Nor in my earthly temple apprehend rightly
His wisdom, and the heav'nly purpose eternal;
Therefor will I be bound to no studied system
Nor argument, nor with delusion enslave me,
Nor seek to please Him in any foolish invention,
Which my spirit within me, that loveth beauty
And hateth evil, hath reprov'd as unworthy:

But I cherish my freedom in loving service,
Gratefully adoring for delight beyond asking
Or thinking, and in hours of anguish and darkness
Confiding always on His excellent greatness.

50

Il me faut, comme à l'univers, un Dieu, qui me
sauve du chaos et de l'anarchie de mes idées . . . Son
idée délivre notre esprit de ses longs tourments, et notre
cœur de sa vaste solitude.

51

You are young, my son, and, as the years go by,
time will change and even reverse many of your present

opinions. Refrain therefore awhile from setting yourself up as a judge of the highest matters.

And this which you now deem of no moment is the
very highest of all : that is whether you have a right
idea of the gods, whereby you may live your life well
or ill. But first I would point out to you something
bearing on this question, which you will hardly dispute ;
—it is thus :

Neither you nor your friends are the first to hold
atheistical opinions ; there have always been plenty of
persons suffering from this disease—and I can tell you
how it has gone with a good many of them who were
in your condition : how not one of them who took up
in his youth with this opinion that there are no gods,
ever continued until old age faithful to his conviction ;
although I grant that the other two diseased notions
concerning the gods may and do persist with a few
persons : the notion I mean that gods exist but that
they regard not human affairs, and that other notion
that they regard human affairs but are easily persuaded
by sacrifice and prayer.

Whatever doctrine then concerning the gods may
have won your immature conviction, you will, if you
listen to me, await before seeking even to examine it,
whether it be false or true.

52

. . Do you believe in a future life ? he asked.
In a future life ? repeated Prince André : but Pierre
gave him no time to answer, taking this repetition of his
own words for a negation all the more readily because

in earlier days he had known the Prince's atheistical convictions.

You say that you cannot see the kingdom of goodness and truth on earth. Neither have I seen it : nor is it possible for any one to see it who looks upon this life as the sum and end of all. On the earth, that is to say on this earth (Pierre pointed to the fields), there is no truth ; all is falsehood and evil : but in the universe, in the whole universe, truth has its kingdom ; and we who are now children of the earth are none the less children of the universe. Do not I feel in my soul that I am actually a member of this vast harmonious whole ? Do not I feel that in this countless assemblage of beings, wherein the Divinity, the First Cause—or however you may term it— is manifested, I make one link, one step between the lower beings and the higher ? If I see, and clearly see the ladder leading from plant to man, then why must I suppose that it breaks off at me, and does not lead on further and beyond ? I feel not only that I cannot utterly perish, since nothing in the universe is annihilated, but that I always shall be, and always was. I feel that besides me are spirits that live above me, and that in this universe there is truth.

Yes, that is Herder's doctrine, said Prince André ; but it is not that, my friend, that will convince me,— life and death — they are what convince a man. The sort of thing that convinces a man is when he sees a being dear to him, with whose life he has been intimately bound up, to whom he has done a wrong, and has wished to make atonement (Prince André's voice trembled and he turned away), and suddenly this being suffers, is tortured and ceases to be.—Why ? It cannot

be that there is no answer. And I believe that there
is one. That is what convinces a man. That is what
has convinced me, said Prince André.

Why, certainly, that is it, said Pierre: is not that
just what I was saying?

No. I only say that it is not arguments that convince
one of the necessity of a future life, but the fact that one
has been going thro' life in fond companionship with
another, and suddenly that dear one vanishes *there, into
the nowhere*; and you yourself are left on the brink of
the chasm looking down into it. And I have looked.

Well, and what then? You have known a *There* and a
Someone. The *There* is the future life, the *Someone* is God.

Prince André did not reply. The carriage and horses
had long been led out on to the further bank, and were
already harnessed, the sun was half-sunken beneath the
horizon, and the evening frost was beginning to incrust
the little pools on the shore with starry crystals, while
Pierre and André, to the astonishment of the servants
coachmen and ferry-men, still stood in the boat talking.

If God and the future life exist, then truth and virtue
exist; and man's highest happiness consists in striving
for their attainment. One must live, said Pierre, one must
love, one must believe that we live not merely now on
this patch of earth, but that we have lived and shall live
eternally there in the universe. He pointed to the sky.

Prince André stood leaning on the rail of the ferry-
boat and listening to Pierre. He never moved his eyes,
but gazed at the red reflection of the sun in the dark-
blue flood. Pierre ceased speaking. All was silent.
The ferry-boat lay drifted along the bank, and only the
ripples of the current could be heard lapping feebly

against its sides. Prince André fancied that this patter
of the water babbled a refrain to Pierre's words 'That
is sooth, accept it : that is sooth, accept it'.

53

GOD mastering me ;
Giver of breath and bread ;
World's strand, sway of the sea ;
Lord of living and dead ;
Thou hast bound bones and veins in me, fasten'd me flesh,
And after at times almost unmade me with dread,
Thy doing ; and dost Thou touch me afresh ?
Over again I feel thy finger and find Thee . . .

54

Not with doubting, but with assured consciousness
do I love thee, O Lord. Thou didst strike my heart
with thy word and I loved thee. And the heavens too,
and the earth and all therein, manifestly on every side
they bid me love thee ; nor cease to say so unto all,
that there may be no excuse . . . .

But what do I love when I love Thee ? Not grace
of bodies, nor the beauty of the seasons, nor the brightness of the light, so gladsome to these eyes ; nor inex-
haustible melodies of sweet song, nor the fragrant smell
of flowers, of ointments and spices, not manna and
honey, not limbs acceptable to embracements of the
flesh. None of these love I when I love my God : and
yet I love a kind of light, and of melody and of fragrance,
a kind of food, and a manner of embracement, when I

love my God; the embracement, food, fragrance, melody, and light of my inner man: where there shineth unto my soul what space containeth not, and there soundeth what time snatcheth not, and there smelleth what breath disperseth not, and there tasteth what eating cloyeth not, and there clingeth what satiety divorceth not. This is it which I love when I love my God.

And what is this? I asked the earth and it said, ' I am not He ': and whatsoever is in it confessed the same. I asked the sea and the deeps, and all that swimming or creeping live therein, and they answered 'We are not thy God, seek above us'. I asked the wandering winds; and the whole air with his inhabitants spoke 'Anaximenes was deceived, I am not God'. I asked the heavens, sun, moon and stars, 'Nor (say they) are we the God whom thou seekest'. And I replied unto all those things which encompass the door of my flesh, 'Ye have told me of my God, that ye are not he: tell me something of him'. And they cried all with a great voice, 'He made us'. My questioning them was my mind's desire, and their Beauty was their answer.

55

HE asked: Who standeth at my door? I said: Thy indigent slave.

He asked: What dost thou here? I said: I am come to greet Thee, O my Lord.

He asked: How long wilt thou persist? I said: Until Thou call me in.

He asked: How long wilt thou desire it? I said: Till the last day of time, O Lord.

I laid claim to his Love; I took solemn oath that for
    love of Him I had renounc't wealth and power.
He asked: Doth not a judge demand a witness to prove
    a claim?
  I said: Tears are my witnesses, and my pale face the
    evidence.
He asked: Is thy witness trustworthy, when thine eyes
    are wayward?
  I said: I swear by thy great Justice, they are pure
    and free from sin.
He asked: What desirest thou of me? I said: Thy
    Constancy and Friendship . . .
He asked: Who was thy Comrade? I said: The
    thought of Thee, O King.
He asked: Who call'd thee hither? I said: The
    rumour of thy Feast . . .

O ask ye no more of me. Were I to tell you more
    words of his,
  Ye would burst your bonds; no roof nor door could
    restrain you.

56

LOVE bade me welcome; yet my soul drew back,
    Guilty of dust and sin.
But quick-eyed Love, observing me grow slack
    From my first entrance in,
Drew nearer to me, sweetly questioning
    If I lack'd anything.

'A guest', I answered, 'worthy to be here.'
    Love said, 'You shall be he.'
'I, the unkind, ungrateful? Ah, my dear,
    I cannot look on Thee.'
Love took my hand and smiling did reply,
    'Who made the eyes but I?'

'Truth, Lord; but I have marr'd them: let my shame
    Go where it doth deserve.'
'And know you not', says Love, 'who bore the blame?'
    'My dear, then I will serve.'
'You must sit down', says Love, 'and taste my meat.'
    So I did sit and eat.

57

HOW could the Love between Thee and me sever?
As the leaf of the Lotus abideth on the water,
    so Thou art my Lord and I am thy servant.
As the moon-bird chakor gazeth all night at the moon,
    so Thou art my Lord and I am thy servant.
From the beginning until the end of Time there is love
    between Thee and me;
    and how shall such love be extinguished?

KABIR saith, As a river arriving unto the Ocean,
    so my heart toucheth Thee.

58

I CANNOT ope mine eyes,
But Thou art ready there to catch
My morning soul and sacrifice . . .

59

WHAT pearl art Thou, that no man may pay thy price?
What doth the World offer, which is not a gift from Thee!
What punishment is greater, than to dwell afar from thy Face?
Torture not thy slave, tho' he be unworthy of Thee!

Adoration

Whoever is whelm'd in the waves of Chance, can never escape,
    if he look not to Thee as Friend.
The World hath no permanence : what it hath
    I esteem as perishable, for it is strange to thy permanence ..
My wish ever is to fling my heart and my soul at thy Feet.
Dust be on the head of the soul, that hath received not the dust
    of thy Feet ! . . .
I will not shun thy stroke : for impure is the heart that hath not
    burn'd in the flame of thine Affliction.
No end is there, O Lord, to thy praises, and no count of thy
    Praisers.
What atom is there that danceth not with abandon in thy praise ?

SHAMS-I-TABRIZ, beauty and pride of the skies, saith :
What king is there, but with heart and soul is a beggar of Thee ?

O

    I GOT me flowers to straw thy way,
    I got me boughs off many a tree :
    But thou wast up by break of day,
    And brought'st thy sweets along with thee . . .

I

    'TWAS at the season when the Earth upsprings
    From slumber ; as a spherèd angel's child,
    Shadowing its eyes with green and golden wings,
      Stands up before its mother bright and mild,
    Of whose soft voice the air expectant seems—
    So stood before the sun, which shone and smiled
      To see it rise thus joyous from its dreams,
    The fresh and radiant Earth.   The hoary grove

Praise

Waxed green, and flowers burst forth like starry beams;
    The grass in the warm sun did start and move,
And sea-buds burst under the waves serene.
How many a one, though none be near to love,
    Loves then the shade of his own soul, half seen
In any mirror—or the spring's young minions,
The wingèd leaves amid the copses green:
    How many a spirit then puts on the pinions
Of fancy, and outstrips the lagging blast,
And his own steps, and over wide dominions
    Sweeps in his dream-drawn chariot, far and fast,
More fleet than storms. The wide world shrinks below,
When winter and despondency are past . . .

62

Epictetus. What else can I do, a lame old man, but sing hymns
to God? If then I were a nightingale, I would do the
nightingale's part; if I were a swan, I would do as a
swan. But now I am a rational creature, and I ought to
praise God: this is my work; I do it, nor will I desert
my post, so long as I am allowed to keep it: and I exhort
you to join in this same song.

63

THE shepherds sing; and shall I silent be?
    My God, no hymne for thee?
My soul's a shepherd too; a flock it feeds
    Of thoughts and words and deeds:
The pasture is thy word; the streams thy grace,
    Enriching all the place.
Shepherd and flock shall sing, and all my powers
    Out-sing the day-light houres.

64

Great art thou, O Lord, and highly to be praised:
great is thy power and thy wisdom is infinite . . .
Thou awakest us to delight in thy praise; for thou
madest us for thyself, and our heart is unquiet till it
rest in thee. . .

65

O LORD our Governour,
  How excellent is thy name in all the world,
  Thou that hast set thy glory above the heavens!
Out of the mouth of very babes and sucklings
  hast thou establish'd strength because of thine adversaries,
  that thou mightest still the enemy and the avenger.
When I consider thy heavens, the work of thy fingers,
  the moon and the stars which thou hast ordained—
What is man, that thou art mindful of him,
  and the son of man, that thou regardest him?
Thou hast set him but little lower than godhead,
  to crown him with glory and worship:
Thou makest him to have dominion over the works of thy hands;
  thou hast put all things under his feet;
All sheep and oxen,
  yea and the beasts of the field,
The fowls of the air and the fishes of the sea
  and whatsoever goeth thro' the paths of the sea.

O Lord our Governour,
  How excellent is thy name in all the world!

Book II

❦

66

DANCE, my heart; O dance to-day with joy!
The hymn of Love filleth the days and the nights
with music, & the world hearkeneth to the melody.

Mad with joy, Life and Death dance to the rhythm of
this music.
The hills and the sea and the earth dance:
The world of man danceth in laughter and tears.

Why put on the robe of the monk, and live aloof from
the world in lonely pride?

Behold my heart danceth in the delight of a hundred arts,
and the Creator is well-pleased.

67

A THING of beauty is a joy for ever:
Its loveliness increases; it will never
Pass into nothingness; but still will keep
A bower quiet for us, and a sleep
Full of sweet dreams, and health, and quiet breathing.
Therefore, on every morrow, are we wreathing
A flowery band to bind us to the earth,
Spite of despondence, of the inhuman dearth
Of noble natures, of the gloomy days,
Of all the unhealthy and o'er-darken'd ways

Made for our searching: yes, in spite of all,
Some shape of beauty moves away the pall
From our dark spirits. . .

68

. . The echoes of the human world, which tell
Of the low voice of love, almost unheard,
And dove-eyed pity's murmured pain, and music,
Itself the echo of the heart, and all
That tempers or improves man's life, now free;*
And lovely apparitions, dim at first,
Then radiant—as the mind arising bright
From the embrace of Beauty (whence the forms
Of which these are the phantoms) casts on them
The gathered rays which are reality—
Shall visit us, the progeny immortal
Of Painting, Sculpture, and rapt Poesy,
And arts, tho' unimagined, yet to be.
The wandering voices and the shadows these
Of all that man becomes, the mediators
Of that best worship, Love,—by him and us
Given and returned; swift shapes and sounds, which grow
More fair and soft as man grows wise and kind,
And, veil by veil, evil and error fall. . .

* that is
after the
deliverance
of Prome-
theus.

69

For the absolute good is the cause and source of all
beauty, just as the sun is the source of all daylight, and
it cannot therefore be spoken or written; yet we speak
and write of it, in order to start and escort ourselves on
the way, and arouse our minds to the vision: like as when

one showeth a pilgrim on his way to some shrine that he
would visit: for the teaching is only of whither and how
to go, the vision itself is the work of him who hath willed
to see.

70

Omnia praeclara tam difficilia quam rara.

71

I have relapsed into those abstractions which are my
only life.—I feel escaped from a new strange and threat-
ing sorrow, and am thankful for it. There is an awful
warmth about my heart like a load of immortality. . . .
The roaring of the wind is my wife, and the stars through
the window-pane are my children. The mighty abstract
Idea of Beauty stifles the more divided and minute
domestic happiness.

72

I AM here for thee,
    Art thou there for me?
Or, traitress to my watchful heart,
Dost thou from rock and wave depart,
    And from the desolate sea? . .

I am here for thee,
    Art thou there for me?
Spirit of brightness, shy and sweet!
My eyes thy glimmering robe would meet
    Above the glimmering sea.

The Muses

My little skill,
My passionate will
Are here : where art thou ? Spirit, bow
From darkening cloud thy heavenly brow,
Ere sinks the ebbing sea.

73

PANTHEA

Look, sister, where a troop of spirits gather,
Like flocks of clouds in spring's delightful weather,
Thronging in the blue air !

IONE

And see ! more come,
Like fountain-vapours when the winds are dumb,
That climb up the ravine in scatter'd lines.
And hark ! is it the music of the pines ?
Is it the lake ?   Is it the waterfall ?

PANTHEA

Tis something sadder, sweeter far than all.

CHORUS OF SPIRITS

From unremember'd ages we
Gentle guides and guardians be
Of heaven-oppressed mortality :
And we breathe, and sicken not,
The atmosphere of human thought ;—
Be it dim and dank and grey
Like a storm-extinguish'd day,
Travel'd o'er by dying gleams ;
Be it bright as all between
Cloudless skies and windless streams,
Silent, liquid, and serene ;—
As the birds within the wind,
As the fish within the wave,
As the thoughts of man's own mind

Float thro' all above the grave,
We make there our liquid lair,
Voyaging cloudlike and unpent
Through the boundless element. . .

74

. . Or as on Vesta's sceptre a swift flame,
Or on blind Homer's heart a wingèd thought . . .

75

ORPHEUS with his lute made trees,
And the mountain tops that freeze,
  Bow themselves, when he did sing:
To his music plants and flowers
Ever sprung; as sun and showers
  There had made a lasting spring.

Everything that heard him play,
Even the billows of the sea,
  Hung their heads, and then lay by.
In sweet music is such art;
Killing care and grief of heart
  Fall asleep, or hearing, die.

76

. . Such sweet compulsion doth in musick lie,
To lull the daughters of *Necessity*,
And keep unsteddy Nature to her law,
And the low world in measur'd motion draw,
After the heavenly tune, which none can hear
Of human mould with grosse unpurged ear. . .

77

I PANT for the music which is divine,
   My heart in its thirst is a dying flower;
Pour forth the sound like enchanted wine,
   Loosen the notes in a silver shower;
Like a herbless plain, for the gentle rain,
I gasp, I faint, till they wake again.

Let me drink of the spirit of that sweet sound,
   More, oh more,—I am thirsting yet;
It loosens the serpent which care has bound
   Upon my heart to stifle it;
The dissolving strain, through every vein,
Passes into my heart and brain. . .

78

. . And ever, against eating cares,
Lap me in soft *Lydian* Aires,
Married to immortal verse
Such as the meeting soul may pierce
In notes, with many a winding bout
Of linked sweetness long drawn out,
With wanton heed, and giddy cunning,
The melting voice through mazes running,
Untwisting all the chains that tie
The hidden soul of harmony.

79

. . The Shepherds on the Lawn,
Or ere the point of dawn,

Music

Sat simply chatting in a rustick **row**;
    Full little thought they than
    That the mighty *Pan*
Was kindly com to live with them below:
Perhaps their loves, or els their sheep,
Was all that did their silly thoughts so busie keep.

    When such musick sweet
    Their hearts and ears did greet,
As never was by mortal finger strook.
    Divinely-warbled voice
    Answering the stringed noise,
As all their souls in blisfull rapture took:
The air, such pleasure loth to lose,
With thousand echoes still prolongs each heav'nly close...

    Such Musick (as 'tis said)
    Before was never made,
But when of old the sons of morning sung,
    While the Creator Great
    His constellations set,
And the well-balanc't world on hinges hung,
And cast the dark foundations deep,
And bid the weltering waves their oozy channel keep...

80

IF music be the food of love, play on;
Give me excess **of** it; that, surfeiting,
The appetite may sicken, and so die.
That strain again! it had a dying fall:
O, it came o'er my ear like the sweet south
That breathes upon a bank of violets,
Stealing and giving odour. Enough; no more:
'Tis not so sweet now as it was before.

O spirit of love, how quick and fresh art thou,
That, notwithstanding thy capacity
Receiveth as the sea, nought enters there,
Of what validity and pitch soe'er,
But falls into abatement and low price,
Even in a minute : so full of shapes is fancy,
That it alone is high fantastical.

81

. . Those instruments with which high Spirits call
The future from its cradle, and the past
Out of its grave, and make the present last
In thoughts and joys which sleep, but cannot die,
Folded within their own eternity . . .

82

. . Now, therein, of all sciences (I speak still of
human) according to the human conceits, is our Poet the
Monarch. For he doth not only show the way, but
giveth so sweet a prospect into the way, as will entice
any man to enter into it. Nay he doth, as if your
journey should lie through a fair Vineyard, at the first,
give you a cluster of Grapes, that, full of that taste,
you may long to pass further. He beginneth not with
obscure definitions, which must blur the margent with
interpretations, and load the memory with doubtfulness;
but he cometh to you with words set in delightful proportion, either accompanied with, or prepared for the
well-enchanting skill of Music ; and with a tale forsooth
he cometh unto you, with a tale which holdeth children
from play, and old men from the chimney-corner. . .

83

.. The poet writes under one restriction only, namely, the necessity of giving immediate pleasure. . .

Nor let this necessity . . . be considered as a degradation of the Poet's art. It is far otherwise. It is an acknowledgment of the beauty of the universe, an acknowledgment the more sincere because not formal, but indirect; it is a task light and easy to him who looks at the world in the spirit of love; further, it is a homage paid to the native and naked dignity of man, to the grand elementary principle of pleasure, by which he knows and feels and lives and moves. . .

Poetry is the breath and finer spirit of all knowledge; it is the impassioned expression which is in the countenance of all Science. . .

In spite of difference of soil and climate, of language and manners, of laws and customs,—in spite of things silently gone out of mind, and things violently destroyed, the Poet binds together by passion and knowledge the vast empire of human society, as it is spread over the whole earth, and over all time. . . Poetry is the first and last of all knowledge—it is as immortal as the heart of man.

84

So as it appeareth that Poesy serveth and conferreth to magnanimity [and] morality and to delectation. And therefore it was ever thought to have some participation of divineness, because it doth raise and erect the mind, by submitting the shows of things to the desires of the

D

mind : whereas reason doth buckle and bow the mind
unto the nature of things.

85

. . Poetry, the hand that wrings,
Bruised albeit at the strings,
Music from the soul of things. . .

86

Poetry awakens and enlarges the mind by . . .
a thousand unapprehended combinations of thought.
Poetry lifts the veil from the hidden beauty of the
world. . . The great secret of morals is Love ; or a
going out of our own nature, and an identification of ourselves with the beautiful which exists in thought, action,
or person, not our own. A man to be greatly good
must imagine intensely and comprehensively ; he must
put himself in the place of another and of many others ;
the pains and pleasures of his species must become his
own. The great instrument of moral good is the
imagination. . . Poetry enlarges the circumference of
the Imagination . . . . [and] strengthens the faculty
which is the organ of the moral nature of man, in the
same manner as exercise strengthens a limb.

87

. . O lovely lily clean,
O lily springing green,
O lily bursting white,

Poetic Dream

Dear lily of delight,
Spring in my heart agen
That I may flower to men ! . .

88

MOST sweet it is with unuplifted eyes
To pace the ground, if path be there or none,
While a fair region round the traveller lies
Which he forbears again to look upon ;
Pleased rather with some soft ideal scene,
The work of Fancy, or some happy tone
Of meditation, slipping in between
The beauty coming and the beauty gone. . .

89

On a poet's lips I slept
Dreaming like a love-adept
In the sound his breathing kept ;
Nor seeks nor finds he mortal blisses,
But feeds on the aereal kisses
Of shapes that haunt thought's wildernesses.
He will watch from dawn till gloom
The lake-reflected sun illume
The yellow bees in the ivy-bloom,
Nor heed nor see what things they be ;
But from these create he can
Forms more real than living man,
Nurselings of immortality.
One of these awaken'd me
And I sped to succour thee.

90

. . Thou art light and thou art free,
And to live rejoiceth thee,
Where the splendours greatest be. . .

Thou a seraph art to go
All undaunted to and fro
Where the fiercest ardours glow. . .

Thou an angel art, and well
It sufficeth thee to dwell
In the smallest creature's cell. . .

Thou a spirit art most sweet,
And to make all life complete
Everywhere thou hast thy seat.

91

SHALL I compare thee to a summer's day ?
Thou art more lovely and more temperate :
Rough winds do shake the darling buds of May,
.And summer's lease hath all too short a date :
Sometime too hot the eye of heaven shines,
And often is his gold complexion dimm'd ;
And every fair from fair sometime declines
By chance or nature's changing course untrimm'd ;
But thy eternal summer shall not fade
Nor lose possession of that fair thou ow'st ;
Nor shall Death brag thou wander'st in his shade,
When in eternal lines to time thou grow'st :
   So long as men can breathe or eyes can see,
   So long lives this and this gives life to thee.

92

NOT marble, nor the gilded monuments
Of princes, shall outlive this powerful rime;
But you shall shine more bright in these contents
Than unswept stone besmear'd with sluttish time.
When wasteful war shall statues overturn,
And broils root out the work of masonry,
Nor Mars his sword nor war's quick fire shall burn
The living record of your memory.
'Gainst death and all-oblivious enmity
Shall you pace forth: your praise shall still find room
Even in the eyes of all posterity
That wear this world out to the ending doom.
  So, till the judgement that yourself arise,
  You live in this, and dwell in lovers' eyes.

93

  . The nodding promontories, and blue isles,
    And cloud-like mountains, and dividuous waves
Of Greece, basked glorious in the open smiles
    Of favouring heaven: from their enchanted caves
Prophetic echoes flung dim melody . . .
    And, like unfolded flowers beneath the sea,
      Like the man's thought dark in the infant's brain,
    Like aught that is which wraps what is to be,
      Art's deathless dreams lay veiled by many a vein
Of Parian stone; and, yet a speechless child,
    Verse murmured, and Philosophy did strain
    Her lidless eyes for thee; when o'er the Ægean **main**

        thee, i.e.
        Liberty.

Athens arose: a city such as vision
    Builds from the purple crags and silver towers

Architecture

Of battlemented cloud, as in derision
   Of kingliest masonry : the ocean-floors
Pave it ; the evening sky pavilions it ; . . .
       Athens, diviner yet,
    Gleam'd with its crest of columns, on the will
Of man, as on a mount of diamond, set ;
    For thou wert, and thine all-creative skill
Peopled, with forms that mock the eternal dead
   In marble immortality, that hill
    Which was thine earliest throne and latest oracle.

Within the surface of Time's fleeting river
   Its wrinkled image lies, as then it lay
Immovably unquiet, and for ever

* See note.   It trembles, but it cannot pass away !* . . .

94

THEY dreamt not of a perishable home
Who thus could build.   Be mine, in hours of fear
Or grovelling thought, to seek a refuge here ;
Or through the aisles of Westminster to roam ;
Where bubbles burst, and folly's dancing foam
Melts, if it cross the threshold. . .

95

I WAS thy neighbour once, thou rugged Pile !
Four summer weeks I dwelt in sight of thee :
I saw thee every day ; and all the while
Thy Form was sleeping on a glassy sea.

So pure the sky, so quiet was the air !
So like, so very like, was day to day !
Whene'er I looked, thy Image still was there ;
It trembled, but it never passed away. . .

Sculpture

Ah! THEN, if mine had been the Painter's hand,
To express what then I saw ; and add the gleam,
The light that never was, on sea or land,
The consecration, and the Poet's dream. . .

THOU still unravished bride of quietness,
    Thou foster-child of Silence and slow Time,
Sylvan historian, who canst thus express
    A flowery tale more sweetly than our rhyme :
What leaf-fringed legend haunts about thy shape
    Of deities or mortals, or of both,
        In Tempe or the dales of Arcady ?
    What men or gods are these ? What maidens loath ?
What mad pursuit ?   What struggle to escape ?
        What pipes and timbrels ?   What wild ecstasy ?

Heard melodies are sweet, but those unheard
    Are sweeter ; therefore, ye soft pipes, play on ;
Not to the sensual ear, but, more endear'd,
    Pipe to the spirit ditties of no tone :
Fair youth, beneath the trees, thou canst not leave
    Thy song, nor ever can those trees be bare ;
        Bold Lover, never, never canst thou kiss,
Though winning near the goal—yet, do not grieve ;
        She cannot fade, though thou hast not thy bliss,
    For ever wilt thou love, and she be fair ! . . .

Cold Pastoral !
When old age shall this generation waste,
Thou shalt remain in midst of other woe
Than ours, a friend to man, to whom thou say'st
' Beauty is Truth, Truth Beauty '—That is all
Ye know on earth, and all ye need to know.

97

MUCH have I travell'd in the realms of gold
And many goodly states and kingdoms seen ;
Round many western islands have I been
Which bards in fealty to Apollo hold.
Oft of one wide expanse had I been told
That deep-brow'd Homer ruled as his demesne :
Yet did I never breathe its pure serene
Till I heard Chapman speak out loud and bold :

Then felt I like some watcher of the skies
When a new planet swims into his ken ;
Or like stout Cortez when with eagle eyes
He stared at the Pacific—and all his men
Look'd at each other with a wild surmise—
Silent, upon a peak in Darien.

98

HOW happy wou'd a man be cou'd he imitate *Hero-dotus* !   I do not say in all his perfections, for that
wou'd be too great a wish, but either in the beauty of
his discourse, or in the gravity of his sentences, or in
the delicacy of his *Ionique* tongue, or (to be short) in
a thousand other advantages, which make all those that
wou'd attempt it, despairing, drop their Pens.

99

Soyons vrais, là est le secret de l'éloquence et de la
vertu, là est l'autorité morale, c'est la plus haute maxime
de l'art et de la vie.

100

   .˙. I am certain of nothing but of the holiness of the heart's affections, and the truth of Imagination. What the Imagination seizes as Beauty must be Truth. . . The Imagination may be compared to Adam's dream; —he awoke and found it truth. . .

101

   TRUE Thomas lay on Huntlie bank;
      A ferlie he spied wi' his ee;
And there he saw a lady bright
      Come riding down by the Eildon Tree.

Her skirt was o' the grass-green silk,
      Her mantle of the velvet fine;
At ilka tett of her horse's mane,
      Hung fifty siller bells and nine.

True Thomas he pu'd aff his cap
      And louted low down to his knee:
' All hail, thou mighty Queen of heaven!
      For thy peer on earth I never did see.'

' O no, O no, Thomas, (she said)
      That name does not belang to me;
I'm but the Queen o' fair Elfland,
      That am hither come to visit thee.

' Harp and carp, Thomas, (she said);
      Harp and carp along wi' me;
And if ye dare to kiss my lips,
      Sure of your bodie I will be.'—

True Thomas

' Betide me weal, betide me woe,
    That weird shall never daunten me.'
Syne he has kiss'd her rosy lips,
    All underneath the Eildon Tree.

' Now ye maun go wi' me (she said),
    True Thomas, ye maun go wi' me;
And ye maun serve me seven years,
    Thro' weal or woe as may chance to be.'

She mounted on her milk-white steed,
    She's ta'en true Thomas up behind:
And aye, whene'er her bridle rang,
    The steed flew swifter than the wind.

O they rade on, and farther on,
    The steed gaed swifter than the wind:
Until they reach'd a desert wide,
    And living land was left behind.

' Light down, light down now, true Thomas,
    And lean your head upon my knee:
Abide and rest a little space,
    And I will show you ferlies three.

' O see ye not yon narrow road,
    So thick beset wi' thorns and briers?
That is the Path of Righteousness,
    Tho' after it but few enquires.

' And see ye not that braid, braid road,
    That lies across yon lily leven?
That is the Path of Wickedness,
    Tho' some call it the Road to Heaven.

' And see ye not that bonny road
    That winds about the fernie brae?

Elfland

That is the Road to fair Elfland,
    Where thou and I this night maun gae.

' But, Thomas, ye sall haud your tongue,
    Whatever ye may hear or see :
For if ye speak word in Elflyn-land,
    Ye'll ne'er get back to your ain countrie.'

O they rade on, and farther on,
    And they waded thro' rivers abune the knee :
And they saw neither sun nor mune,
    But they heard the roaring of the sea.

It was mirk mirk night, there was nae sternlight,
    They waded thro' red blude to the knee :
For a' the blude that 's shed on earth
    Rins thro' the springs o' that countrie.

Syne they came to a garden green,
    And she pu'd an apple frae a tree :
' Take this for thy wages, true Thomas ;
    It will give the tongue that can never lee '—

' My tongue is mine ain (true Thomas said) :
    A gudely gift ye wad gie to me !
I neither dought to buy nor sell
    At fair or tryst where I may be.

' I dought neither speak to prince or peer,
    Nor ask of grace from fair ladye ! '—
' Now hold thy peace, Thomas (she said),
    For as I say, so must it be.'

He has gotten a coat of the even cloth
    And a pair o' shoon of velvet green :
And till seven years were gane and past,
    True Thomas on earth was never seen.

102

COME unto these yellow sands,
   And then take hands:
Court'sied when you have, and kiss'd
   The wild waves whist,
Foot it featly here and there;
And, sweet sprites, the burden bear.
   Hark, hark!
     Bowgh, wowgh.
   The watch-dogs bark:
     Bowgh, wowgh.
   Hark, hark!   I hear
The strain of strutting chanticleer
     Cry, Cock-a-diddle-do.

103

HE stood among a crowd at Drumahair;
   His heart hung all upon a silken dress,
   And he had known at last some tenderness,
Before earth made of him her sleepy care;
But when a man poured fish into a pile,
   It seemed they raised their little silver heads,
   And sang how day a Druid twilight sheds
Upon a dim, green, well-beloved isle,
Where people love beside star-laden seas;
   How Time may never mar their faery vows
   Under the woven roofs of quicken boughs:
The singing shook him out of his new ease.

As he went by the sands of Lisadill,
   His mind ran all on money cares and fears,
   And he had known at last some prudent years
Before they heaped his grave under the hill;

Elfland

But while he passed before a plashy place,
    A lug-worm with its gray and muddy mouth
    Sang how somewhere to north or west or south
There dwelt a gay, exulting, gentle race;
And how beneath those three-times blessed skies
    A Danaan fruitage makes a shower of moons,
    And as it falls awakens leafy tunes:
And at that singing he was no more wise.

He mused beside the well of Scanavin,
    He mused upon his mockers: without fail
    His sudden vengeance were a country tale,
Now that deep earth has drunk his body in;
But one small knot-grass growing by the pool
    Told where, ah, little, all-unneeded voice!
    Old Silence bids a lonely folk rejoice,
And chaplet their calm brows with leafage cool;
And how, when fades the sea-strewn rose of day,
    A gentle feeling wraps them like a fleece,
    And all their trouble dies into its peace;
The tale drove his fine angry mood away.

He slept under the hill of Lugnagall;
    And might have known at last unhaunted sleep
    Under that cold and vapour-turbaned steep,
Now that old earth had taken man and all:
Were not the worms that spired about his bones
    A-telling with their low and reedy cry,
    Of how God leans His hands out of the sky,
To bless that isle with honey in His tones;
That none may feel the power of squall and wave,
    And no one any leaf-crowned dancer miss
    Until He burn up Nature with a kiss:
The man has found no comfort in the grave.

104

WHERE the bee sucks, there suck I;
In a cowslip's bell I lie;
There I couch when owls do cry.
On the bat's back I do fly
After summer merrily:
Merrily, merrily, shall I live now,
Under the blossom that hangs on the bough.

105

. . These were tame pleasures; she would often climb
    The steepest ladder of the crudded rack
Up to some beakèd cape of cloud sublime,
    And like Arion on the dolphin's back
Ride singing through the shoreless air;—oft-time
    Following the serpent lightning's winding track,
She ran upon the platforms of the wind,
And laughed to hear the fire-balls roar behind. . .

106

. . And where within the surface of the river
    The shadows of the massy temples lie,
And never are erased—but tremble ever
    Like things which every cloud can doom to die,
Through lotus-paven canals, and wheresoever
    The works of man pierced that serenest sky
With tombs, and towers, and fanes, 'twas her delight
To wander in the shadow of the night. . .

107

CALME was the day, and through the trembling ayre
Sweet-breathing Zephyrus did softly play—

Romance

A gentle spirit, that lightly did delay
Hot Titans beams, which then did glyster fayre:
When I* (whom sullen care,   * Edmund
Through discontent of my long fruitless stay   Spenser.
In Princes court, and expectation vayne
Of idle hopes, which still do fly away,
Like empty shadows, did afflict my brayne,)
Walkt forth to ease my payne
Along the shore of silver-streaming Themmes;
Whose rutty Bank, the which his river hemmes,
Was painted all with variable flowers,
And all the meads adornd with dainty gemmes,
Fit to deck maidens bowers,
And crown their Paramours
Against the Bridale day, which is not long:
Sweet Themmes! run softly, till I end my Song. . .

At length they all to mery London came,
To mery London, my most kindly nurse,
That to me gave this lifes first native source,
Tho' from another place I take my name,
An house of ancient fame:
There when they came, whereas those bricky towers
The which on Themmes broad aged back do ride,
Where now the studious Lawyers have their bowers,
There whylom wont the Templer Knights to bide,
Till they decayd through pride;
Next whereunto there stands a stately place,
Where oft I gained gifts and goodly grace
Of that great lord, which therein wont to dwell:
Whose want too well now feels my friendless case;
But ah! here fits not well
Old woes, but joys to tell
Against the Bridale day, which is not long:
Sweet Themmes! run softly, till I end my song. . .

108

HOW sweet the moonlight sleeps upon this bank!
Here will we sit, and let the sounds of music
Creep in our ears: soft stillness and the night
Become the touches of sweet harmony.
Sit, Jessica: look, how the floor of heaven
Is thick inlaid with patines of bright gold:
There's not the smallest orb which thou behold'st
But in his motion like an angel sings,
Still quiring to the young-eyed cherubins:
Such harmony is in immortal souls;
But whilst this muddy vesture of decay
Doth grossly close it in, we cannot hear it. . .

109

O never rudely will I blame his faith
In the might of stars and angels! 'Tis not merely
The human being's pride that peoples space
With life and mystical predominance;
Since likewise for the stricken heart of Love
This visible nature, and this common world
Is all too narrow . . .
For fable is Love's world, his home, his birthplace:
Delightedly dwells he mong fays and talismans,
And spirits; and delightedly believes
Divinities, being himself divine.
The intelligible forms of ancient poets,
The fair humanities of old religion,
The power, the beauty and the majesty
That had their haunts in dale or piny mountain
Or forest, by slow stream or pebbly spring
Or chasms and watery depths: all these have vanish'd,

They live no longer in the faith of reason:
But still the heart doth need a language, still
Doth the old instinct bring back the old names;
And to yon starry world they now are gone,
Spirits or gods, that used to share this earth
With man as with their friend. . .

110

. . I have been still led like a child
My heedless wayward path and wild
Thro' this rough world by feebler clues,
So they were bright, than rainbow-dews
Spun by the insect gossamer
To climb with thro' the ropy air. . .

111

THERE was a man whom Sorrow named his friend,
And he, of his high comrade Sorrow dreaming,
Went walking with slow steps along the gleaming
And humming sands, where windy surges wend:
And he called loudly to the stars to bend
From their pale thrones and comfort him, but they
Among themselves laugh on and sing alway:
And then the man whom Sorrow named his friend
Cried out, *Dim sea, hear my most piteous story !*
The sea swept on and cried her old cry still,
Rolling along in dreams from hill to hill;
He fled the persecution of her glory
And, in a far-off, gentle valley stopping,
Cried all his story to the dewdrops glistening,
But naught they heard, for they are always listening,
The dewdrops, for the sound of their own dropping.

And then the man whom Sorrow named his friend
Sought once again the shore, and found a shell
And thought, *I will my heavy story tell*
Till my own words, re-echoing, shall send
Their sadness through a hollow, pearly heart ;
And my own tale again for me shall sing,
And my own whispering words, be comforting :
And lo ! my ancient burden may depart.
Then he sang softly nigh the pearly rim ;
But the sad dweller by the sea-ways lone
Changed all he sang to inarticulate moan
Among her wildering whorls, forgetting him.

112

THERE lived a wife at Usher's well,
  And a wealthy wife was she ;
She had three stout and stalwart sons,
  And sent them o'er the sea.

They hadna been a week from her,
  A week but barely ane,
When word came to the carlin wife
  That her three sons were gane.

They hadna been a week from her
  A week but barely three,
When word came to the carlin wife
  That her sons she'd never see.—

' I wish the wind may never cease
  Nor fishes in the flood,
Till my three sons come hame to me,
  In earthly flesh and blood ! '

It fell about the Martinmas
  When nights are long and mirk,

The Ancient Burden

The carlin wife's three sons came hame,
    And their hats were o' the birk.

It neither grew in syke nor ditch,
    Nor yet on any sheugh;
But at the gates of Paradise
    That birk grew fair eneugh.—

'Blow up the fire, my maidens!
    Bring water from the well!
For a' my house shall feast this night,
    Since my three sons are well.'—

And she has made to them a bed,
    She's made it large and wide;
And she's ta'en her mantle her about,
    Sat down at the bedside.

Up then crew the red red cock,
    And up and crew the grey;
The eldest to the youngest said,
    'Tis time we were away.'—

The cock he had not craw'd but once
    And clapp'd his wings at a',
When the youngest to the eldest said,
    'Brother we must awa.

The cock doth craw, the day doth daw,
    The channerin worm doth chide;
Gin we be miss'd out o' our place
    A sair pain we maun bide.'—

'Fare ye weel, my mother dear!
    Fareweel to barn and byre!
And fare ye weel, the bonny lass
    That kindles my mother's fire!'

Revenge

I WISH I were where Helen lies,
Night and day on me she cries:
O that I were where Helen lies,
   On fair Kirconnell lea!

Curst be the heart that thought the thought,
And curst the hand that fired the shot,
When in my arms burd Helen dropt,
   And died to succour me!

O think na ye my heart was sair,
When my Love dropt and spak nae mair?
There did she swoon wi' meikle care,
   On fair Kirconnell lea.

As I went down the waterside
None but my foe to be my guide,
None but my foe to be my guide,
   On fair Kirconnell lea;

I lighted down, my sword did draw,
I hackèd him in pieces sma',
I hackèd him in pieces sma',
   For her sake that died for me.

O Helen fair beyond compare!
I'll make a garland of thy hair,
Shall bind my heart for evermair
   Until the day I dee.

O that I were where Helen lies!
Night and day on me she cries;
Out of my bed she bids me rise,
   Says, ' Haste and come to me.'

O Helen fair! O Helen chaste!
If I were with thee I were blest,

The Wild Stream

Where thou lies low, and takes thy rest
　　On fair Kirconnell lea.

I wish my grave were growing green,
A winding sheet drawn owre my een,
And I in Helen's arms lying
　　On fair Kirconnell lea.

I wish I were where Helen lies!
Night and day on me she cries:
And I am weary of the skies
　　For her sake that died for me.

14

. . O wild and desert stream ! . .
Gloomy and dark art thou—the crowded firs
Spire from thy shores, and stretch across thy bed,
Making thee doleful as a cavern-well :
Save when the shy king-fishers build their nest
On thy steep banks, no loves hast thou, wild stream !

15

LA Rivière de Cassis roule ignorée
　　En des vaux étranges :
La voix de cent corbeaux l'accompagne, vraie
　　Et bonne voix d'anges :
Avec les grands mouvements des sapinaies
　　Quand plusieurs vents plongent.

Tout roule avec des mystères révoltants
　　De campagnes d'anciens temps :
De donjons visités, de parcs importants :
　　C'est en ces bords qu'on entend
Les passions mortes des chevaliers errants :
　　Mais que salubre est le vent !

Dryads

Que le piéton regarde à ces clairevoies :
  Il ira plus courageux.
Soldats des forêts que le Seigneur envoie,
  Chers corbeaux délicieux !
Faites fuir d'ici le paysan matois
  Qui trinque d'un moignon vieux.

116

. . And so this man returned with axe and saw
At evening close from killing the tall treen,
The soul of whom by nature's gentle law
  Was each a wood-nymph, and kept ever green
The pavement and the roof of the wild copse,
Chequering the sunlight of the blue serene
  With jaggèd leaves,—and from the forest tops
Singing the winds to sleep—or weeping oft
Fast showers of aëreal water drops
  Into their mother's bosom, sweet and soft,
Nature's pure tears which have no bitterness ;—
Around the cradles of the birds aloft
  They spread themselves into the loveliness
Of fan-like leaves, and over pallid flowers
Hang like moist clouds :—or, where high branches kiss,
  Make a green space among the silent bowers,
Like a vast fane in a metropolis,
Surrounded by the columns and the towers
  All overwrought with branch-like traceries
In which there is religion—and the mute
Persuasion of unkindled melodies,
  Odours and gleams and murmurs . . .

The world is full of Woodmen who expel
Love's gentle Dryads from the haunts of life,
And vex the nightingales in every dell.

Fantastic Forms

O Lily-lady,
Dreaming serenely alone in cloud-garden shady,
No longer may'st thou muse, no more repose,
O lily-lady
In thy garden shady.

The great rose
Now waking, his crimson splendour doth loftily dispose;
Now is thy calm day done, now the star-daisies close,
O lily-lady
In thy garden shady.

. . . Fantastic forms, whither are ye fled? Or if the like of you exist, why exist they no more for me ?. . . In those days I saw gods, as ' old men covered with a mantle ', walking upon the earth. Let the dreams of classic idolatry perish,—extinct be the fairies and fairy trumpery of legendary fabling,—in the heart of childhood there will for ever spring up a well of innocent or wholesome superstition—the seeds of exaggeration will be busy there, and vital—from everyday forms educing the unknown and the uncommon. In that little Goshen there will be light, when the grown world flounders about in the darkness of sense and materiality. While childhood, and while dreams reducing childhood, shall be left, imagination shall not have spread her holy wings totally to fly the earth.

119

         I am the powr
Of this fair Wood, and live in Oak'n bowr,
To nurse the Saplings tall, and curl the grove
With Ringlets quaint, and wanton windings wove.
And all my Plants I save from nightly ill,
Of noisom winds, and blasting vapours chill;
And from the Boughs brush off the evil dew,
And heal the harms of thwarting thunder blew,
Or what the cross dire-looking Planet smites,
Or hurtfull Worm with canker'd venom bites.
When Eev'ning gray doth rise, I fetch my round
Over the mount, and all this hallow'd ground,
And early ere the odorous breath of morn
Awakes the slumbring leaves, or tasseld horn
Shakes the high thicket, haste I all about,
Number my ranks, and visit every sprout
With puissant words, and murmurs made to bless,
But els in deep of night when drowsines
Hath lockt up mortal sense, then listen I
To the celestial *Sirens* harmony,
That sit upon the nine enfolded Sphears,
And sing to those that hold the vital shears,
And turn the Adamantine spindle round,
On which the fate of gods and men is wound.

120

IN Xanadu did Kubla Khan
A stately pleasure-dome decree:
Where Alph, the sacred river, ran
Through caverns measureless to man,
    Down to a sunless sea.

Kubla Khan

So twice five miles of fertile ground
With walls and towers were girdled round:
And there were gardens bright with sinuous rills
Where blossomed many an incense-bearing tree;
And here were forests ancient as the hills,
Enfolding sunny spots of greenery.

But oh! that deep romantic chasm which slanted
Down the green hill athwart a cedarn cover!
A savage place! as holy and enchanted
As e'er beneath a waning moon was haunted
By woman wailing for her demon-lover!
And from this chasm, with ceaseless turmoil seething,
As if this earth in fast thick pants were breathing,
A mighty fountain momently was forced:
Amid whose swift half-intermitted burst
Huge fragments vaulted like rebounding hail,
Or chaffy grain beneath the thresher's flail:
And mid these dancing rocks at once and ever
It flung up momently the sacred river
Five miles meandering with a mazy motion
Through wood and dale the sacred river ran,
Then reached the caverns measureless to man,
And sank in tumult to a lifeless ocean:
And mid this tumult Kubla heard from far
Ancestral voices prophesying war!

    The shadow of the dome of pleasure
    Floated midway on the waves;
    Where was heard the mingled measure
    From the fountain and the caves.
It was a miracle of rare device,
A sunny pleasure-dome with caves of ice!

    A damsel with a dulcimer
    In a vision once I saw:

It was an Abyssinian maid,
And on her dulcimer she play'd,
Singing of Mount Abora.
Could I revive within me
Her symphony and song,
To such a deep delight 'twould win me,
That with music loud and long,
I would build that dome in air,
That sunny dome ! those caves of ice !
And all who heard should see them there
And all should cry, Beware ! Beware !
His flashing eyes, his floating hair !
Weave a circle round him thrice,
And close your eyes with holy dread,
For he on honey-dew hath fed,
And drunk the milk of Paradise.

121

OFTEN rebuked, yet always back returning
To those first feelings that were born with me,
And leaving busy chase of wealth and learning
For idle dreams of things which cannot be. . .

I'll walk where my own nature would be leading—
It vexes me to choose another guide—
Where the grey flocks in ferny glens are feeding,
Where the wild wind blows on the mountain-side. . .

122

I DREAMED that, as I wandered by the way,
Bare Winter suddenly was changed to Spring,

Visionary Flowers

And gentle odours led my steps astray,
   Mixed with a sound of waters murmuring
Along a shelving bank of turf, which lay
   Under a copse, and hardly dared to fling
Its green arms round the bosom of the stream,
But kissed it and then fled, as thou mightest in dream.

There grew pied wind-flowers and violets,
   Daisies, those pearled Arcturi of the earth,
The constellated flower that never sets ;
   Faint oxslips ; tender bluebells, at whose birth
The sod scarce heaved ; and that tall flower that wets—
   Like a child, half in tenderness and mirth—
Its mother's face with heaven's collected tears,
When the low wind, its playmate's voice, it hears.

And in the warm hedge grew lush eglantine,
   Green cowbind and the moonlight-coloured may,
And cherry-blossoms, and white cups, whose wine
   Was the bright dew, yet drained not by the day ;
And wild roses, and ivy serpentine,
   With its dark buds and leaves, wandering astray ;
And flowers azure, black, and streaked with gold,
Fairer than any wakened eyes behold.

And nearer to the river's trembling edge
   There grew broad flag-flowers, purple prankt with white,
And starry river buds among the sedge,
   And floating water-lilies, broad and bright,
Which lit the oak that overhung the hedge
   With moonlight beams of their own watery light ;
And bulrushes, and reeds of such deep green
As soothed the dazzled eye with sober sheen.

Methought that of these visionary flowers
   I made a nosegay, bound in such a way

That the same hues, which in their natural bowers
  Were mingled or opposed, the like array
Kept these imprisoned children of the Hours
  Within my hand,—and then, elate and gay,
I hastened to the spot whence I had come,
That I might there present it!—oh! to whom?

123

HAD I the heavens' embroidered cloths,
Enwrought with golden and silver light,
The blue and the dim and the dark cloths
Of night and light and the half-light;
I would spread the cloths under your feet:
But I, being poor, have only my dreams;
I have spread my dreams under your feet;
Tread softly because you tread on my dreams.

124

Ere Babylon was dust,
The Magus Zoroaster, my dead child,
Met his own image walking in the garden.
That apparition, sole of men, he saw.
For know there are two worlds of life and death
One that which thou beholdest; but the other
Is underneath the grave, where do inhabit
The shadows of all forms that think and live
Till death unite them and they part no more;
Dreams and the light imaginings of men,
And all that faith creates or love desires,
Terrible, strange, sublime and beauteous shapes

Tawny Trees

LOV'ST thou tawny trees?
I can show thee soon
Stranger sights than these.

Throngs of wilder'd kings
  Their power who sold,
Wearing its ruddy price
  In coins of gold.

Lov'st thou lilies white,
Untrod vales where bask
Fields of scented light?

Come where cloister'd queens
  By thousands sing
Their virgin saintliness
  Warm-sheltering.

Wilt thou strength and life?
Wilt thou beauteous ease
Far from soiling strife?

When thy powers surrender
  Their glory tall,
When thy calm soft-closeth
  At evening fall,

When no joys shall please,
I can still devise
Fairer things than these.

O BLEST unfabled Incense Tree,
That burns in glorious Araby,

The Phoenix

With red scent chalicing the air,
Till earth-life grow Elysian there!

Half buried to her flaming breast
In this bright tree she makes her nest,
Hundred-sunned Phoenix! when she must
Crumble at length to hoary dust;

Her gorgeous death-bed, her rich pyre
Burnt up with aromatic fire;
Her urn, sight-high from spoiler men,
Her birthplace when self-born again.

The mountainless green wilds among,
Here ends she her unechoing song:
With amber tears and odorous sighs
Mourned by the desert where she dies.

127

*these
joys are
the mere
luxuries
of poetry.

. . And can I ever bid these joys* farewell?
Yes, I must pass them for a nobler life,
Where I may find the agonies, the strife
Of human hearts: for lo! I see afar,
O'er-sailing the blue cragginess, a car
And steeds with streamy manes—the charioteer
Looks out upon the winds with glorious fear:
And now the numerous tramplings quiver lightly
Along a huge cloud's ridge; and now with sprightly
Wheel downward come they into fresher skies,
Tipt round with silver from the sun's bright eyes.
Still downward with capacious whirl they glide;
And now I see them on a green hill-side
In breezy rest among the nodding stalks.
The charioteer with wondrous gesture talks

The Charioteer

To the trees and mountains ; and there soon appear
Shapes of delight, of mystery, and fear,
Passing along before a dusky space
Made by some mighty oaks—as they would chase
Some ever-fleeting music, on they sweep.
Lo! how they murmur, laugh, and smile, and weep
Some with upholden hand and mouth severe ;
Some with their faces muffled to the ear
Between their arms ; some clear in youthful bloom,
Go glad and smilingly athwart the gloom ;
Some looking back, and some with upward gaze. . .

                            Most awfully intent
The driver of those steeds is forward bent,
And seems to listen : O that I might know
All that he writes with such a hurrying glow !

The visions all are fled—the car is fled
Into the light of heaven, and in their stead
A sense of real things comes doubly strong,
And, like a muddy stream, would bear along
My soul to nothingness : but I will strive
Against all doubtings, and will keep alive
The thought of that same chariot, and the strange
Journey it went. . .

28

. . A man's life of any worth is a continual Allegory,
and very few eyes can see the Mystery of his life. . .

29

. . Qui veut voir parfaitement clair avant de se déter-
miner ne se détermine jamais. Qui n'accepte pas le
regret n'accepte pas la vie.

.. Yet not the more
Cease I to wander where the Muses haunt
Cleer Spring, or shadie Grove, or Sunnie Hill,
Smit with the love of sacred song ; but chief
Thee *Sion* and the flowrie Brooks beneath
That wash thy hallowd feet, and warbling flow,
Nightly I visit : nor somtimes forget
Those other two equal'd with me in Fate,
So were I equal'd with them in renown,
Blind *Thamyris* and blind *Mæonides*,
And *Tiresias* and *Phineus* Prophets old.
Then feed on thoughts, that voluntarie move
Harmonious numbers ; as the wakeful Bird
Sings darkling, and in shadiest Covert hid
Tunes her nocturnal Note.   Thus with the Year
Seasons return, but not to me returns
Day, or the sweet approach of Ev'n or Morn,
Or sight of vernal bloom, or Summers Rose,
Or flocks, or herds, or human face divine ;
But cloud in stead, and ever-during dark
Surrounds me, from the chearful waies of men
Cut off, and for the Book of knowledg fair
Presented with a Universal blanc
Of Natures works to mee expung'd and ras'd,
And wisdome at one entrance quite shut out.
So much the rather thou Celestial light
Shine inward, and the mind through all her powers
Irradiate, there plant eyes, all mist from thence
Purge and disperse, that I may see and tell
Of things invisible to mortal sight. . .

131

.. Raising me on ethereal wing
Lighter than the lark can spring
When drunk with dewlight, which the Morn
Pours from her translucent horn
To steep his sweet throat in the corn. . .

132

.. Now every human soul must have seen the realities of that other world, else could she not have entered
into this body.

But to recall those things by means of the things of
this world is not easy for every soul. It may be that
some, when in the other world, had too brief a vision of
it ; and others, when they fell hitherward, met with ill
fortune, and, through various companionships being turned
to iniquity, forgat the holy things which they had seen
aforetime. Few indeed are left who have a ready and
sufficient memory ; and they, when they behold here any
likeness of the things there, are amazed and cannot con-
tain themselves. But what this emotion really is they
know not, because their perception is too indistinct.

133

THERE was a time when meadow, grove, and stream,
The earth, and every common sight
        To me did seem
    Apparell'd in celestial light,
The glory and the freshness of a dream.

E

Man's Heritage

It is not now as it hath been of yore ;—
    Turn wheresoe'er I may,
      By night or day,
The things which I have seen I now can see no more. . .

Whither is fled the visionary gleam ?
Where is it now, the glory and the dream ?

Our birth is but a sleep and a forgetting ;
The Soul that rises with us, our life's Star,
    Hath had elsewhere its setting,
      And cometh from afar :
    Not in entire forgetfulness,
    And not in utter nakedness,
But trailing clouds of glory do we come
    From God, who is our home :
Heaven lies about us in our infancy !
Shades of the prison-house begin to close
    Upon the growing Boy,
But he beholds the light, and whence it flows,
    He sees it in his joy ;
The Youth, who daily farther from the east
    Must travel, still is Nature's Priest,
    And by the vision splendid
    Is on his way attended ;
At length the Man perceives it die away,
And fade into the light of common day. . .

    O joy ! that in our embers
    Is something that doth live,
    That nature yet remembers
    What was so fugitive !
The thought of our past years in me doth breed
Perpetual benediction : not indeed

Childhood

For that which is most worthy to be blest;
Delight and liberty, the simple creed
Of Childhood, whether busy or at rest,
With new-fledged hope still fluttering in his breast:—
  Not for these I raise
  The song of thanks and praise;
  But for those obstinate questionings
  Of sense and outward things,
  Fallings from us, vanishings;
  Blank misgivings of a Creature
Moving about in worlds not realised,
High instincts before which our mortal Nature
Did tremble like a guilty Thing surprised:
  But for those first affections,
  Those shadowy recollections,
  Which, be they what they may,
Are yet the fountain-light of all our day,
Are yet a master-light of all our seeing;
 Uphold us, cherish, and have power to make
Our noisy years seem moments in the being
Of the eternal Silence: truths that wake,
  To perish never:
Which neither listlessness, nor mad endeavour,
  Nor Man nor Boy,
Nor all that is at enmity with joy,
Can utterly abolish or destroy!
  Hence in a season of calm weather
  Though inland far we be,
Our Souls have sight of that immortal sea
  Which brought us hither,
  Can in a moment travel thither,
And see the Children sport upon the shore,
And hear the mighty waters rolling evermore.

Childhood

TELL me, tell me, smiling child,
What the Past is like to thee.
—An Autumn evening soft and mild
With a wind that sighs mournfully.

Tell me what is the Present hour.
—A green and flowery spray,
Where a young bird sits gathering its power
To mount and fly away.

And what is the Future, happy one?
—A sea beneath a cloudless sun:
A mighty glorious dazzling sea
Stretching into Infinity.

The inspiring music's thrilling sound,
The glory of the festal day,
The glittering splendor rising round,
Have pass'd like all earth's joys away.

Forsaken by that lady fair
She glides unheeding thro' them all;
Covering her brow to hide the tear
That still, tho' check'd, trembles to fall.

She hurries thro' the outer hall,
And up the stairs thro' galleries dim,
That murmur to the breezes' call,
The night-wind's lonely vesper-hymn.

135

IT is a beauteous evening, calm and free,
The holy time is quiet as a Nun
Breathless with adoration ; the broad sun
Is sinking down in its tranquillity ;
The gentleness of heaven broods o'er the Sea :
Listen ! the mighty Being is awake,
And doth with his eternal motion make
A sound like thunder—everlastingly.
Dear Child ! dear Girl ! that walkest with me here,
If thou appear untouched by solemn thought,
Thy nature is not therefore less divine :
Thou liest in Abraham's bosom all the year ;
And worshipp'st at the Temple's inner shrine,
God being with thee when we know it not.

136

MON petit fils qui n'as encor rien vu,
A ce matin, ton père te salue ;
Vien-t-en, vien voir ce monde bien pourvu
D'honneurs et biens qui sont de grant value ;
Vien voir la paix en France descendue,
Vien voir François, notre roy et le tien,
Qui a la France ornée et défendue ;
Vien voir le monde où y a tant de bien.

Jan, petit Jan, vien voir ce tant beau monde,
Ce ciel d'azur, ces estoiles luisantes,
Ce soleil d'or, cette grant terre ronde,
Cette ample mer, ces rivières bruyantes,
Ce bel air vague et ces nuës courantes,

Ces beaux oyseaux qui chantent à plaisir,
Ces poissons frais et ces bestes paissantes;
Vien voir le tout à souhait et désir.

Petit enfant! peux-tu le bien venu
Estre sur terre, où tu n'apportes rien,
Mais où tu viens comme un petit ver nu?
Tu n'as de drap, ne linge qui soit tien,
Or ny argent, n'aucun bien terrien;
A père et mère apportes seulement
Peine et soucy, et voilà tout ton bien.
Petit enfant, tu viens bien povrement!

De ton honneur ne veuil plus être chiche,
Petit enfant de grand bien jouissant,
Tu viens au monde aussi grand, aussi riche
Comme le roy, et aussi florissant.
Ton héritage est le ciel splendissant;
Tes serviteurs sont les anges sans vice;
Ton trésorier, c'est le Dieu tout-puissant:
Grâce divine est ta mère nourrice.

137

. . I cannot paint
What then I was.   The sounding cataract
Haunted me like a passion : the tall rock,
The mountain, and the deep and gloomy wood,
Their colours and their forms, were then to me
An appetite ; a feeling and a love,
That had no need of a remoter charm,
By thought supplied, nor any interest
Unborrowed from the eye.—That time is past,
And all its aching joys are now no more,

The Rainbow

And all its dizzy raptures.   Not for this
Faint I, nor mourn nor murmur; other gifts
Have followed; for such loss, I would believe,
Abundant recompense.   For I have learned
To look on nature, not as in the hour
Of thoughtless youth; but hearing oftentimes
The still, sad music of humanity,
Nor harsh nor grating, though of ample power
To chasten and subdue.   And I have felt
A presence that disturbs me with the joy
Of elevated thoughts; a sense sublime
Of something far more deeply interfused,
Whose dwelling is the light of setting suns,
And the round ocean and the living air,
And the blue sky, and in the mind of man:
A motion and a spirit, that impels
All thinking things, all objects of all thought,
And rolls through all things. . .

138

The true harvest of my daily life is somewhat as
intangible and indescribable as the tints of morning or
evening.   It is a little star-dust caught, a segment of
the rainbow which I have clutched.

139

. . Making a couplement of proud compare
With sun and moon, with earth and sea's rich gems,
With April's first-born flowers, and all things rare
That heaven's air in this huge rondure hems. . .

140

DEAR Friend, seest thou not
    that whatever we look on here
Is but an image, shadows only
    of a beauty hid from our eyes?

Dear friend, hear'st thou not
    this jarring tumult of life
Is but a far discordant echo
    of heavn's triumphant harmonies?

Dear friend, know'st thou not
    that the only truth in the world
Is what one heart telleth another
    in speechless greetings of love?

141

THY bosom is endeared with all hearts
Which I by lacking have supposed dead;
And there reigns love and all love's loving parts,
And all those friends which I thought buried.
How many a holy and obsequious tear
Hath dear religious love stol'n from mine eye,
As interest of the dead, which now appear
But things removed that hidden in thee lie!
Thou art the grave where buried love doth live,
Hung with the trophies of my lovers gone,
Who all their parts of me to thee did give:
That due of many now is thine alone:
    Their images I loved I view in thee,
    And thou, all they, hast all the all of me.

142

WHEN in the chronicle of wasted time
I see descriptions of the fairest wights,
And beauty making beautiful old rime
In praise of ladies dead and lovely knights,
Then, in the blazon of sweet beauty's best,
Of hand, of foot, of lip, of eye, of brow,
I see their antique pen would have express'd
Even such a beauty as you master now.
So all their praises are but prophecies
Of this our time, all you prefiguring;
And, for they look'd but with divining eyes,
They had not skill enough your worth to sing:
    For we, which now behold these present days,
    Have eyes to wonder, but lack tongues to praise.

143

NOW at thy soft recalling voice I rise
Where thought is lord o'er Time's complete estate,
Like as a dove from out the gray sedge flies
To tree-tops green where cooes his heavenly mate.
From these clear coverts high and cool I see
How every time with every time is knit,
And each to all is mortised cunningly,
And none is sole or whole, yet all are fit.
Thus, if this Age but as a comma show
'Twixt weightier clauses of large-worded years,
My calmer soul scorns not the mark: I know
This crooked point Time's complex sentence clears.
Yet more I learn while, Friend! I sit by thee:
Who sees all time, sees all eternity.

144

.. With thee conversing I forget all time,
All seasons and thir change, all please alike.
Sweet is the breath of morn, her rising sweet,
With charm of earliest Birds ; pleasant the Sun
When first on this delightful Land he spreads
His orient Beams, on herb, tree, fruit, and flour,
Glistring with dew ; fragrant the fertil earth
After soft showers ; and sweet the coming on
Of grateful Eevning milde, then silent Night
With this her solemn Bird and this fair Moon,
And these the Gemms of Heav'n, her starrie train :
But neither breath of Morn when she ascends
With charm of earliest Birds, nor rising Sun
On this delightful land, nor herb, fruit, floure,
Glistring with dew, nor fragrance after showers,
Nor grateful Evening mild, nor silent Night
With this her solemn Bird, nor walk by Moon,
Or glittering Starr-light without thee is sweet. . .

145

ART thou gone so far,
Beyond the poplar tops, beyond the sunset-bar,
Beyond the purple cloud that swells on high
In the tender fields of sky ? . . .
O come thou again ! . . .
Be heard in the voice that across the river comes
From the distant wood, even when the stilly rain
Is made to cease by light winds : come again,
As out of yon grey glooms,
When the cloud grows luminous and shiftily riven,
Forth comes the moon, the sweet surprise of heaven,
And her footfall light

Drops on the multiplied wave : her face is seen
In evening's pallor green :
And she waxes bright
With the death of the tinted air : yea, brighter grows
In sunset's gradual close.
To earth from heaven comes she,
So come thou to me. . . .

146

FROM you have I been absent in the spring,
When proud-pied April, dress'd in all his trim,
Hath put a spirit of youth in every thing,
That heavy Saturn laugh'd and leap'd with him.
Yet nor the lays of birds nor the sweet smell
Of different flowers in odour and in hue
Could make me any summer's story tell,
Or from their proud lap pluck them where they grew :
Nor did I wonder at the lily's white,
Nor praise the deep vermilion in the rose ;
They were but sweet, but figures of delight,
Drawn after you, you pattern of all those.
    Yet seem'd it winter still, and, you away,
    As with your shadow I with these did play.

147

L'héroïsme, l'extase, la prière, l'amour, l'enthousiasme
tracent l'auréole autour d'un front, parce qu'ils dégagent
l'âme, qui rend transparente son enveloppe et rayonne
ensuite autour d'elle. *La beauté est donc un phénomène de
spiritualisation de la matière* . . . Comme un puissant
courant électrique peut rendre les métaux lumineux et ré-
vèle leur essence par la couleur de leur flamme, de même

la vie intense et la joie suprême embellissent jusqu'à
l'éblouissement un simple mortel.

148

    .. Radiant Sister of the Day,
    Awake! arise! and come away!
    To the wild woods and the plains,
    And the pools where winter rains
    Image all their roof of leaves,
    Where the pine its garland weaves
    Of sapless green and ivy dun
    Round stems that never kiss the sun;
    Where the lawns and pastures be
    And the sandhills of the sea;—
    Where the melting hoar-frost wets
    The daisy-star that never sets,
    And wind-flowers, and violets,
    Which yet join not scent to hue,
    Crown the pale year weak and new;
    When the night is left behind
    In the deep east, dun and blind,
    And the blue noon is over us,
    And the multitudinous
    Billows murmur at our feet,
    Where the earth and ocean meet,
    And all things seem only one
    In the universal sun. . .

149

HOW like a winter hath my absence been
From thee, the pleasure of the fleeting year!

Ideal Love

What freezings have I felt, what dark days seen!
What old December's bareness everywhere!
And yet this time remov'd was summer's time;
The teeming autumn big with rich increase,
Bearing the wanton burthen of the prime,
Like widow'd wombs after their lord's decease:
Yet this abundant issue seem'd to me
But hope of orphans and unfather'd fruit;
For summer and his pleasures wait on thee,
And, thou away, the very birds are mute;
    Or, if they sing, 't is with so dull a cheer
    That leaves look pale, dreading the winter's near.

150

. . The only strength for me is to be found in the sense
of a personal presence everywhere, it scarcely matters
whether it be called human or divine; a presence which
only makes itself felt at first in this and that particular
form and feature. . . Into this presence we come, not
by leaving behind what are usually called earthly things,
or by loving them less, but by living more intensely in
them, and loving more what is really loveable in them;
for it is literally true that this world *is* everything to us,
if only we choose to make it so, if only we 'live in the
present' *because* it is eternity. . .

151

WHEN in disgrace with fortune and men's eyes,
I all alone beweep my outcast state,
And trouble deaf heaven with my bootless cries,
And look upon myself and curse my fate,

Wishing me like to one more rich in hope,
Featured like him, like him with friends possess'd,
Desiring this man's art, and that man's scope,
With what I most enjoy contented least;
   Yet in these thoughts myself almost despising,
Haply I think on thee,—and then my state
(Like to the lark at break of day arising
From sullen earth) sings hymns at heaven's gate;
   For thy sweet love remember'd such wealth brings,
That then I scorn to change my state with kings.

152

. . O Love, they wrong thee much
That say thy sweet is bitter,
When thy rich fruit is such
As nothing can be sweeter.
Fair house of joy and bliss,
Where truest pleasure is,
I do adore thee;
I know thee what thou art,
I serve thee with my heart
And fall before thee.

153

. . Love's very pain is sweet,
But its reward is in the world divine,
Which, if not here, it builds beyond the grave. . .

154

ALL things uncomely and broken,
   all things worn out and old,

Ideal Love

The cry of a child by the roadway,
    the creak of a lumbering cart,
The heavy steps of the ploughman,
    splashing the wintry mould,
Are wronging your image that blossoms
    a rose in the deeps of my heart.

The wrong of unshapely things
    is a wrong too great to be told;
I hunger to build them anew
    and sit on a green knoll apart,
With the earth and the sky and the water
    remade, like a casket of gold
For my dreams of your image that blossoms
    a rose in the deeps of my heart.

155

WHEN to the sessions of sweet silent thought
I summon up remembrance of things past,
I sigh the lack of many a thing I sought,
And with old woes new wail my dear time's waste:
Then can I drown an eye, unused to flow,
For precious friends hid in death's dateless night,
And weep afresh love's long since cancell'd woe,
And moan the expense of many a vanish'd sight:
Then can I grieve at grievances foregone,
And heavily from woe to woe tell o'er
The sad account of fore-bemoaned moan,
Which I new pay as if not paid before.
    But if the while I think on thee, dear friend,
    All losses are restored and sorrows end.

156

MUSIC, when soft voices die,
Vibrates in the memory—
Odours, when sweet violets sicken,
Live within the sense they quicken.
Rose leaves, when the rose is dead,
Are heaped for the belovèd's bed ;
And so thy thoughts, when thou art gone
Love itself shall slumber on.

157

THERE is a soul above the soul of each,
A mightier soul, which yet to each belongs :
There is a sound made of all human speech,
And numerous as the concourse of all songs :
And in that soul lives each, in each that soul,
Though all the ages are its lifetime vast ;
Each soul that dies, in its most sacred whole
Receiveth life that shall for ever last.
    And thus for ever with a wider span
Humanity o'erarches time and death ;
Man can elect the universal man,
And live in life that ends not with his breath,
And gather glory that increaseth still
Till Time his glass with Death's last dust shall fill.

158

A SWIFT dark dream from the outer lands,
From the folk whose talk none understands,

Dark Messages

Along my smooth sleep travelling,
Yet tampering not with my ken's rest,
Pass'd as undisturbingly
As a nightjar o'er the quietude
Of the clear'd middle of a pine-wood
Seemeth to haunt the evening,
And leave the blue air yet more whist.

And yesternight it haunted me;
Again, suddenly, quietly,
Shadowy wings above my clear sleep.
But swift, so swift it might scarce be seen;
Not as with me it had to do,
But eagerly, as though it flew
From mystery to mystery,
And my sleep lay in between;—
Once before, and yesternight.

So twice I have felt its noiseless flight;
Twice has my sleep been the road
The dark message took in journeying
From the one to the other secret reign;—
Out of the dark lying behind,
Into that lying before, man's mind,
My sleep was the only bridge for the thing
Whereon to cross Reality.

But the third time, if it come again,
A stranger, unkindly from the abode
Of Beginnings sent to the place of Dooms,
Shewing me thus so easily
Way thro' the skirts of time to the glooms
That march both sides our bodily place,—
My soul will up and give it chase;
Out of my sleep my soul will slip
And ere that duty vanisheth
I'll o'ertake its moth-wing'd speed.
And be it a bird softlier fledge

Than white owl or brown nightjar,
Be softer the down on the wing's edge
Than combing crests of a snowdrift are
Which the smooth wind holloweth,
Of its shadowing I will be more aware
Than a mirror is of a swoon'd man's breath,
To find the guidance that I need. . .

159

TO see a world in a grain of sand,
    And a heaven in a wild flower;
Hold infinity in the palm of your hand,
    And eternity in an hour.

160

Mortal though I be, yea ephemeral, if but a moment
    I gaze up to the night's starry domain of heaven,
Then no longer on earth I stand; I touch the Creator,
    And my lively spirit drinketh immortality.

161

. . And for magnitude, as Alexander the Great, after
that he was used to great armies, and the great conquests
of the spacious provinces in Asia, when he received
letters out of Greece, of some fights and services there
. . . he said, It seemed to him that he was advertised
of the battles of the frogs and the mice, that the old tales
went of.   So certainly, if a man meditate much upon the
universal frame of nature, the earth with men upon it (the

divineness of souls except) will not seem much other than an ant-hill, whereas some ants carry corn, and some carry their young, and some go empty, and all to and fro a little heap of dust. . .

162

> . . But at my back I always hear
> Time's winged chariot hurrying near ;
> And yonder all before us lie
> Deserts of vast eternity.

163

Le silence éternel de ces espaces infinis m'effraie.

164

Science carries us into zones of speculation, where there is no habitable city for the mind of man.

165

If a man were to ask Nature for what purpose she produces, and if she chose to attend and reply to him, she would say 'You should never have asked ; you ought to have understood in silence, even as I keep silence and am wont to say nothing. What is it then that you should have understood ? This ; that whatever is produced is a sight for me (Nature) to look upon in silence, a vision naturally produced ; and that I, who am myself the child of such a vision, am of my nature a lover of sights; and that which sees in me produces the vision, as a geometrician draws the figure which his mind sees. I do not indeed draw; but, as I look, the forms of the bodily world fall off, as it were, from my gaze, and take substance. . . . I owe my life not to any action, but to the being of thoughts greater than I, contemplating themselves.'

* ψυχη

What then should this mean? It means that what we call Nature, being a Life-soul* and born of a prior soul that lives a more potent life than hers, stands quietly at gaze within herself, looking neither at what is above her nor at what is below, but steadfast in her own place, and in a sort of self-conscience; and that with this intelligence and conscience of herself she sees her own effects as far as it is given her to see, and is content to do nothing more than perfect the vision bright and fair. But the intelligence and sense which we may, if we will, attribute to her, are not like those of other sensible and intelligent beings: compared with them they are as sleeping is to waking: for . . . as she gazes on the vision of herself she rests, and her gaze is unruffled, but dim.

166

* thou,
i. e.
Nature.

. . But if thou * scorn us not, though keeping still
Thy silence to our askings, even herein
Some part at least our quest thou dost fulfil,
Thy gravity charms us from man's world of sin. . .
   O thou art grave; pointest with steadfast aim
At us a warning hand, and in our eyes
Thou lookest with but one look, ever the same.
   The shafted beam that breaks from summer skies,

Man in Nature

The unclouded sun, all things 'twixt sun and shade,
That into that which we call thee arise,
They are thy temple, builded and display'd
For worship fair. . .

167

. . Dieu est présent dans la nature, mais la nature
n'est pas Dieu ; il y a une nature en Dieu, mais ce n'est
pas Dieu même . . .

168

. . Certes, la Nature est inique, sans pudeur, sans
probité et sans foi.   Elle ne veut connaître que la faveur
gratuite et l'aversion folle, et n'entend compenser une
injustice que par une autre.   Le bonheur de quelques-
uns s'expie par le malheur d'un plus grand nombre. —
Inutile d'ergoter contre une force aveugle . . .

Il n'est nullement nécessaire que l'univers soit, mais
il est nécessaire que justice se fasse, et l'athéisme est
tenu d'expliquer l'opiniâtreté absolue de la conscience sur
ce point.   La Nature n'est pas juste ; nous sommes les
produits de la Nature : pourquoi réclamons-nous et pro-
phétisons-nous la justice ? pourquoi l'effet se redresse-
t-il contre sa cause ? le phénomène est singulier.   Cette
revendication provient-elle d'un aveuglement puéril de la
vanité humaine ?   Non, elle est le cri le plus profond de
notre être . . .

Tel est le credo du genre humain.   La Nature sera
vaincue par l'Esprit ; l'éternel aura raison du temps . . .

Poor soul, here for so little, cast among so many
hardships, filled with desires so incommensurate and so
inconsistent, savagely surrounded, savagely descended,
irremediably condemned to prey upon his fellow lives :
who sh^d have blamed him had he been of a piece with
his destiny and a being merely barbarous ? And we
look and behold him instead filled with imperfect virtues :
. . . sitting down, amidst his momentary life, to debate
of Right and Wrong and the attributes of the Deity. . .
. . To touch the heart of his mystery, we find in him
. . . the thought of Duty ; the thought of something
owing to himself, to his neighbour, to his God : an
ideal of decency, to which he would rise if it were
possible ; a limit of shame, below which, if it be possible,
he will not stoop. . . . .   It matters not where we
look, under what climate we observe him, in what stage
of society, in what depth of ignorance, burthened with
what erroneous morality ; by camp-fires in Assiniboia,
the snow powdering his shoulders, the wind plucking
his blanket, as he sits, passing the ceremonial calumet
and uttering his grave opinions like a Roman senator ;
in ships at sea, a man inured to hardships and vile
pleasures ; . . . in the slums of cities, moving among
indifferent millions to mechanical employments, . .
a fool, a thief, the comrade of thieves, even here keeping
the point of honour and the touch of pity, often repaying
the world's scorn with service, often standing firm upon
a scruple, and at a certain cost rejecting riches :—everywhere some virtue cherished or affected, everywhere

some decency of thought and carriage, everywhere the
ensign of man's ineffectual goodness :—ah ! if I could
show you this ! if I could show you these men and
women, all the world over, in every stage of history,
under every abuse of error, under every circumstance of
failure, without hope, without help, without thanks, still
obscurely fighting the lost fight of virtue, still clinging,
in the brothel or on the scaffold, to some rag of honour,
the poor jewel of their souls ! They may seek to escape,
and yet they cannot ; it is not alone their privilege and
glory, but their doom ; they are condemned to some
nobility ; all their lives long, the desire of good is at
their heels, the implacable hunter. . . . .

170

. . I have seen the travail which God hath given to
the sons of men to be exercised therewith. He hath
made everything beautiful in its time ; he hath also set
the world in their heart, and yet so that man cannot find
out the work that God hath wrought from the beginning
even unto the end. . . I know that whatsoever God
doeth shall be for ever ; nothing can be put to it, nor
anything taken from it ; and God hath done it that he
be drad.

171

        . . Every night and every morn
        Some to misery are born ;
        Every morn and every night

Some are born to sweet delight ;
Some are born to sweet delight,
Some are born to endless night.
Joy and woe are woven fine,
A clothing for the soul divine :
Under every grief and pine
Runs a joy with silken twine.
It is right it should be so :
Man was made for joy and woe ;
And when this we rightly know
Safely through the world we go. .

172

. . nous devons chercher la consolation à nos maux,
non pas dans nous-mêmes, non pas dans les hommes, non
pas dans tout ce qui est créé, mais dans Dieu. Et la
raison en est que toutes les créatures ne sont pas la
première cause des accidents que nous appelons maux ;
mais que la providence de Dieu en étant l'unique et
véritable cause, l'arbitre et la souveraine, il est indubitable
qu'il faut recourir directement à la source et remonter
jusqu'à l'origine, pour trouver un solide allégement.
Que si nous suivons ce précepte, et que nous envisagions
cet événement, non pas comme un effet du hasard, non
pas comme une nécessité fatale de la nature, non pas
comme le jouet des éléments et des parties qui composent
l'homme . . mais comme une suite indispensable, in-
évitable, juste, sainte, . . . non pas dans lui-même et
hors de Dieu, mais hors de lui-même et dans l'intime
de la volonté de Dieu, dans la justice de son arrêt, dans
l'ordre de sa providence, qui en est la véritable cause,

sans qui il ne fût pas arrivé, par qui seul il est arrivé et
de la manière dont il est arrivé ; nous adorerons dans un
humble silence . . . nous bénirons la conduite de sa providence ; et unissant notre volonté à celle de Dieu même,
nous voudrons avec lui, en lui et pour lui, la chose qu'il
a voulue en nous et pour nous de toute éternité.

173

I am at one with everything, O Universe,
which is well-fitting in thee.
Nothing to me is early or late which is timely with thee.
All is fruit to me that thy seasons bring.
O Nature, from thee are all things,
in thee are all things,
to thee all things return.
The poet saith, Dear city of Cecrops ;
shall not I say, Dear City of God.

174

Chaque être peut arriver à l'harmonie : quand il y est,
il est dans l'ordre, et il représente la pensée divine aussi
clairement pour le moins qu'une fleur ou qu'un système
solaire. L'harmonie ne cherche rien en dehors d'elle-
même. Elle est ce qu'elle doit être ; elle exprime le
bien, l'ordre, la loi, le vrai ; elle est supérieure au temps
et représente l'éternel . . .

. . J'éprouve avec intensité que l'homme, dans tout ce
qu'il fait ou peut faire de beau, de grand, de bon, n'est

que l'organe et le véhicule de quelque chose ou de quel-
qu'un de plus haut que lui.   Ce sentiment est religion.
L'homme religieux assiste avec un tremblement de joie
sacrée à ces phénomènes dont il est l'intermédiaire sans
en être l'origine, dont il est le théâtre sans en être
l'auteur. . . . . .

175

. . This world is the City of Truth :
its maze of paths enchanteth the heart . . .

176

. . And, day and night, aloof, from the high towers
And terraces, the Earth and Ocean seem
To sleep in one another's arms, and dream
Of waves, flowers, clouds, woods, rocks, and all that we
Read in their smiles, and call reality. . .

177

TO one who has been long in city pent,
   'Tis very sweet to look into the fair
   And open face of heaven,—to breathe a prayer
Full in the smile of the blue firmament.
Who is more happy, when, with heart's content,
   Fatigued he sinks into some pleasant lair
   Of wavy grass, and reads a debonair
And gentle tale of love and languishment ?
Returning home at evening, with an ear
   Catching the notes of Philomel,—an eye

Surrender

Watching the sailing cloudlet's bright career,
   He mourns that day so soon has glided by,
E'en like the passage of an angel's tear
   That falls through the clear ether silently.

AUX branches claires des tilleuls
Meurt un maladif hallali.
Mais des chansons spirituelles
Voltigent partout les groseilles.
Que notre sang rie en nos veines,
Voici s'enchevêtrer les vignes.
Le ciel est joli comme un ange,
Azur et Onde communient.
Je sors ! Si un rayon me blesse,
Je succomberai sur la mousse.

Qu'on patiente et qu'on s'ennuie,
C'est si simple ! — Fi de ces peines.
Je veux que l'été dramatique
Me lie à son char de fortune.
Que par toi beaucoup, ô Nature,
— Ah moins nul et moins seul ! je meure . . .

Je veux bien que les Saisons m'usent.
A toi, Nature ! je me rends,
Et ma faim et toute ma soif ;
Et s'il te plaît, nourris, abreuve.
Rien de rien ne m'illusionne :
C'est rire aux parents qu'au soleil :
Mais moi je ne veux rire à rien
Et libre soit cette infortune.

Sweet Content

HOW sweet is the shepherd's sweet lot!
From the morn to the evening he strays;
He shall follow his sheep all the day,
And his tongue shall be filled with praise.

For he hears the lambs innocent call,
And he hears the ewes tender reply;
He is watchful while they are in peace,
For they know when their shepherd is nigh.

180

ART thou poor, yet hast thou golden slumbers?
   O sweet content!
Art thou rich, yet is thy mind perplex'd?
   O punishment!
Dost thou laugh to see how fools are vex'd
To add to golden numbers golden numbers?
  O sweet content! O sweet, O sweet content!
Work apace, apace, apace, apace;
Honest labour bears a lovely face;
Then hey nonny nonny—hey nonny nonny!

Canst drink the waters of the crispèd spring?
   O sweet content!
Swim'st thou in wealth, yet sink'st in thine own tears?
   O punishment!
Then he that patiently want's burden bears,
No burden bears, but is a king, a king!
  O sweet content! O sweet, O sweet content!
Work apace, apace, apace, apace;
Honest labour bears a lovely face;
Then hey nonny nonny—hey nonny nonny!

181

.. Look thou within : within thee is the fountain of good,
and it will ever spring, if thou wilt ever delve.

182

GO NOT, O go not into the garden of flowers;
Friend, go not thither.
In thy body is the garden of flowers.
Take thy seat on the thousand-petalled Lotus,
And gaze thence on the infinite Beauty.

183

I LOVE to rise in a summer morn,
When the birds sing on every tree ;
The distant huntsman winds his horn,
And the skylark sings with me :
    O what sweet company ! . . .

184

To hear the Lark begin his flight,
And singing startle the dull night,
From his watch-towre in the skies,
Till the dappled dawn doth rise ;
Then to com in spight of sorrow,
And at my window bid good morrow,
Through the Sweet-Briar, or the Vine,
Or the twisted Eglantine.
While the Cock with lively din,
Scatters the rear of darknes thin,
And to the stack, or the Barn dore,
Stoutly struts his Dames before,
Oft list'ning how the Hounds and horn

Chearly rouse the slumbring morn,
From the side of som Hoar Hill,
Through the high wood echoing shrill.
Som time walking not unseen
By Hedge-row Elms, on Hillocks green,
Right against the Eastern gate,
Wher the great Sun begins his state,
Rob'd in flames, and Amber light,
The clouds in thousand Liveries dight.
While the Plowman neer at hand,
Whistles ore the Furrow'd Land,
And the Milkmaid singeth blithe,
And the Mower whets his sithe,
And every Shepherd tells his tale
Under the Hawthorn in the dale.

185

WITH love exceeding a simple love of the things
    That glide in grasses and rubble of woody wreck ;
Or change their perch on a beat of quivering wings
    From branch to branch, only restful to pipe and peck ;
Or, bristled, curl at a touch their snouts in a ball ;
    Or cast their web between bramble and thorny hook ;
The good physician Melampus, loving them all,
    Among them walk'd, as a scholar who reads a book.

For him the woods were a home and gave him the key
    Of knowledge, thirst for their treasures in herbs and flowers.
The secrets held by the creatures nearer than we
    To earth he sought, and the link of their life with ours :
And where alike we are, unlike where, and the vein'd
    Division, vein'd parallel, of a blood that flows
In them, in us, from the source by man unattain'd
    Save marks he well what the mystical woods disclose. . .

LA froidure paresseuse
De l'yver a fait son temps :
Voicy la saison joyeuse
Du délicieux printems.

La terre est d'herbes ornée,
L'herbe de fleuretes l'est :
La feuillure retournée
Fait ombre dans la forest.

De grand matin, la pucelle
Va devancer la chaleur,
Pour de la rose nouvelle
Cueillir l'odorante fleur.

Pour avoir meilleure grace,
Soit qu'elle en pare son sein,
Soit que présent elle en fasse
A son amy, de sa main ;

Qui, de sa main l'ayant uë
Pour souvenance d'amour,
Ne la perdra point de vuë,
La baisant cent fois le jour . . .

La mer est calme et bonasse :
Le ciel est serein et cler :
La nef jusqu'aux Indes passe ;
Un bon vent la fait voler.

Les menageres avetes
Font çà et là un doux fruit,
Voletant par les fleuretes
Pour cueillir ce qui leur duit.

Spring-time

En leur ruche elles amassent
Des meilleures fleurs la fleur,
C'est à fin qu'elles en fassent
Du miel la douce liqueur.

Tout resonne des voix nettes
De toutes races d'oyseaux,
Par les chams des alouetes,
Des cygnes dessus les eaux.

Aux maisons les arondelles,
Les rossignols dans les boys,
En gayes chansons nouvelles
Exercent leurs belles voix . .

Et si le chanter m'agrée,
N'est-ce pas avec raison,
Puis qu'ainsi tout se recrée
Avec la gaye saison?

187

Thousand threads of rain and fine white wreathing of air-mist
    Hide from us earth's greenness, hide the enarching azure.
Yet will a breath of spring homeward convoying attend us,
    And the mellow flutings of passionate Philomel.

188

SPRING, the sweet Spring, is the year's pleasant king;
Then blooms each thing, then maids dance in a ring,
Cold doth not sting, the pretty birds do sing,
Cuckoo, jug, jug, pu we, to witta woo.

The palm and may make country houses gay,
Lambs frisk and play, the shepherds pipe all day,
And we hear aye birds tune this merry lay,
Cuckoo, jug, jug, pu we, to witta woo.

Spring-time

The fields breathe sweet, the daisies kiss our feet,
Young lovers meet, old wives a sunning sit,
In every street these tunes our ears do greet,
Cuckoo, jug, jug, pu we, to witta woo.
      Spring, the sweet Spring!

189

HARK! hark! the lark at heaven's gate sings,
   And Phoebus 'gins arise,
His steeds to water at those springs
   On chaliced flowers that lies;
And winking Mary-buds begin
   To ope their golden eyes;
With every thing that pretty bin:
   My lady sweet, arise;
     Arise, arise.

190

LE Tems a laissié son manteau
De vent, de froidure et de pluye,
Et s'est vestu de broderye
De soleil riant, cler et beau.

Il n'y a beste ne oiseau
Qu'en son jargon ne chante ou crye:
Le Tems a laissié son manteau.

Riviere, fontaine et ruisseau
Portent en livrée jolye
Goutes d'argent d'orfaverie;
Chascun s'abille de nouveau:
Le Tems a laissié son manteau.

F

191

IT was a lover and his lass,
  With a hey, and a ho, and a hey nonino!
That o'er the green corn-field did pass
  In the Spring time, the only pretty ring time,
When birds do sing, hey ding a ding, ding;
    Sweet lovers love the Spring.

Between the acres of the rye,
  With a hey, and a ho, and a hey nonino!
These pretty country folks would lie,
  In Spring time, &c.

This carol they began that hour,
  With a hey, and a ho, and a hey nonino!
How that life was but a flower
  In Spring time, &c.

And therefore take the present time,
  With a hey, and a ho, and a hey nonino!
For love is crownèd with the prime,
  In Spring time, the only pretty ring time;
When birds do sing, hey ding a ding, ding;
    Sweet lovers love the Spring.

192

O HURRY where by water among trees
The delicate-stepping stag and his lady sigh,
When they have but looked upon their images,—
O that none ever loved but you and I!

Or have you heard that sliding silver-shoed
Pale silver-proud queen-woman of the sky,
When the sun looked out of his golden hood,—
O that none ever loved but you and I!

Spring Lovers

O hurry to the ragged wood, for there
I'll hollo all those lovers out and cry—
O my share of the world, O yellow hair!
No one has ever loved but you and I.

193

JEUNES amoureux nouveaulx,
En la nouvelle saison,
Par les rues, sans raison,
Chevauchant faisans les saulx;

Et font saillir des carreaulx
Le feu, comme de charbon:
Jeunes amoureux nouveaulx
En la nouvelle saison.

Je ne sçay se leurs travaulx
Ilz employent bien ou non;
Mais piqués de l'esperon
Sont autant que leurs chevaulx,
Jeunes amoureux nouveaulx.

194

LO where the Virgin veiléd in airy beams,
All-holy Morn, in splendor awakening,
  Heav'ns gate hath unbarrèd, the golden
    Aerial lattices set open.

With music endeth night's prisoning terror,
With flow'ry incense : Haste to salute the sun,
  That for the day's chase, like a huntsman,
    With flashing arms cometh o'er the mountain.

195

WHAN that April with his shourës sote
The droghte of Marche hath percèd to the rote,
And bathèd every veyne in swich licour,
Of which vertu engendred is the flour;
Whan Zephirus eek with his sweetë breeth
Inspirèd hath in every holt and heeth
The tendre croppës, and the yongë sonne
Hath in the Ram his halfë cours y-ronne,
And smalë fowlës maken melodyë
That slepen al the night with open yë,
(So priketh hem Nature in hir corages)
Than longen folk to goon on pilgrimages. . .

196

O MISTRESS mine, where are you roaming?
O, stay and hear! your true love's coming,
   That can sing both high and low:
Trip no further, pretty sweeting;
Journeys end in lovers' meeting,
   Every wise man's son doth know.

What is love? 'tis not hereafter;
Present mirth hath present laughter;
   What's to come is still unsure:
In delay there lies no plenty;
Then come kiss me, sweet-and-twenty,
   Youth's a stuff will not endure.

197

UNDER the greenwood tree,
Who loves to lie with me,
And tune his merry note
Unto the sweet bird's throat,
Come hither, come hither, come hither!
Here shall we see
No enemy
But winter and rough weather.

Who doth ambition shun
And loves to live i' the sun,
Seeking the food he eats
And pleased with what he gets,
Come hither, come hither, come hither!
Here shall he see
No enemy
But winter and rough weather.

198

BLOW, blow, thou winter wind,
Thou art not so unkind
As man's ingratitude;
Thy tooth is not so keen
Because thou art not seen,
Although thy breath be rude.
Heigh ho! sing, heigh ho! unto the green holly:
Most friendship is feigning, most loving mere folly:
Then, heigh ho! the holly!
This life is most jolly.

Freeze, freeze, thou bitter sky,
Thou dost not bite so nigh
    As benefits forgot :
Though thou the waters warp,
Thy sting is not so sharp
    As friend remember'd not.
Heigh ho ! sing, heigh ho ! unto the green holly :
Most friendship is feigning, most loving mere folly :
    Then, heigh ho ! the holly !
    This life is most jolly.

199

CRABBED Age and Youth
Cannot live together :
Youth is full of pleasance,
Age is full of care ;
Youth like summer morn,
Age like winter weather ;
Youth like summer brave,
Age like winter bare.
Youth is full of sport,
Age's breath is short ;
Youth is nimble, Age is lame ;
Youth is hot and bold,
Age is weak and cold ;
Youth is wild, and Age is tame.
Age, I do abhor thee ;
Youth, I do adore thee :
O, my Love, my Love is young !
Age, I do defy thee :
O sweet shepherd, hie thee !
For methinks thou stay'st too long.

The Human Seasons

200

. . To be a Prodigal's Favourite—then, worse truth,
A Miser's Pensioner—behold our lot !
O Man, that from thy fair and shining youth
Age might but take the things Youth needed not !

201

FOUR Seasons fill the measure of the year ;
    There are four seasons in the mind of man :
He has his lusty Spring, when fancy clear
    Takes in all beauty with an easy span :
He has his Summer, when luxuriously
    Spring's honey'd cud of youthful thought he loves
To ruminate, and by such dreaming high
    Is nearest unto Heaven : quiet coves
His soul has in its Autumn, when his wings
    He furleth close ; contented so to look
On mists in idleness—to let fair things
    Pass by unheeded as a threshold brook :—
He has his Winter too of pale misfeature,
Or else he would forego his mortal nature.

202

. . And O, ye Fountains, Meadows, Hills, and Groves,
Forebode not any severing of our loves !
Yet in my heart of hearts I feel your might ;
I only have relinquished one delight
To live beneath your more habitual sway.
I love the Brooks which down their channels fret,
Even more than when I tripped lightly as they ;

The innocent brightness of a new-born Day
        Is lovely yet;
The Clouds that gather round the setting sun
Do take a sober colouring from an eye
That hath kept watch o'er man's mortality;
Another race hath been, and other palms are won.
Thanks to the human heart by which we live,
Thanks to its tenderness, its joys, and fears,
To me the meanest flower that blows can give
Thoughts that do often lie too deep for tears.

203

TWO children in two neighbour villages
Playing mad pranks along the heathy leas;
Two strangers meeting at a festival;
Two lovers whispering by an orchard wall;
Two lives bound fast in one with golden ease;
Two graves grass-green beside a gray church-tower,
Wash'd with still rains and daisy-blossomèd;
Two children in one hamlet born and bred;
So runs the round of life from hour to hour.

204

. . O yonge fresshe folkes, he or she,
In which that love upgroweth with your age,
Repayreth hoom from worldly vanitee,
And of your herte up-casteth the visage
To thilke god that after his image
Yow made, and thinketh al nis but a fayre
This world, that passeth sone as floures fayre;

The Fall of the Year

And loveth him, the which that right for love
Upon a cros, our soules for to beye,
First starf, and roos, and sit in heven above ;
For he nil falsen no wight, dar I seye,
That wol his herte al hoolly on him leye.
And sin he best to love is, and most meke,
What nedeth feyned loves for to seke ? . .

205

YE have been fresh and green,
Ye have been fill'd with flowers,
And ye the walks have been
Where maids have spent their hours.

You have beheld how they
With wicker arks did come
To kiss and bear away
The richer cowslips home.

You've heard them sweetly sing,
And seen them in a round :
Each virgin like a spring,
With honeysuckles crown'd.

But now we see none here
Whose silvery feet did tread
And with dishevell'd hair
Adorn'd this smoother mead.

Like unthrifts, having spent
Your stock and needy grown,
You're left here to lament
Your poor estates, alone.

F 2

206

MY silks and fine array,
　　My smiles and languish'd air,
By love are driven away:
　　And mournful lean Despair
Brings me yew to deck my grave:
Such end true lovers have.

His face is fair as heaven
　　When springing buds unfold;
O why to him was't given
　　Whose heart is wintry cold?
His breast is love's all-worshipp'd **tomb**,
Where all love's pilgrims come.

Bring me an axe and spade,
　　Bring me a winding sheet;
When I my grave have made,
　　Let winds and tempests beat:
Then down I'll lie, as cold as clay.
True love doth pass away.

207

. . I compare human life to a large Mansion of Many
apartments, two of which I can only describe, the doors
of the rest being as yet shut upon me. The first we step
into we call the infant or thoughtless Chamber, in which
we remain as long as we do not think. We remain
there a long while, and notwithstanding the doors of the
second Chamber remain wide open, showing a bright
appearance, we care not to hasten to it; but are at length

imperceptibly impelled by the awakening of the thinking
principle within us. We no sooner get into the second
Chamber, which I shall call the Chamber of Maiden-
Thought, than we become intoxicated with the light and
the atmosphere; we see nothing but pleasant wonders,
and think of delaying there for ever in delight. However, among the effects this breathing is father of, is
that tremendous one of sharpening one's vision into the
heart and nature of Man—of convincing one's nerves
that the world is full of Misery and Heart-break, Pain,
Sickness, and Oppression—whereby this Chamber of
Maiden-Thought becomes gradually darkened, and at
the same time, on all sides of it, many doors are set
open—but all dark—all leading to dark passages—We
see not the balance of good and evil—we are in a mist—
we are now in that state—We feel the 'burden of the
Mystery.'. .

208

TELL me where is Fancy bred,
Or in the heart, or in the head?
How begot, how nourishèd?
        Reply, reply.

It is engender'd in the eyes,
With gazing fed; and Fancy dies
In the cradle where it lies:
Let us all ring Fancy's knell;
I'll begin it,—Ding, dong, bell.
    Ding, dong, bell.

Book III

209

STOP and consider!   Life is but a day;
A fragile dewdrop on its perilous way
From a tree's summit; a poor Indian's sleep
While his boat hastens to the monstrous steep
Of Montmorenci.   Why so sad a moan?
Life is the rose's hope while yet unblown;
The reading of an ever-changing tale;
The light uplifting of a maiden's veil;
A pigeon tumbling in clear summer air;
A laughing school boy, without grief or care,
Riding the springy branches of an elm. . .

210

JE vous envoie un bouquet que ma main
Vient de trier de ces fleurs epanies;
Qui ne les eust à ce vespre cueillies,
Cheutes à terre elles fussent demain.

    Cela vous soit un exemple certain
Que vos beautez, bien qu'elles soient fleuries,
En peu de temps cherront toutes fletries,
Et, comme fleurs, periront tout soudain.

    Le temps s'en va, le temps s'en va, ma dame,
Las! le temps non, mais nous, nous en allons,
Et tost serons estendus sous la lame:

    Et des amours desquelles nous parlons,
Quand serons morts, ne sera plus nouvelle:
Pour ce, aymez-moy, ce pendant qu'estes belle.

211

THE feathers of the willow
Are half of them grown yellow
  Above the swelling stream;
And ragged are the bushes,
And rusty now the rushes,
  And wild the clouded gleam.

The thistle now is older,
His stalk begins to moulder,
  His head is white as snow;
The branches all are barer,
The linnet's song is rarer,
  The robin pipeth now.

212

WHEN I do count the clock that tells the time,
And see the brave day sunk in hideous night;
When I behold the violet past prime,
And sable curls all silver'd o'er with white;
When lofty trees I see barren of leaves
Which erst from heat did canopy the herd,
And summer's green, all girded up in sheaves,
Borne on the bier with white and bristly beard;
Then of thy beauty do I question make,
That thou among the wastes of time must go,
Since sweets and beauties do themselves forsake
And die as fast as they see others grow;
  And nothing 'gainst Time's scythe can make defence
  Save breed, to brave him when he takes thee hence.

213

A SPIRIT haunts the year's last hours
Dwelling amid these yellowing bowers :
    To himself he talks ;
For at eventide listening earnestly,
At his work you may hear him sob and sigh
    In the walks :
Earthward he boweth the heavy stalks
    Of the mouldering flowers :
  Heavily hangs the broad sunflower
    Over its grave i' the earth so chilly ;
  Heavily hangs the hollyhock,
    Heavily hangs the tiger lily. . .

214

I MET a traveller from an antique land
Who said : Two vast and trunkless legs of stone
Stand in the desert.   Near them, on the sand,
Half sunk, a shattered visage lies, whose frown,
And wrinkled lip, and sneer of cold command,
Tell that its sculptor well those passions read
Which yet survive, stamped on these lifeless things,
The hand that mocked them and the heart that fed :
And on the pedestal these words appear :
' My name is Ozymandias, king of kings :
Look on my works, ye Mighty, and despair ! '
Nothing beside remains.   Round the decay
Of that colossal wreck, boundless and bare
The lone and level sands stretch far away.

215

THESE grey stones have rung with mirth and lordly carousel:
  Here proud kings mingled Poetry and ruddy wine.
All hath pass'd long ago; nought but this ruin abideth,
  Sadly in eyeless trance gazing upon the river.
Wou'dst thou know who here visiteth, dwelleth and singeth also,
  Ask the swallows flying from sunny-wall'd Italy.

216

THE curfew tolls the knell of parting day,
The lowing herd wind slowly o'er the lea,
The ploughman homeward plods his weary way,
And leaves the world to darkness and to me.

Now fades the glimmering landscape on the sight,
And all the air a solemn stillness holds,
Save where the beetle wheels his droning flight,
And drowsy tinklings lull the distant folds:

Save that from yonder ivy-mantled tower
The moping owl does to the moon complain
Of such as wand'ring near her secret bower
Molest her ancient solitary reign.

Beneath those rugged elms, that yew-tree's shade,
Where heaves the turf in many a mould'ring heap,
Each in his narrow cell for ever laid,
The rude Forefathers of the hamlet sleep.

The breezy call of incense-breathing Morn,
The swallow twittering from the straw-built shed,
The cock's shrill clarion, or the echoing horn,
No more shall rouse them from their lowly bed.

The Country Churchyard

For them no more the blazing hearth shall burn,
Or busy housewife ply her evening care:
No children run to lisp their sire's return,
Or climb his knees the envied kiss to share.

Oft did the harvest to their sickle yield,
Their furrow oft the stubborn glebe has broke;
How jocund did they drive their team afield!
How bow'd the woods beneath their sturdy stroke!

Let not Ambition mock their useful toil,
Their homely joys, and destiny obscure;
Nor Grandeur hear with a disdainful smile
The short and simple annals of the poor.

The boast of heraldry, the pomp of power,
And all that beauty, all that wealth e'er gave,
Awaits alike th' inevitable hour.
The paths of glory lead but to the grave. . .

Perhaps in this neglected spot is laid
Some heart once pregnant with celestial fire;
Hands, that the rod of empire might have sway'd,
Or waked to ecstasy the living lyre.

But Knowledge to their eyes her ample page
Rich with the spoils of time did ne'er unroll;
Chill Penury repress'd their noble rage,
And froze the genial current of the soul.

Full many a gem of purest ray serene,
The dark unfathom'd caves of ocean bear:
Full many a flower is born to blush unseen,
And waste its sweetness on the desert air.

Some village=Hampden, that with dauntless breast
The little tyrant of his fields withstood;
Some mute inglorious Milton here may rest,
Some Cromwell guiltless of his country's blood.

Elegy

Th' applause of list'ning senates to command,
The threats of pain and ruin to despise,
To scatter plenty o'er a smiling land,
And read their history in a nation's eyes,

Their lot forbad : nor circumscribed alone
Their growing virtues, but their crimes confin'd;
Forbad to wade through slaughter to a throne,
And shut the gates of mercy on mankind. . .

Far from the madding crowd's ignoble strife,
Their sober wishes never learn'd to stray;
Along the cool sequester'd vale of life
They kept the noiseless tenour of their way. . .

Their name, their years, spelt by th' unletter'd Muse,
The place of fame and elegy supply :
And many a holy text around she strews,
That teach the rustic moralist to die. . .

For thee, who mindful of th' unhonour'd Dead,
Dost in these lines their artless tale relate;
If chance, by lonely contemplation led,
Some kindred spirit shall inquire thy fate,

Haply some hoary-headed swain may say,
' Oft have we seen him at the peep of dawn
Brushing with hasty steps the dews away
To meet the sun upon the upland lawn.

There at the foot of yonder nodding beech
That wreathes its old fantastic roots so high,
His listless length at noontide would he stretch,
And pore upon the brook that babbles by.

Hard by yon wood, now smiling as in scorn,
Mutt'ring his wayward fancies he would rove,
Now drooping, woeful wan, like one forlorn,
Or crazed with care, or cross'd in hopeless love.

Mortality

One morn I miss'd him on the custom'd hill,
Along the heath, and near his favourite tree ;
Another came ; nor yet beside the rill,
Nor up the lawn, nor at the wood was he ;

The next, with dirges due in sad array
Slow through the church-way path we saw him borne,—
Approach and read (for thou canst read) the lay,
Graved on the stone beneath yon aged thorn.

There scatter'd oft, the earliest of the year,
By hands unseen are show'rs of violets found ;
The redbreast loves to build and warble there,
And little footsteps lightly print the ground.'

The Epitaph

Here rests his head upon the lap of Earth
A Youth, to Fortune and to Fame unknown ;
Fair Science frown'd not on his humble birth,
And Melancholy mark'd him for her own.

Large was his bounty, and his soul sincere,
Heav'n did a recompense as largely send :
He gave to Misery all he had, a tear,
He gain'd from Heaven ('twas all he wish'd) a friend.

No farther seek his merits to disclose,
Or draw his frailties from their dread abode,
(There they alike in trembling hope repose,)
The bosom of his Father and his God.

CETTE verrière a vu dames et hauts barons
Étincelants d'azur, d'or, de flamme et de nacre,
Incliner, sous la dextre auguste qui consacre,
L'orgueil de leurs cimiers et de leurs chaperons ;

Mortality

Lorsqu'ils allaient, au bruit du cor ou des clairons,
Ayant le glaive au poing, le gerfaut ou le sacre,
Vers la plaine ou le bois, Byzance ou Saint-Jean d'Acre,
Partir pour la croisade ou le vol des hérons.

Aujourd'hui, les seigneurs auprès des châtelaines,
Avec le lévrier à leurs longues poulaines,
S'allongent aux carreaux de marbre blanc et noir;

Ils gisent là sans voix, sans geste et sans ouïe,
Et de leurs yeux de pierre ils regardent sans voir
La rose du vitrail toujours épanouie.

218

THE glories of our blood and state
    Are shadows, not substantial things;
There is no armour against fate;
    Death lays his icy hand on kings:
        Sceptre and crown
        Must tumble down,
And in the dust be equal made
With the poor crooked scythe and spade.

Some men with swords may reap the field,
    And plant fresh laurels where they kill;
But their strong nerves at last must yield;
    They tame but one another still:
        Early or late
        They stoop to fate,
And must give up their murmuring breath
When they, pale captives, creep to death.

The garlands wither on your brow;
    Then boast no more your mighty deeds:
Upon Death's purple altar now
    See where the victor-victim bleeds!

Mortality

Your heads must come
To the cold tomb:
Only the actions of the just
Smell sweet, and blossom in their dust.

219

MAN with his burning soul
Has but an hour of breath
To build a ship of truth
In which his soul may sail—
Sail on the sea of death,
For death takes toll
Of beauty, courage, youth,
Of all but truth . . .

220

QUAND vous serez bien vieille, au soir, à la chandelle,
Assise auprès du feu, devisant, et filant,
Direz, chantant mes vers, en vous esmerveillant :
' Ronsard me celebroit du temps que j'estois belle.'

Lors, vous n'aurez servante oyant cette nouvelle,
Desjà sous le labeur à demy sommeillant,
Qui, au bruit de mon nom, ne s'aille reveillant,
Benissant vostre nom de louange immortelle.

Je seray sous la terre, et, fantosme sans os,
Par les ombres myrteux je prendray mon repos ;
Vous serez au foyer une vieille accroupie,

Regrettant mon amour et vostre fier desdain.
Vivez, si m'en croyez, n'attendez à demain ;
Cueillez dès aujourd'huy les roses de la vie.

221

HIS icicle upon the frozen bough
Stern Winter hangs, where hung the leaf ere now:
In soft diffusion doth the morning creep
Along the clouded heaven from mound to mound,
So faint and wan, the woods are still asleep,
And pallid shadows scarcely mark the ground. . .

222

NO longer mourn for me when I am dead
Than you shall hear the surly sullen bell
Give warning to the world that I am fled
From this vile world, with vilest worms to dwell:
Nay, if you read this line, remember not
The hand that writ it; for I love you so
That I in your sweet thoughts would be forgot,
If thinking on me then should make you woe.
O, if, I say, you look upon this verse
When I perhaps compounded am with clay,
Do not so much as my poor name rehearse,
But let your love even with my life decay;
   Lest the wise world should look into your moan
   And mock you with me after I am gone.

223

FULL fathom five thy father lies:
   Of his bones are coral made;
Those are pearls that were his eyes:
   Nothing of him that doth fade,
But doth suffer a sea-change
Into something rich and strange.

Sea-nymphs hourly ring his knell:
Hark! now I hear them,—ding-dong, bell.

224

. . His helmet now shall make a hive for bees;
　And, lovers' sonnets turn'd to holy psalms,
A man-at-arms must now serve on his knees,
　And feed on prayërs, which are Age his alms;
But though from court to cottage he depart,
His Saint is sure of his unspotted heart. . .

225

THAT time of year thou mayst in me behold
When yellow leaves, or none, or few, do hang
Upon those boughs which shake against the cold,
Bare ruin'd choirs where late the sweet birds sang.
In me thou see'st the twilight of such day
As after sunset fadeth in the west;
Which by and by black night doth take away,
Death's second self, that seals up all in rest.
In me thou see'st the glowing of such fire
That on the ashes of his youth doth lie,
As the death-bed whereon it must expire,
Consumed with that which it was nourish'd by.
　This thou perceiv'st, which makes thy love more strong,
　To love that well which thou must leave ere long.

226

FALL, leaves, fall; die, flowers, away;
Lengthen night and shorten day:
Every leaf speaks bliss to me,
Fluttering from the autumn tree:

I shall smile when wreaths of snow
Blossom where the rose should grow:
I shall sing when night's decay
Ushers in the drearier day.

Ballade des
dames du
temps
jadis.

DICTES-MOY où, n'en quel pays,
Est Flora, la belle Romaine,
Archipiada, ne Thaïs,
Qui fut sa cousine germaine;
Echo, parlant quant bruyt on maine
Dessus rivière ou sus estan,
Qui beauté eut trop plus qu'humaine?—
Mais où sont les neiges d'antan!

Où est la très sage Heloïs,
Pour qui fut chastré, et puis moyne
Pierre Esbaillart à Sainct-Denys
(Pour son amour eut cest essoyne)?
Semblablement, où est la royne
Qui commanda que Buridan
Fut jetté en ung sac en Seine?—
Mais où sont les neiges d'antan !

La royne Blanche comme ung lys,
Qui chantoit à voix de sereine;
Berthe au grand pied, Bietris, Allys;
Harembourges, qui tint le Mayne,
Et Jeanne, la bonne Lorraine,
Qu'Anglois bruslèrent à Rouen;
Où sont-ils, Vierge souveraine?—
Mais où sont les neiges d'antan !

Mortality

Envoi.

Prince, n'enquerez, de sepmaine,
Où elles sont, ne de cest an,
Que ce refrain ne vous remaine :
Mais où sont les neiges d'antan !

228

HOW should I your true love know
    From another one ?
By his cockle hat and staff,
    And his sandal shoon.

He is dead and gone, lady,
    He is dead and gone ;
At his head a grass-green turf,
    At his heels a stone.

White his shroud as the mountain snow,
    Larded all with sweet flowers,
Which bewept to the grave did go
    With true-love showers.

229

WHY fadest thou in death,
        Oh yellow waning tree ?
Gentle is autumn's breath,
        And green the oak by thee.

But with each wind that sighs
        The leaves from thee take wing ;
And bare thy branches rise
        Above their drifted ring.

230

SIT beneath the poplars here, traveller, when thou art weary, and drawing nigh drink of our spring; and even far away remember the fountain that Simus sets by the side of Gillus his dead child.

231

THEY die—the dead return not—Misery
   Sits near an open grave and calls them over,
A Youth with hoary hair and haggard eye—
   They are the names of kindred, friend and lover,
Which he so feebly calls—they all are gone—
Fond wretch, all dead! Those vacant names alone,
      This most familiar scene, my pain—
      These tombs—alone remain.

Misery, my sweetest friend—oh, weep no more!
   Thou wilt not be consoled—I wonder not!
For I have seen thee from thy dwelling's door
   Watch the calm sunset with them, and this spot
Was even as bright and calm, but transitory,
And now thy hopes are gone, thy hair is hoary;
      This most familiar scene, my pain—
      These tombs—alone remain.

232

. . Grey recumbent tombs of the dead in desert places,
   Standing stones on the vacant wine-red moor,
Hills of sheep, and the howes of the silent vanished races,
   And winds, austere and pure:

Death

Be it granted me to behold you again in dying,
    Hills of home! and to hear again the call;
Hear about the graves of the martyrs the peewees crying,
    And hear no more at all.

233

  . . Far from her moon had Phœbe wandered;
And many else were free to roam abroad,
But for the main, here found they covert drear:
Scarce images of life, one here, one there,
Lay vast and edgeways; like a dismal cirque
Of Druid stones, upon a forlorn moor,
When the chill rain begins at shut of eve,
In dull November, and their chancel vault,
The heaven itself, is blinded throughout night. . .

234

SALISBURY
      Pardon me, madam,
I may not go without you to the kings.
      CONSTANCE
Thou may'st, thou shalt: I will not go with thee.
I will instruct my sorrows to be proud;
For grief is proud, and makes his owner stoop.
To me and to the state of my great grief
Let kings assemble; for my grief's so great
That no supporter but the huge firm earth
Can hold it up: here I and sorrows sit;
Here is my throne, bid kings come bow to it.
        (*She seats herself on the ground*) . . .

Grief

. . And, father cardinal, I have heard you say
That we shall see and know our friends in heaven:
If that be true, I shall see my boy again;
For since the birth of Cain, the first male child,
To him that did but yesterday suspire,
There was not such a gracious creature born.
But now will canker sorrow eat my bud,
And chase the native beauty from his cheek,
And he will look as hollow as a ghost,
As dim and meagre as an ague's fit,
And so he'll die; and, rising so again,
When I shall meet him in the court of heaven
I shall not know him: therefore never, never
Must I behold my pretty Arthur more.

PANDULPH

You hold too heinous a respect of grief.

CONSTANCE

He talks to me that never had a son.

K. PHILIP

You are as fond of grief as of your child.

CONSTANCE

Grief fills the room up of my absent child,
Lies in his bed, walks up and down with me,
Puts on his pretty looks, repeats his words,
Remembers me of all his gracious parts,
Stuffs out his vacant garments with his form:
Then, have I reason to be fond of grief?
Fare you well: had you such a loss as I,
I could give better comfort than you do.
I will not keep this form upon my head
When there is such disorder in my wit.

                    [*Tearing off her head-dress.*
O Lord! my boy, my Arthur, my fair son!
My life, my joy, my food, my all the world!
My widow-comfort, and my sorrows cure!   [*Exit.*

Grief

K. PHILIP

I fear some outrage, and I'll follow her.   [*Exit.*

LEWIS

There's nothing in this world can make me joy.
Life is as tedious as a twice-told tale
Vexing the dull ear of a drowsy man;
And bitter shame hath spoiled the sweet world's taste
That it yields nought but shame and bitterness. . .

235

For never touch of gladness stirs my heart,
But timorously beginning to rejoice
Like a blind Arab, that from sleep doth **start**
In lonesome tent, I listen for thy voice.
Beloved! 'tis not thine; thou art not there!
Then melts the bubble into idle air,
And wishing without hope I restlessly despair.

236

. . How frequently does his form visit my mind's eye in
slumber and in wakefulness, in the light of day, and in
the night watches; but last night I saw him in his beauty
and his strength; he was about to speak, and my ear was
on the stretch, when at once I awoke, and there was
I alone, and the night storm was howling amidst the
branches of the pines which surround my lonely dwelling:
'Listen to the moaning of the pine, at whose root thy
hut is fastened,'—a saying that, of wild Finland, in
which there is wisdom; I listened, and thought of life
and death.

237

Ah! he is gone, and yet will not depart!—
Is with me still, yet I from him exiled!
For still there lives within my secret heart
The magic image of the magic Child,
Which there he made up-grow by his strong art,
As in that crystal orb—wise Merlin's feat,—
The wondrous 'World of Glass', wherein inisled
All long'd for things their beings did repeat;—
And there he left it, like a Sylph beguiled,
To live and yearn and languish incomplete!

238

A WIDOW bird sate mourning for her love
   Upon a wintry bough;
The frozen wind crept on above,
   The freezing stream below.

There was no leaf upon the forest bare,
   No flower upon the ground,
And little motion in the air
   Except the mill-wheel's sound.

239

YE hasten to the grave! What seek ye there,
Ye restless thoughts and busy purposes
Of the idle brain, which the world's livery wear?
Oh thou quick heart, which pantest to possess
All that pale Expectation feigneth fair!

Mortality

Thou vainly curious mind which wouldest guess
Whence thou didst come, and whither thou must go,
And all that never yet was known wouldst know—
Oh, whither hasten ye, that thus ye press,
With such swift feet life's green and pleasant path,
Seeking, alike from happiness and woe,
A refuge in the cavern of gray death?
O heart, and mind, and thoughts! what thing do you
Hope to inherit in the grave below?

240

LIKE as the waves make towards the pebbled shore,
So do our minutes hasten to their end;
Each changing place with that which goes before,
In sequent toil all forwards do contend.
Nativity, once in the main of light,
Crawls to maturity, wherewith being crown'd,
Crooked eclipses 'gainst his glory fight,
And Time that gave doth now his gift confound.
Time doth transfix the flourish set on youth
And delves the parallels in beauty's brow,
Feeds on the rarities of nature's truth;
And nothing stands but for his scythe to mow:
    And yet to times in hope my verse shall stand,
    Praising thy worth, despite his cruel hand.

241

SINCE all that beat about in Nature's range,
Or veer or vanish; why shouldst thou remain
The only constant in a world of change,
O yearning thought! that livest but in the brain?
Call to the hours, that in the distance play,

Phantoms

The faery people of the future day—
Fond thought! not one of all that shining swarm
Will breathe on thee with life-enkindling breath,
Till when, like strangers sheltering from a storm,
Hope and Despair meet in the porch of Death! . . .

And art thou nothing?   Such thou art, as when
The woodman winding westward up the glen
At wintry dawn, where o'er the sheep-track's maze
The viewless snow-mist weaves a glistening haze,
Sees full before him, gliding without tread,
An image with a glory round its head;
The enamour'd rustic worships its fair hues,
Nor knows he makes the shadow he pursues!

242

                . . Thou art slow, my son;
The Anarchs of the world of darkness keep
A throne for thee, round which thine empire lies
Boundless and mute; and for thy subjects thou,
Like us, shalt rule the ghosts of murdered life,
The phantoms of the powers who rule thee now—
Mutinous passions, and conflicting fears,
And hopes that sate themselves on dust, and die!—
Stript of their mortal strength, as thou of thine. . .

243

AT dead of unseen night ghosts of the departed assembling
    Flit to the graves, where each in body had burial.
Ah, then revisiting my sad heart, their desolate tomb,
    Troop the desires and loves vainly buried long-ago.

244

METHOUGHT I saw my late espoused Saint
    Brought to me like *Alcestis* from the grave,
    Whom *Joves* great Son to her glad Husband gave,
    Rescu'd from death by force though pale and faint.
Mine as whom washt from spot of child-bed taint,
    Purification in the old Law did save,
    And such, as yet once more I trust to have
    Full sight of her in Heaven without restraint,
Came vested all in white, pure as her mind:
    Her face was vail'd, yet to my fancied sight,
    Love, sweetness, goodness, in her person shin'd
So clear, as in no face with more delight.
    But O as to embrace me she enclin'd
    I wak'd, she fled, and day brought back my night

245

        IF grief for grief can touch thee,
            If answering woe for woe,
        If any ruth can melt thee,
            Come to me now!

        I cannot be more lonely,
            More drear I cannot be:
        My worn heart throbs so wildly
            'Twill break for thee.

        And when the world despises,
            When heaven repels my prayer,
        Will not mine angel comfort?
            Mine idol hear?

G

Bereavement

Yes, by the tears I've poured,
   By all my hours of pain,
O I shall surely win thee,
   Beloved, again.

246

AWAY! the moor is dark beneath the moon,
Rapid clouds have drunk the last pale beam of even:
Away! the gathering winds will call the darkness soon,
And profoundest midnight shroud the serene lights of heaven.
Pause not! The time is past! Every voice cries, Away!
Tempt not with one last tear thy friend's ungentle mood:
Thy lover's eye, so glazed and cold, dares not entreat thy stay:
Duty and dereliction guide thee back to solitude.

Away, away! to thy sad and silent home;
Pour bitter tears on its desolated hearth;
Watch the dim shades as like ghosts they go and come,
And complicate strange webs of melancholy mirth.
The leaves of wasted autumn woods shall float around thine head:
The blooms of dewy spring shall gleam beneath thy feet:
But thy soul or this world must fade in the frost that binds the dead,
Ere midnight's frown & morning's smile, ere thou & peace may meet.

The cloud shadows of midnight possess their own repose,
For the weary winds are silent, or the moon is in the deep:
Some respite to its turbulence unresting ocean knows;
Whatever moves, or toils, or grieves, hath its appointed sleep.
Thou in the grave shalt rest—yet till the phantoms flee

Which that house & heath & garden made dear to thee erewhile,
Thy remembrance, & repentance, & deep musings are not free
From the music of two voices & the light of one sweet smile.

247

      THE world is young to-day:
        Forget the gods are old,
        Forget the years of gold
      When all the months were May.

      A little flower of Love
        Is ours, without a root,
        Without the end of fruit,
      Yet—take the scent thereof.

      There may be hope above,
        There may be rest beneath;
        We see them not, but Death
      Is palpable—and Love.

248

      O WORLD! O life! O time!
      On whose last steps I climb,
Trembling at that where I had stood before;
  When will return the glory of your prime?
      No more—Oh, never more!

      Out of the day and night
      A joy has taken flight;
Fresh spring and summer and winter hoar
  Move my faint heart with grief, but with delight
      No more—Oh, never more!

249

Qui rend justice à la gaieté ? les âmes tristes. Celles-ci savent que la gaieté est un élan et une vigueur, que d'ordinaire elle est de la bonté dissimulée, et que, fût-elle pure affaire de tempérament et d'humeur, elle est un bienfait.

La grandeur de l'homme est grande en ce qu'il se connaît misérable. Un arbre ne se connaît pas misérable. C'est donc être misérable que de se connaître misérable ; mais c'est être grand que de connaître qu'on est misérable. Toutes ces misères-là même prouvent sa grandeur. Ce sont misères de grand seigneur, misères d'un roi dépossédé.

250

RARELY, rarely, comest thou,
   Spirit of Delight !
Wherefore hast thou left me now
   Many a day and night ?
Many a weary night and day
'Tis since thou art fled away.

How shall ever one like me
   Win thee back again ?
With the joyous and the free
   Thou wilt scoff at pain.
Spirit false ! thou hast forgot
All but those who need thee not.

As a lizard with the shade
   Of a trembling leaf,
Thou with sorrow art dismayed ;
   Even the sighs of grief
Reproach thee, that thou art not near,
And reproach thou wilt not hear.

Melancholy

Let me set my mournful ditty
    To a merry measure;
Thou wilt never come for pity,
    Thou wilt come for pleasure.
Pity then will cut away
Those cruel wings, and thou wilt stay.

I love all that thou lovest,
    Spirit of Delight!
The fresh Earth in new leaves drest,
    And the starry night;
Autumn evening, and the morn
When the golden mists are born. . .

I love Love—though he has wings,
    And like light can flee,
But above all other things,
    Spirit, I love thee—
Thou art love and life!   Oh, come,
Make once more my heart thy home.

251

. . She dwells with Beauty—Beauty that must die;
    And Joy, whose hand is ever at his lips
Bidding adieu; and aching Pleasure nigh,
    Turning to poison while the bee-mouth sips:
Ay, in the very temple of Delight
    Veil'd Melancholy has her sovran shrine,
Tho' seen of none save him whose strenuous tongue
    Can burst Joy's grape against his palate fine;
His soul shall taste the sadness of her might
    And be among her cloudy trophies hung.

252

BEHOLD her, single in the field,
Yon solitary Highland Lass!
Reaping and singing by herself;
Stop here, or gently pass!
Alone she cuts and binds the grain,
And sings a melancholy strain;
O listen! for the Vale profound
Is overflowing with the sound.

No Nightingale did ever chaunt
More welcome notes to weary bands
Of travellers in some shady haunt,
Among Arabian sands:
A voice so thrilling ne'er was heard
In spring-time from the Cuckoo-bird,
Breaking the silence of the seas
Among the farthest Hebrides.

Will no one tell me what she sings?—
Perhaps the plaintive numbers flow
For old, unhappy, far-off things,
And battles long ago:
Or is it some more humble lay,
Familiar matter of to-day?
Some natural sorrow, loss, or pain,
That has been, and may be again? . . .

253

. . Perhaps the self-same song that found a path
Through the sad heart of Ruth, when, sick for home,
She stood in tears amid the alien corn;
The same that oft-times hath

Charm'd magic casements, opening on the foam
Of perilous seas, in faery lands forlorn. . .

254

. . [The] silver sand
Broader and broader yet doth gleam
Spreading into ocean's strand,
Over whose white verge the storm
With his wide-swaying loomy arm
Weaves his mournful tapestry
Slowly let down from sky to sea. . .

255

CE sont de grandes lignes paisibles qui se confondent
tantôt avec le ciel, tantôt avec la terre.
Elles n'apportent plus à mon cœur solitaire
cette paix d'autrefois que je croyais profonde.

Ainsi va s'en aller le charme des vallées.
Ainsi va s'en aller le charme de mon cœur.
Qu'aurai-je regretté ?   Peut-être la douleur,
peut-être la douleur qui s'en est en allée.

Les coups d'un bûcheron sont sourds dans le coteau.
L'aulne mâle fleurit.   Le printemps va venir.
Mais, cette fois, mon Dieu, ni rêve ni soupir
ne passent dans le vent sur cette flaque d'eau.

256

MY Love lies in the gates of foam,
The last dear wreck of shore :
The naked sea-marsh binds her home,
The sand her chamber door.

Resignation

The grey gull flaps the written stones,
  The ox-birds chase the tide:
And near that narrow field of bones
  Great ships at anchor ride. . .

In peace the swallow's eggs are laid
  Along the belfry walls;
The tempest does not reach her shade,
  The rain her silent halls. . .

Strong and alone, my Dove, with thee;
  And tho' mine eyes be wet,
There's nothing in the world to me
  So dear as my regret. . .

Sleep and forget all things but one,
  Heard in each wave of sea,—
How lonely all the years will run
  Until I rest by thee.

257

COME, be happy!—sit near me,
Shadow-vested Misery! . .
All the wide world beside us
Show like multitudinous
Puppets passing from a scene;
What but mockery can they mean,
Where I am—where thou hast been?

258

. . Je ne demande pas d'être exempt des douleurs, car
c'est la récompense des saints; mais je demande de n'être
pas abandonné aux douleurs de la nature sans les consolations de votre esprit . . .

Consolation

Je ne demande pas d'avoir une plénitude de consolation sans aucune souffrance ; car c'est la vie de la gloire.

Je ne demande pas aussi d'être dans une plénitude de maux sans consolation . . . Mais je demande, Seigneur, de ressentir tout ensemble et les douleurs de la nature pour mes péchés, et les consolations de votre esprit par votre grâce . . .

Que je ne sente pas des douleurs sans consolation ; mais que je sente des douleurs et de la consolation tout ensemble, pour arriver enfin à ne sentir plus que vos consolations sans aucune douleur . . .

259

THE sun descending in the West,
The evening star doth shine ;
The birds are silent in their nest,
And I must seek for mine.
 The moon, like a flower
 In heaven's high bower,
 With silent delight
Sits and smiles on the night.

Farewell, green fields and happy groves,
Where flocks have took delight.
Where Lambs have nibbled, silent moves
The feet of angels bright ;
 Unseen they pour blessing,
 And joy without ceasing,
 On each bud and blossom,
 And each sleeping bosom. . .

And there the lion's ruddy eyes
Shall flow with tears of gold,
And pitying the tender cries,

Consolation

And walking round the fold,
Saying: Wrath by His meekness,
And, by His health, sickness,
Is driven away
From our immortal day. . .

260

. . I will complain, yet praise;
I will bewail, approve:
And all my sowre-sweet dayes
I will lament and love.

261

MANY are the sayings of the wise,
In ancient and in modern books enroll'd,
Extolling patience as the truest fortitude,
And to the bearing well of all calamities,
All chances incident to man's frail life,—
Consolatories writ
With studied argument, and much persuasion sought,
Lenient of grief and anxious thought;
But with th' afflicted in his pangs their sound
Little prevails, or rather seems a tune
Harsh, and of dissonant mood from his complaint,
Unless he feel within
Some source of consolation from above,
Secret refreshings that repair his strength
And fainting spirits uphold.
    God of our fathers, what is Man!
That thou towards him with hand so various—
Or might I say contrarious—
Temper'st thy providence through his short course. . .

262

.. The Virtue of *Prosperity* is Temperance; the Virtue
of *Adversity* is Fortitude, which in Morals is the more
heroical Virtue. ..

Prosperity is not without many fears and distastes;
and *Adversity* is not without comforts and hopes. We
see in Needle-works and Embroideries, it is more pleasing
to have a lively work upon a sad and solemn ground, than
to have a dark and melancholy work upon a lightsome
ground. Judge therefore of the pleasure of the Heart,
by the pleasure of the Eye. Certainly Virtue is like
precious Odours, most fragrant when they are incensed
or crushed: For *Prosperity* doth best discover Vice,
but *Adversity* doth best discover Virtue.

263

DEEP in the shady sadness of a vale
Far sunken from the healthy breath of morn,
Far from the fiery noon, and eve's one star,
Sat grey-hair'd Saturn, quiet as a stone,
Still as the silence round about his lair;
Forest on forest hung about his head
Like cloud on cloud. No stir of air was there,
Not so much life as on a summer's day
Robs not one light seed from the feather'd grass,
But where the dead leaf fell, there did it rest.
A stream went voiceless by, still deaden'd more
By reason of his fallen divinity
Spreading a shade: the Naiad 'mid her reeds
Press'd her cold finger closer to her lips.

It seem'd no force could wake him from his place;
But there came one, who with a kindred hand
Touch'd his wide shoulders, after bending low
With reverence, though to one who knew it not.
She was a Goddess of the infant world;
By her in stature the tall Amazon
Had stood a pigmy's height: she would have ta'en
Achilles by the hair and bent his neck;
Or with a finger stay'd Ixion's wheel.
Her face was large as that of Memphian sphinx,
Pedestal'd haply in a palace-court,
When sages look'd to Egypt for their lore.
But oh! how unlike marble was that face:
How beautiful, if sorrow had not made
Sorrow more beautiful than Beauty's self.
There was a listening fear in her regard,
As if calamity had but begun;
As if the vanward clouds of evil days
Had spent their malice, and the sullen rear
Was with its stored thunder labouring up. . .

264

BEFORE thy shrine I kneel, an unknown worshipper,
Chanting strange hymns to thee and sorrowful litanies,
Incense of dirges, prayers that are as holy myrrh.

Ah! goddess, on thy throne of tears and faint low sighs,
Weary at last to theeward come the feet that err,
And empty hearts grown tired of the world's vanities.

How fair this cool deep silence to a wanderer
Deaf with the roar of winds along the open skies!
Sweet, after sting and bitter kiss of sea-water,

Sorrow

The pale Lethean wine within thy chalices!—
I come before thee, I, too tired wanderer
To heed the horror of the shrine, the distant cries,

And evil whispers in the gloom, or the swift whirr
Of terrible wings—I, least of all thy votaries,
With a faint hope to see the scented darkness stir,

And, parting, frame within its quiet mysteries
One face, with lips than autumn-lilies tenderer,
And voice more sweet than the far plaint of viols is,

Or the soft moan of any grey-eyed lute-player.

265

. . To Sorrow
I bade good morrow,
And thought to leave her far away behind;
But cheerly, cheerly,
She loves me dearly;
She is so constant to me, and so kind:
I would deceive her,
And so leave her,
But ah! she is so constant and so kind.

Beneath my palm-trees, by the river side,
I sat a-weeping: in the whole world wide
There was no one to ask me why I wept—
And so I kept
Brimming the water-lily cups with tears
Cold as my fears. . .

Come then, Sorrow,
Sweetest Sorrow!
Like an own babe I nurse thee on my breast:

Sorrow

I thought to leave thee,
And deceive thee,
But now of all the world I love thee best.

There is not one,
No, no, not one
But thee to comfort a poor lonely maid;
Thou art her mother,
And her brother,
Her playmate, and her wooer in the shade.

266

O, the dark feeling of mysterious dread which comes over the mind, and which the lamp of reason, though burning bright the while, is unable to dispel! Art thou, as leeches say, the concomitant of disease? . . Nay, rather the principle of woe itself, the fountain head of all sorrow co-existent with man, whose influence he feels when yet unborn; . . . for . . . woe doth he bring with him into the world, even thyself, dark one, terrible one, causeless, unbegotten, without a father. . . Then is it not lawful for man to exclaim, 'Better that I had never been born!' Fool, for thyself thou wast not born, but to fulfil the inscrutable decrees of thy Creator; and how dost thou know that this dark principle is not . . . thy best friend; that it is not that which tempers the whole mass of thy corruption? It may be, for what thou knowest, the mother of wisdom, and of great works: it is the dread of the horror of the night that makes the pilgrim hasten on his way. When thou feelest it nigh, let thy safety word be 'Onward'; if thou tarry, thou art overwhelmed.

Courage! build great works—'tis urging thee—it is ever nearest the favourites of God—the fool knows little of it. Thou wouldst be joyous, wouldst thou? then be a fool. What great work was ever the result of joy, the puny one? Who have been the wise ones, the mighty ones, the conquering ones of this earth? the joyous? I believe (it) not.

267

O SAISONS, ô châteaux,
Quelle âme est sans défauts?

O saisons, ô châteaux,

J'ai fait la magique étude
Du bonheur, que nul n'élude.

O vive lui, chaque fois
Que chante le coq gaulois.

Mais je n'aurai plus d'envie,
Il s'est chargé de ma vie.

Ce charme! il prit âme et corps,
Et dispersa tous efforts.

Que comprendre à ma parole?
Il fait qu'elle fuit et vole!

O saisons, ô châteaux.

Conscience

268

. . Ce qui nous fait sortir du palais des songes, c'est la douleur, la douleur personnelle ; c'est aussi le sentiment de l'obligation, ou ce qui réunit les deux, *la douleur du péché* ; c'est encore l'amour ; en un mot c'est l'ordre moral. Ce qui nous arrache aux enchantements de Maïa, c'est la conscience. La conscience dissipe les vapeurs du kief, les hallucinations de l'opium et la placidité de l'indifférence contemplative. Elle nous pousse dans l'engrenage terrible de la souffrance humaine et de la responsabilité humaine. C'est le réveille-matin, c'est le cri du coq qui met en fuite les fantômes, c'est l'archange armé du glaive qui chasse l'homme du paradis artificiel . . . Hélas ! Hélas !

269

SOME candle clear burns somewhere I come by.
I muse at how its being puts blissful back
With a yellowy moisture mild night's blear-all black ;
Or to-fro tender trambeams truckle at the eye.
   At that window what task what fingers ply,
I plod wondering, a-wanting, just for lack
Of answer the eagerer awanting Jessy or Jack
There, God to aggrandise, God to glorify.—
   Come you indoors, come home ; your fading fire
Mend first and vital candle in close heart's vault :
You there are master, do your own desire ;
What hinders ?   Are you beam-blind, yet to a fault
In a neighbour deft-handed ?   Are you that liar ?
And cast by conscience out, spendsavour salt ?

The Irrevocable

EARTH, sad earth, thou roamest
　　Through the day and night ;
Weary with the darkness,
　　Weary with the light.

Clouds of hanging judgment,
　　And the cloud that weeps for me,
Swell above the mountain,
　　Strive above the sea.

But, sad earth, thou knowest
　　All my love for thee ;
Therefore thou dost welcome
　　The cloud that weeps for me.

THE Dawn is touching the heavens,
The light winds blow,
And over the dewy clover
In shivers of silver go ;
And I cry to my soul, and I cry again and again
　　'Tis the morning of the world
　　And tired time hath upfurl'd
Upon himself, my soul !' And I cry in vain.

Within the central whorl
Of her mazy shell she lies,
Like a snail that doth recoil
From the touch of enemies ;
And my mind blows into her shell, and I cry again
　　'The long years that had come
　　Are crept back into the womb,
And Saturn is not fallen !' And I cry in vain.

Ask God for gladness. Be glad like children, like the birds of heaven. And let not the sin of men dismay you in your doings : Fear not lest it choke your work and hinder its accomplishment. Say not, Sin is powerful, Ungodliness is powerful, bad Conventionalism is powerful ; while we are solitary and powerless : the world will choke us and will frustrate the good work. Away with such despondency, my children. . . If a man cast the blame of his sloth and inefficiency upon others, he will end by sharing the pride of Satan and murmuring against God. Now, about the pride of Satan, I think thus : it is difficult for us on earth to understand it, and therefore it is easy to be ensnared in it, and to share it, and even to imagine all the while that we are doing something great and wonderful. And in the profoundest sensations and impulses of our nature also there is much that we cannot now understand. . . On this earth we truly wander, and are as it were lost ; so that were it not for the glorious figure of Christ before us, we should perish utterly. . . Much on earth is hidden from us, but there is given us in recompense the secret conviction of our living bond with another world, a celestial and loftier world : and the very roots of our thoughts and sensations are not here but there, in other worlds. And that is why the philosophers say that on earth it is impossible to know the essence of things.

273

. . Mean while upon the firm opacous Globe
Of this round World, whose first convex divides

Satan

The luminous inferior Orbs, enclos'd
From *Chaos* and th' inroad of Darkness old,
Satan alighted walks: a Globe farr off
It seem'd, now seems a boundless Continent
Dark, waste, and wild, under the frown of Night
Starless expos'd, and ever-threatning storms
Of *Chaos* blustring round, inclement skie;
Save on that side which from the wall of Heav'n
Though distant farr som small reflection gaines
Of glimmering air less vext with tempest loud:
Here walk'd the Fiend at large in spacious field.
As when a Vultur on *Imaus* bred,
Whose snowie ridge the roving *Tartar* bounds,
Dislodging from a Region scarce of prey
To gorge the flesh of Lambs or yeanling Kids
On hills where Flocks are fed, flies toward the Springs
Of *Ganges* or *Hydaspes*, *Indian* streams;
But in his way lights on the barren plaines
Of *Sericana*, where *Chineses* drive
With Sails and Wind thir canie Waggons light:
So on this windie Sea of Land, the Fiend
Walk'd up and down alone bent on his prey,
Alone, for other Creature in this place
Living or liveless to be found was none,
None yet, but store hereafter from the earth
Up hither like Aereal vapours flew
Of all things transitorie and vain, when Sin
With vanity had filld the works of men:
Both all things vain, and all who in vain things
Built their fond hopes of Glorie or lasting fame,
Or happiness in this or th' other life;
All who have thir reward on Earth, the fruits
Of painful Superstition and blind Zeal,
Naught seeking but the praise of men, here find
Fit retribution, emptie as thir deeds;

All th' unaccomplisht works of Natures hand,
Abortive, monstrous, or unkindly mixt,
Dissolvd on earth, fleet hither, and in vain,
Till final dissolution, wander here. . .

274

. . But neither can Reason nor Religion exist or co-
exist as Reason and Religion, except as far as they are
actuated by the Will. . .

In its state of immanence (or indwelling) in reason and
religion, the Will appears indifferently as Wisdom or as
Love : two names of the same power, the former more
intelligential, the latter more spiritual.   But in its utmost
abstraction and consequent state of reprobation, the Will
becomes satanic pride and rebellious self-idolatry in the
relations of the spirit to itself, and remorseless despotism
relatively to others ; the more hopeless as the more ob-
durate by its subjugation of sensual impulses, by its superi-
ority to toil and pain and pleasure : in short, by the fearful
resolve to find in itself alone the one absolute motive of
action, under which all other motives from within and
from without must be either subordinated or crushed.

This is the character which Milton has so philoso-
phically as well as sublimely embodied in the Satan of
his *Paradise Lost.*   Alas ! too often has it been embodied in real life !   Too often has it given a dark and
savage grandeur to the historic page !   And wherever
it has appeared, under whatever circumstances of time
and country, . . it has been identified by the same
attributes.   Hope, in which there is no cheerfulness ;
steadfastness within and immovable resolve, with outward

restlessness and whirling activity ; violence with guile ; temerity with cunning ; and, as the result of all, interminableness of object with perfect indifference of means : .. these are the marks that have characterised the masters of mischief, the liberticides and mighty hunters of mankind, from Nimrod to Napoleon. And . . . even men of honest intentions too frequently become fascinated. Nay, whole nations have been so far duped . . . as to regard with palliative admiration, instead of . . . abhorrence, the Molochs of human nature, who . . . dare to say with their whole heart 'Evil, be thou my good !' All system so far is power ; and a systematic criminal, self-consistent and entire in wickedness, who entrenches villany within villany, and barricadoes crime by crime, has removed a world of obstacles by the mere decision that he will have no obstacles but those of force and brute matter.

75

TYGER, Tyger, burning bright
In the forests of the night,
What immortal hand or eye
Could frame thy fearful symmetry ?

In what distant deeps or skies
Burnt the fire of thine eyes ?
On what wings dare he aspire ?
What the hand dare seize the fire ?

And what shoulder and what art
Could twist the sinews of thy heart ?
And when thy heart began to beat,
What dread hand and what dread feet ?

The Traitor Angel

What the hammer? what the chain?
In what furnace was thy brain?
What the anvil? what dread grasp
Dare its deadly terrors clasp?

When the stars threw down their spears,
And water'd heaven with their tears,
Did He smile his work to see?
Did He who made the lamb make thee?

Tyger, Tyger, burning bright
In the forests of the night,
What immortal hand or eye
Dare frame thy fearful symmetry?

276

.. To whom the Goblin full of wrauth reply'd,
Art thou that Traitor Angel, art thou hee,
Who first broke peace in Heav'n and Faith, till then
Unbrok'n, and in proud rebellious Arms
Drew after him the third part of Heav'ns Sons
Conjur'd against the highest, for which both Thou
And they outcast from God, are here condemn'd
To waste Eternal daies in woe and pain?
And reck'n'st thou thy self with Spirits of Heav'n,
Hell-doomd, and breath'st defiance here and scorn,
Where I reign King, and to enrage thee more,
Thy King and Lord? Back to thy punishment,
False fugitive, and to thy speed add wings,
Least with a whip of Scorpions I pursue
Thy lingring, or with one stroke of this Dart
Strange horror seise thee, and pangs unfelt before. ..

The Shame of Sin

.. O sorrow of Sinfulness! the gate
To Pain, kept wide by watchful Hate!
Sloping aloft with cliffy sides
Thro' the burnt air the porchway rides:
Demoniac shapes, devices grim,
Trenching the storied panels dim.

Alas! what scalding sand-wind rolls
Me to the sulphury rack of souls
Fierce on, and scarfs my victim eyes
With careless wreaths for sacrifice?

.. For we know that the Law is spiritual; but I am
carnal, sold under sin. . . For the good that I would
I do not; but the evil which I would not, that I do.

Now if I do that I would not, it is no more I that do
it, but sin that dwelleth in me.

I find then a law, that when I would do good, evil
is present with me. For I delight in the law of God
after the inward man; but I see another law in my
members, warring against the law of my mind, and
bringing me into captivity to the law of sin, which is in
my members.

O wretched man that I am! Who shall deliver me
from the body of this death?

I thank God through Jesus Christ our Lord.

.. Lo, all my heart's field red and torn,
And Thou wilt bring the young green corn.

Toujours et partout le salut est une torture, la délivrance est une mort, l'apaisement est dans l'immolation ; ... Il faut reconnaître que chacun de nous porte en soi son bourreau, son démon, son enfer, dans son péché, et que son péché c'est son idole, et que cette idole qui séduit les volontés de son cœur est sa malédiction.

Mourir au péché ! ce prodigieux mot du christianisme, demeure bien la plus haute solution théorique de la vie intérieure. C'est là seulement qu'est la paix de la conscience, et sans cette paix il n'y a point de paix ... Vivre en Dieu et faire ses œuvres, voilà la religion, le salut, la vie éternelle.

O LORD my God, when sore bested
　　My evil life I do bewail,
What times the life I might have led
　　Arising smites me like a flail :

When I regard the past of sin,
　　Till sorrow drown me like despair ;
The saint in me that might have been
　　With that I am when I compare :

Then grant the life that might have been
　　To be in fact through penitence ;
All my past years discharged of sin,
　　And spent in grace and innocence :

And grant that I, when I forecast,
　　And shrink in fear of coming things,
May take this comfort of the past,
　　And lay it on my imaginings.

. . Things that I longed for in vain and things that I got—let them pass. Let me but truly possess the things that I ever spurned and overlooked.

283

THE expense of spirit in a waste of shame
Is lust in action; and till action, lust
Is perjured, murderous, bloody, full of blame,
Savage, extreme, rude, cruel, not to trust;
Enjoy'd no sooner but despised straight;
Past reason hunted, and no sooner had,
Past reason hated, as a swallow'd bait
On purpose laid to make the taker mad:
Mad in pursuit and in possession so;
Had, having, and in quest to have, extreme;
A bliss in proof, and proved, a very woe;
Before a joy proposed; behind a dream.
    All this the world well knows; yet none knows well
    To shun the heaven that leads men to this hell.

284

. . Prisoner, tell me who was it that wrought this un-breakable chain? It was I, said the prisoner, who forged this chain very carefully. I thought my invincible power would hold the world captive, leaving me in a freedom undisturbed. Thus night and day I worked at the chain with huge fires and cruel hard strokes. When at last the work was done and the links were complete and unbreakable, I found that it held me in its grip.

285

. . O, that Fire ! before whose face
Heav'n and earth shall find no place :
O, those Eyes ! whose angry light
Must be the day of that dread Night. . .

But Thou giv'st leave, dread Lord, that we
Take shelter from Thyself in Thee ;
And with the wings of thine own dove
Fly to thy sceptre of soft love.

Dear, remember in that day
Who was the cause Thou cam'st this way :
Thy sheep was stray'd, and Thou wouldst be
Even lost Thyself in seeking me !

Shall all that labour, all that cost
Of love, and ev'n that loss, be lost ?
And this lov'd soul judg'd worth no less
Than all that way and weariness ? . .

O, when thy last frown shall proclaim
The flocks of goats to folds of flame,
And all thy lost sheep found shall be,
Let 'Come ye blessed' then call me !

286

WILT thou forgive that sin where I begun,
   Which was my sin, tho' it were done before ?
Wilt thou forgive that sin thro' which I run,
   And do run still, tho' I do still deplore ?
When thou hast done, thou hast not done ;
      For I have more. . .

Confession

C'est comme à la mort d'un ami, on s'accuse de l'avoir trop peu et trop mal aimé. C'est comme à sa propre mort, on sent qu'on a mal employé sa vie.

288

ACCEPT the sacrifice of my confessions from the ministry of my tongue, which thou hast formed and aroused to confess unto thy name. . . . . . Let my soul praise thee, that it may love thee ; and let it confess unto thee thy mercy, that it may praise thee. Thy whole Creation ceaseth not nor is silent in thy praise : neither the spirit of man with speech directed unto thee ; nor things animate nor inanimate by the mouth of them that meditate thereon : that so our souls may from their weariness arise toward thee, and leaning on those things which thou hast made, pass to thyself, who madest all wonderfully ; and in whom is refreshment and true strength.

289

. . Consider too that thou thyself often sinnest, and however thou differ from others, thou art yet of the same stuff as they.

And if may be thou refrain from certain sins, yet thou hast at least the disposition to commit them ;

Even though thro' cowardice or concern for thy reputation or for some such mean motive thou may'st refrain. . .

Milton is
advocating
the liberty
of the press.

. .They are not skilful considerers of human things, who imagin to remove sin by removing the matter of sin; for besides that it is a huge heap increasing under the very act of diminishing, though some part of it may for a time be withdrawn from some persons, it cannot from all, in such a universal thing as books are; and when this is done yet the sin remains entire. Though ye take from a covetous man all his treasure, he has yet one jewel left, ye cannot bereave him of his covetousness. Banish all objects of lust, shut up all youth into the severest discipline that can be exercis'd in any hermitage, ye cannot make them chaste, that came not thither so; such great care and wisdom is requir'd to the right managing of this point. Suppose we could expell sin by this means; look how much we thus expell of sin, so much we expell of vertue: for the matter of them both is the same; remove that, and ye remove them both alike. This justifies the high providence of God, who though he command us temperance, justice, continence, yet pours out before us ev'n to a profuseness all desirable things, and gives us minds that can wander beyond all limit and satiety. . .

291

. . Quand je me confeſſe à moy religieuſement, je trouve que la meilleure bonté que j'aye, a quelque teinture vicieuſe. Et crains que Platon en ſa plus nette vertu (moy qui en ſuis autant ſincere & loyal eſtimateur, & des vertus de ſemblable marque, qu'autre puiſſe eſtre), s'il y euſt eſcouté de prés (& il y eſcoutoit de prés) il y euſt

senty quelque ton gauche, de mixtion humaine : mais ton
obscur, & sensible seulement à soy. L'homme en tout &
par tout, n'est que rappiessement & bigarrure . . .

292

. . The truth of the matter is, that neither he who is
a Fop in the world is a fit man to be alone ; nor he who
has set his heart much upon the world, though he have
never so much understanding ; so that Solitude can be
well fitted and set right, but upon a very few persons.
They must have enough knowledge of the World to see
the vanity of it, and enough Virtue to despise all Vanity ;
if the Mind be possest with any Lust or Passion, a man
had better be in a Fair, than in a Wood alone.   They
may, like petty Thieves, cheat us perhaps, and pick our
pockets, in the midst of company ; but like Robbers, they
use to strip and bind or murder us, when they catch us
alone.   This is but to retreat from Men, and to fall into
the hands of Devils.   It is like the punishment of Parri-
cides among the *Romans*, to be sew'd into a Bag, with
an Ape, a Dog, and a Serpent. . .

293

O Rose, thou art sick !
The invisible worm,
That flies in the night,
In the howling storm,

Has found out thy bed
Of crimson joy ;
And his dark secret love
Does thy life destroy.

294

Malgré tous les efforts d'un siècle philosophique, les empires les plus civilisés seront toujours aussi près de la barbarie que le fer le plus poli l'est de la rouille.

295

Chacun recommence le monde, et pas une faute du premier homme n'a été évitée par son millième successeur. L'expérience collective s'accumule, mais l'expérience individuelle s'éteint avec l'individu. Conséquence : les institutions deviennent plus sages et la science anonyme s'accroît, mais l'adolescent, quoique plus cultivé, est tout aussi présomptueux et non moins faillible aujourd'hui qu'autrefois. Ainsi absolument il y a progrès et relativement il n'y en a pas. Les circonstances s'améliorent, le mérite ne grandit pas. Tout est mieux peut-être, mais l'homme n'est pas positivement meilleur, il n'est qu'autre. Ses défauts et ses vertus changent de forme, mais le bilan total n'établit pas un enrichissement. Mille choses avancent, neuf cent quatre-vingt-dix-huit reculent : c'est là le progrès. Il n'y a pas là de quoi rendre fier, mais bien de quoi consoler.

296

. . And not only are the spiritual vices voluntary, but in some cases also those of the body, and these we censure ; for we see it is not natural difformities that anyone blames, but those that come of sloth and neglect ; and it is the same in case of weakness or maiming, for no one would be disposed to reproach a man who was blind from birth or through disease or wounding, but rather to pity him; while every one would censure him if [his blindness were] due to drunkenness or other profligacy. Thus bodily vices which depend on ourselves are censured, but not those which are out of our power: and if this be so, then in other fields also, the vices which we blame should be in our own power.

But suppose it be objected that all men aim at the apparent good, but cannot control their imagined perception of it, since, such as each is, of the same sort will goodness appear to him.—I answer, if each man be in some way responsible for his habit, he must then be in some way responsible also for this imagination.

But if not, then neither is he ever responsible for his ill doings [which is untenable], but he does wrong through ignorance of the true good, thinking in this way to attain to it: but the end at which he aims is not self-chosen; it is indispensable that he should be born with a gift, as it were, of sight, whereby to judge rightly and choose the good accordant to truth; and a man will be truly well-born who is born with this gift in perfection, for it is the greatest and fairest, and impossible to be learned or acquired from others; but such as it was born in him, such will he keep it, and the possession of it in full excellence would be the birthright of perfect and true nobility.

297

WORLD
. . But if thou wilt,
What thou art I will show to thee.
My thought
Moved in its brooding, and its movement stirred

Misprision

A ripple in the quiet of the waters
Whereunder my thought's Sabbath is moored deep,—
The region of the happening of my Will.
And when my act, this ripple's viewless travel,
In its upheaval reached the upper calm
Laid on the mere, whose waters are my will,
Whose surface is Appearance and broad Place,
Its breaking whirls became a journeying wave,
That at the last became a gathered sea,
A pile of all the waters in one tide.
But it is grown to its height; and now, before
The smooth heapt power tumbles down in surf,
Its head is whiten'd with an age of spray,
Weakness beginning. Lo, that spray is Man,
Crest of the wave, and token of its downfall.
Not stately like the early wave, nor clear,
Nor with an inner lodging for the light,
But troublous, misty, throwing off the light
In glitter, all apieces, loose, uneasy.
Truly my act is near its end when thou,
Man, the loose spray, ride on its stooping neck,
From one firm bulk of waters, one onward gang,
Broken away to be a brawl of drops,
Freedom and hither-thither motions light,
Each drop one to itself, a discrete self.
    Thou freedom, thou high self-acquaintance, thou SIN,
Man, dost thou know me? But now know thyself. . .

    . . How wilt thou measure the portion of the limitless
void of time which is allotted to any man?—So very
quickly is it swallowed up and lost in the Eternal.
    Or what portion he hath of the universal Substance?
    Or what portion of the universal Life?

Reflecting on all this think nothing great, save only to act as thy nature leadeth, and to suffer what the common nature bringeth.

299

THESE are the properties of the rational soul:— It seeth itself: it analyseth itself, and maketh itself such as it will; and all things that happen unto it to appear such as it will: the fruit which it beareth it enjoyeth in itself .. and it attaineth its own end wheresoever the limit of life may be fixed.

300

.. Sure He that made us with such large discourse
Looking before and after, gave us not
That capability and godlike reason
To fust in us unused. ..

301

.. Now concerning the moral virtues we have spoken generally and have shown in outline of what kind they are, that they are mid-states [between evil extremes] and that they are habits; also whence they spring, that they are effects of their own proper actions; that they are in our own power, and voluntary, and such as right Reason would prescribe. ...

.. But what makes men good is held by some to be nature, by others habit (or training), by others instruc-

Aristot. Eth. III 5. 21.*

X. 9. 6

H

tion. As for the goodness that comes by Nature, this is plainly not within our control, but is bestowed by some divine agency on certain people who truly deserve to be called fortunate. . .

VI. 13. 1.   . . All admit that in a certain sense the several kinds of character are bestowed by nature. Justice, a tendency to Temperance, Courage, and the other types of character are exhibited from the moment of birth. Nevertheless we look for developed goodness as something different from this, and expect to find these same qualities in another form. For even in children and brutes these natural virtues are present, but without the guidance of reason [intellect] they are plainly hurtful. So much at least seems to be plain—that just as a strong-bodied creature devoid of sight stumbles heavily when it tries to move, because it cannot see, so it is with this natural virtue; but when it is enlightened by reason [intellect] it acts surpassingly well; and the natural virtue (which before was only like virtue) will then be fully developed virtue.

We find then, that just as there are two forms of the calculative faculty, namely cleverness and prudence, so there are two forms of the moral qualities, namely natural virtue and fully developed virtue, and that the latter is impossible without Prudence [practical intellect] . .

X. 7. 1.   . . But if happiness be the exercise of virtue, it is reasonable to suppose that it will be the exercise of the highest virtue; and that will be the virtue or excellence of the best part of us.

Now that part or faculty—call it reason [intellect] or

what you will—which seems naturally to rule and take the lead, and to apprehend 'things noble and divine— whether it be itself divine, or only the divinest part of us—is the faculty the exercise of which, in its proper excellence, will be perfect happiness.

That this consists in [intellectual] speculation or contemplation we have already said. . .

. . But a life which realized this idea would be some- X. 7. 8. thing more than human; for it would not be the expression of man's nature, but of some divine element in that nature —the exercise of which is as far superior to the exercise of the other kind of virtue (*i.e.* practical or moral virtue), as this divine element is superior to our compound human nature.

If then reason [intellect] be divine as compared with man, the life which consists in the exercise of this faculty will also be divine in comparison with human life. Nevertheless, instead of listening to those who advise us as men and mortals not to lift our thoughts above what is human and mortal, we ought rather, as far as possible, to put off our mortality, and make every effort to live in the exercise of the highest of our faculties; for though it be but a small part of us, yet in power and value it far surpasses all the rest. . .

The life that consists in the exercise of the other X. 8. 1. [practical] kind of virtue is happy in a secondary sense; for the manifestations of moral virtue are emphatically human. Justice (I mean) and Courage and the other moral virtues are displayed in our dealings with one another by the observance in every case of what is due in contracts and services, and all sorts of outward acts,

as well as in our inward feelings. And all these seem
to be emphatically human affairs . . . and being bound
up with the passions must belong to our compound nature;
and the virtues of the compound nature are emphatically
human. Therefore the life which manifests them, and
the happiness which consists in this, must be emphatically
human. . .

VI. 13. 5.*   . . (But it must be remembered that this life of moral
virtue) is also not only in accordance with right Reason,
but implies the possession of right Reason. . .

X. 9. 1.   . . [Surely too] in practical matters the end is not
mere speculative knowledge of what is to be done, but
rather the doing of it. It is not enough to know about
Virtue, then, but we must endeavour to possess it, and
to use it, or to take any other steps that may make us
good.

Now if theories had power of themselves to make us
good 'Many and great rewards would they deserve' as
Theognis says, and such ought we to give; but in fact
it seems that though they are potent to guide and to
stimulate liberal-minded young men, and though a generous disposition, with a sincere love of what is noble, may
by them be opened to the influence of virtue, yet they are
powerless to turn the mass of men to goodness. For
the generality of men are naturally apt to be swayed by
fear rather than by reverence, and to refrain from evil
rather because of the punishment that it brings, than
because of its own foulness. For under the guidance
of their passions they pursue the pleasures that suit their
nature, and the means by which those pleasures may be
obtained, and avoid the opposite pains; while of that

which is noble and truly pleasant they have no conception,
as they have never tasted it. . .

. . But the test of truth in matters of practice is to be X. 8. 12.
found in the facts of life; for it is in them that the supreme
authority resides. The theories which we have advanced
should therefore be tested by comparison with the facts
of life; and if they agree with the facts, they should be
accepted, but if they disagree they should be accounted
mere theories.

302

. . They sat them down upon the yellow sand,
Between the sun and moon upon the shore;
And sweet it was to dream of Fatherland,
Of child and wife and slave; but evermore
Most weary seem'd the sea, weary the oar,
Weary the wandering fields of barren foam.
Then someone said, 'We will return no more';
And all at once they sang, 'Our island home
Is far beyond the wave; we will no longer roam.'

CHORIC SONG

There is sweet music here that softer falls
Than petals from blown roses on the grass,
Or night-dews on still waters between walls
Of shadowy granite, in a gleaming pass;
Music that gentlier on the spirit lies,
Than tir'd eyelids upon tir'd eyes;
Music that brings sweet sleep down from the blissful skies.
Here are cool mosses deep,
And thro' the moss the ivies creep,

Restlessness

And in the stream the long-leaved flowers weep,
And from the craggy ledge the poppy hangs in sleep.

Why are we weigh'd upon with heaviness,
And utterly consumed with sharp distress,
While all things else have rest from weariness?
All things have rest: why should we toil alone,
We only toil, who are the first of things,
And make perpetual moan,
Still from one sorrow to another thrown:
Nor ever fold our wings,
And cease from wanderings,
Nor steep our brows in slumber's holy balm;
Nor harken what the inner spirit sings,
'There is no joy but calm!'
Why should we only toil, the roof and crown of things?..

Hateful is the dark-blue sky,
Vaulted o'er the dark-blue sea.
Death is the end of life; ah, why
Should life all labour be?
Let us alone.   Time driveth onward fast,
And in a little while our lips are dumb.
Let us alone.   What is it that will last?
All things are taken from us, and become
Portions and parcels of the dreadful Past.
Let us alone.   What pleasure can we have
To war with evil?   Is there any peace
In ever climbing up the climbing wave?
All things have rest, and ripen toward the grave
In silence; ripen, fall and cease:
Give us long rest or death, dark death or dreamful ease...

303

.. Light-trooping o'er the distant lea
A band I saw, where Revelry
Seem'd on her bacchant foot to be;
And heard the dry tambour afar
Before her Corybantian car
Booming the rout to winy war. ..

.. Uproar sweet! as when he crost,
Omnipotent Bacchus, with his host,
To farthest Ind; and for his van
Satyrs and other sons of Pan,
With swoln eye-burying cheeks of tan,
Who troll'd him round, which way he ran
His spotted yoke thro' Hindustan,
And with most victorious scorn
The mild foes of wine to warn,
Blew his dithyrambic horn!
That each river to his source
Trembled and sank beneath his course,
Where, 'tis said of many, they
Mourn undiscover'd till this day. ..

304

A MAN'S inability to moderate and control his passions I call servitude. .. The common vulgar opinion seems to be quite otherwise. For most people seem to believe that they are free just in so far as they may obey their lusts, and that they renounce their rights in so far as they are constrained to live according to the precepts of divine law. Wherefore they believe that Piety and Religion [that is to live according to Reason and the knowledge of God] and whatever else regards fortitude of mind, are burdens which they hope to get rid of at death, when they will receive the reward of their servitude, that is of their piety and religion. And it is not only by this hope, but also and principally by the fear of terrible punishments after death, that they are induced to live by the precepts of divine law as far as their meagre and impotent spirit will carry them. And had they not this hope and fear, but believed rather that the mind perished with the body, and would not survive it when they die miserably worn out by the burden of their piety, they would surely return to their inborn disposition, and wish to govern all things by their lusts, submitting everything to the government of fortune rather than to themselves. All this appears to me no less absurd than that a man, because he did not believe that he could keep his body alive for ever by wholesome diet, should stuff himself with poisons and deadly food : or, deeming his mind not to be eternal and immortal, should therefore wish to be mad, and live without reason.

305

. . He therefore who hath always been occupied with the cravings of desire and ambition, and who busieth himself wholly therewith, will of necessity have got all his notions mortal, and as far as possible he will become altogether mortal ; nor will he fall short of this in any way, since he hath fostered his mortal part.

But he who hath earnestly striven after learning and true wisdom, and hath been fully trained and exercised therein, he, if he lay hold on truth, must one would think

of necessity acquire an immortal and heavenly temper;
nay—so far I say again as human nature is capable of it
—he will in no wise fall short of immortality: and since
he is ever serving the divine, and hath the genius which
dwelleth in him ordered aright, he must needs be blessed
exceedingly. . .

306

HOW happy is he born and taught,
That serveth not another's will;
Whose armour is his honest thought,
And simple truth his utmost skill!

Whose passions not his masters are,
Whose soul is still prepar'd for death;
Untied unto the world by care
Of publick fame or private breath. . .

307

. . Blest are those
Whose blood and judgment are so well commingled
That they are not a pipe for Fortune's finger
To sound what stop she please.   Give me that man
That is not passion's slave, and I will wear him
In my heart's core, ay, in my heart of heart,
As I do thee. . .

308

. . I, loving freedom and untried,
No sport of every random gust,
Yet being to myself a guide,
Too blindly have reposed my trust. . .

Me this uncharter'd freedom tires;
I feel the weight of chance desires:
My hopes no more must change their name,
I long for a repose that ever is the same.

309

. . O qu'heureux sont ceux qui avec une liberté entière
et une pente invincible de leur volonté aiment parfaitement
et librement ce qu'ils sont obligés d'aimer nécessaire-
ment ! . . .

310

Ma troisième maxime était de tâcher toujours plutôt
à me vaincre que la fortune, et à changer mes désirs que
l'ordre du monde, et généralement de m'accoutumer à croire
qu'il n'y a rien qui soit entièrement en notre pouvoir que
nos pensées, en sorte qu'après que nous avons fait notre
mieux touchant les choses qui nous sont extérieures, tout
ce qui manque de nous réussir est au regard de nous
absolument impossible.

Et ceci seul me semblait être suffisant pour m'empêcher
de rien désirer à l'avenir que je n'acquisse, et ainsi pour
me rendre content : car, notre volonté ne se portant
naturellement à désirer que les choses que notre entende-
ment lui représente en quelque façon comme possibles, il
est certain que, si nous considérons tous les biens qui
sont hors de nous comme également éloignés de notre
pouvoir, nous n'aurons pas plus de regret de manquer de
ceux qui semblent être dus à notre naissance, lorsque
nous en serons privés sans notre faute, que nous avons de

ne posséder pas les royaumes de la Chine ou de Mexique;
et que, faisant, comme on dit, de nécessité vertu, nous ne
désirerons pas davantage d'être sains étant malades, ou
d'être libres étant en prison, que nous faisons maintenant
d'avoir des corps d'une matière aussi peu corruptible que
les diamants, ou des ailes pour voler comme les oiseaux.

Mais j'avoue qu'il est besoin d'un long exercice et d'une
méditation souvent réitérée pour s'accoutumer à regarder
de ce biais toutes les choses : et je crois que c'est prin-
cipalement en ceci que consistait le secret de ces philoso-
phes qui ont pu autrefois se soustraire de l'empire de la
fortune, et, malgré les douleurs et la pauvreté, disputer
de la félicité avec leurs dieux. Car s'occupant sans cesse
à considérer les bornes qui leur étaient prescrites par la
nature, ils se persuadaient si parfaitement que rien n'était
en leur pouvoir que leurs pensées, que cela seul était
suffisant pour les empêcher d'avoir aucune affection pour
d'autres choses ; et ils disposaient d'elles si absolument,
qu'ils avaient en cela quelque raison de s'estimer plus
riches et plus puissants, et plus libres et plus heureux
qu'aucun des autres hommes, qui, n'ayant point cette
philosophie, tant favorisés de la nature et de la fortune
qu'ils puissent être, ne disposent jamais ainsi de tout ce
qu'ils veulent.

311

   . . I thank thee, Lord Amphinomus, and since
I see thee like thy father, wise and good,
Old Nisus of Dulichium, I will say
What thrice thou hast refused to hear : Attend.
   Of all that moves and breathes upon the earth

Vicissitude

Nothing is found more unstable than man.
Awhile his spirit within him is gay, his limbs
Light, and he saith, No ill shall overtake me.
Then evil comes : and lo ! he beareth it
Patiently, in its turn as God provides.
So I too once looked to be ever happy
And gave the rein to wantonness, and now—
Thou seest me. . . .

312

Quand on se porte bien, on admire comment on pour-
rait faire si on était malade ; quand on l'est on prend
médecine gaiement : le mal y résout. On n'a plus les passions et les désirs de divertissements et de promenades,
que la santé donnait et qui sont incompatibles avec les
nécessités de la maladie. La nature donne alors des
passions et des désirs conformes à l'état présent. Il n'y
a que les craintes que nous nous donnons nous-mêmes
et non pas la nature, qui nous troublent ; parce qu'elles
joignent à l'état où nous sommes les passions de l'état où
nous ne sommes pas.

313

Mon humeur ne dépend guère du temps. J'ai mes
brouillards et mon beau temps au dedans de moi ; le bien
et le mal de mes affaires mêmes y font peu. Je m'efforce
quelquefois de moi-même contre la fortune ; la gloire
de la dompter me la fait dompter gaiement ; au lieu que
je fais quelquefois le dégoûté dans la bonne fortune.

314

. . Je sais que pas un de mes désirs ne sera réalisé,
et il y a longtemps que je ne désire plus. J'accepte seulement ce qui vient à moi, comme la visite d'un oiseau sur
ma fenêtre. Je lui souris, mais je sais bien que le visiteur
a des ailes et ne restera pas longtemps. Le renoncement
par désespérance a une douceur mélancolique . . .

315

HE who bends to himself a joy
Doth the wingèd life destroy:
But he who kisses the joy as it flies
Lives in eternity's sunrise.

316

Nous sommes si malheureux, que nous ne pouvons
prendre plaisir à une chose qu'à condition de nous fâcher
si elle réussit mal : ce que mille choses peuvent faire et
font à toute heure. Qui aurait trouvé le secret de se
réjouir du bien sans se fâcher du mal contraire aurait
trouvé le point. C'est le mouvement perpétuel.

317

. . More safe I Sing with mortal voice, unchang'd
To hoarce or mute, though fall'n on evil dayes,
On evil dayes though fall'n, and evil tongues;
In darkness, and with dangers compast round,
And solitude; yet not alone, while thou
Visit'st my slumbers Nightly, or when Morn

Purples the East: still govern thou my Song,
Urania, and fit audience find, though few.
But drive farr off the barbarous dissonance
Of *Bacchus* and his Revellers, the Race
Of that wilde Rout that tore the *Thracian* Bard
In *Rhodope*, where Woods and Rocks had Eares
To rapture, till the savage clamor dround
Both Harp and Voice; nor could the Muse defend
Her Son. So fail not thou, who thee implores:
For thou art Heav'nlie, shee an empty dreame. . .

318

Beatitudo non est virtutis praemium, sed ipsa virtus.

319

C'EST à la verité une tres-utile et grande partie que
la science: ceux qui la mefprifent tefmoignent affez leur
beftife: mais je n'eftime pas pourtant fa valeur jufques
à cette mefure extreme qu'aucuns luy attribuent, comme
Herillus le Philofophe, qui logeoit en elle le fouverain
bien, et tenoit qu'il fuft en elle de nous rendre fages &
contents; ce que je ne croy pas: ny ce que d'autres ont
dict, que la fcience eft mere de toute vertu, et que tout
vice eft produit par l'ignorance. Si cela eft vray, il eft
fubject à une longue interpretation. Ma maifon a efté
dés longtemps ouverte aux gens de fçavoir, & en eft fort
cogneue; car mon Pere qui l'a commandée cinquante ans
& plus, efchauffé de cette ardeur nouvelle, dequoy le Roy
François premier embraffa les Lettres & les mit en credit,
recherche avec grand foin & defpenfe l'accointance des
hommes doctes, les recevant chez luy, comme perfonnes

iainctes, & ayants quelque particuliere infpiration de fa-
geffe divine ; recueillant leurs fentences, et leurs difcours
comme des oracles, & avec d'autant plus de reverence,
& de religion, qu'il avoit moins de loy d'en juger : car
il n'avoit aucune cognoiffance des Lettres, non plus que
fes predeceffeurs.   Moy je les ayme bien, mais je ne les
adore pas . . .

. . Le philosophe rit, parce qu'il n'est dupe de rien, et
que l'illusion des autres persiste.   Il est pareil au malin
spectateur d'un bal qui aurait adroitement enlevé aux
violons toutes leurs cordes et qui verrait néanmoins se
démener musiciens et danseurs, comme s'il y avait
musique.   L'expérience le réjouirait en démontrant que
l'universelle danse de Saint-Guy est pourtant une aberra-
tion du sens intérieur, et qu'un sage a raison contre
l'universelle crédulité.   Ne suffit-il pas déjà de se boucher
les oreilles dans une salle de danse, pour se croire dans
une maison de fous ?

Pour celui qui a détruit en lui-même l'idée religieuse,
l'ensemble des cultes sur la terre doit produire un effet
tout semblable.   Mais il est dangereux de se mettre hors
la loi du genre humain et de prétendre avoir raison contre
tout le monde.

Rarement les rieurs se dévouent.   Pourquoi le feraient-
ils ?   Le dévouement est sérieux et c'est sortir de son
rôle que de cesser de rire.   Pour se dévouer, il faut
aimer ; pour aimer, il faut croire à la réalité de ce qu'on
aime ; il faut savoir souffrir, s'oublier, se donner, en un
mot devenir sérieux.   Le rire éternel c'est l'isolement

absolu, c'est la proclamation de l'égoïsme parfait.   Pour
faire du bien aux hommes, il faut les plaindre et non les
mépriser ; et dire d'eux, non pas : les imbéciles ! mais :
les malheureux !   Le sceptique pessimiste et nihiliste
paraît moins glacial que l'athée goguenard.   Or que dit
le sombre Ahasvérus ?

> Vous qui manquez de charité,
> Tremblez à mon supplice étrange :
> Ce n'est point sa divinité,
> C'est l'humanité que Dieu venge !

Mieux vaut se perdre que de se sauver tout seul . . .

321

. . Others apart sat on a Hill retir'd,
In thoughts more elevate, and reason'd high
Of Providence, Foreknowledge, Will, and Fate,
Fixt Fate, free will, foreknowledge absolute,
And found no end, in wandring mazes lost.
Of good and evil much they argu'd then,
Of happiness and final misery,
Passion and Apathie, and glory and shame,
Vain wisdom all, and false Philosophie :
Yet with a pleasing sorcerie could charm
Pain for a while or anguish, and excite
Fallacious hope, or arm th' obdured brest
With stubborn patience as with triple steel. . .

322

Stoicism . . was a system put together hastily, violently
to meet a desperate emergency.   Some ring-wall must
be built against chaos.   High over the place where Zeno

talked could be descried the wall, built generations before, under the terror of a Persian attack, built in haste of the materials which lay to hand, the drums of columns fitted together, just as they were, with the more regular stones. That heroic wall still looks over the roofs of modern Athens. To Zeno it might have been a parable of his own teaching.

323

. . Le vice radical de la philosophie, c'est de ne pouvoir parler au cœur. Or, l'esprit est le côté partiel de l'homme ; le cœur est tout . . . Aussi la religion, même la plus mal conçue, est-elle infiniment plus favorable à l'ordre politique, et plus conforme à la nature humaine en général, que la philosophie, parce qu'elle ne dit pas à l'homme d'aimer Dieu *de tout son esprit*, mais *de tout son cœur* : elle nous prend par ce côté *sensible et vaste* qui est à peu près le même dans tous les individus, et non par le côté *raisonneur, inégal et borné*, qu'on appelle *esprit* . . .

324

. . Que l'histoire vous rappelle que partout où il y a mélange de religion et de barbarie, c'est toujours la religion qui triomphe ; mais que partout où il y a mélange de barbarie et de philosophie, c'est la barbarie qui l'emporte . . . En un mot, la philosophie divise les hommes par les opinions, la religion les unit dans les mêmes principes ; il y a donc un contrat éternel entre la politique et la religion. *Tout État, si j'ose le dire, est un vaisseau mystérieux qui a ses ancres dans le Ciel* . . .

325

Dans la physique, ils n'ont trouvé que des objections contre l'Auteur de la nature ; dans la métaphysique, que doute et subtilités ; la morale et la logique ne leur ont fourni que des déclamations contre l'ordre politique, contre les idées religieuses et contre les lois de la propriété ; ils n'ont pas aspiré à moins qu'à la reconstruction du tout, par la révolte contre tout ; et, sans songer qu'ils étaient eux-mêmes dans le monde, ils ont renversé les colonnes du monde . . .

326

It is not strange if we are tempted to despair of good . . . our religions and moralities have been trimmed to flatter us, till they are all emasculate and sentimentalised, and only please and weaken. Truth is of a rougher strain. In the harsh face of life faith can read a bracing gospel.

327

But the greatest error . . . is the mistaking or misplacing of the last or furthest end of knowledge. For men have entered into a desire of learning and knowledge, sometimes upon a natural curiosity and inquisitive appetite; sometimes to entertain their minds with variety and delight ; sometimes for ornament and reputation ; and sometimes to enable them to victory of wit and contradiction ; and most times for lucre and profession ; and seldom sincerely to give a true account of their gift of reason, to the benefit and use of men : As if there were

sought in knowledge a couch whereupon to rest a searching and restless spirit ; or a terrace for a wandering and
variable mind to walk up and down with a fair prospect ;
or a tower of state for a proud mind to raise itself upon ;
or a fort or commanding ground for strife and contention ;
or a shop for profit or sale ; and not a rich storehouse for
the glory of the Creator and the relief of man's estate.

328

      OUT-WORN Heart, in a time out-worn,
      Come clear of the nets of wrong and right ;
      Laugh, heart, again in the grey twilight,
      Sigh, heart, again in the dew of morn . . .

329

    We thought of that inquisitive spirit of self-criticism,
who had made his entry even into our inner chamber.

    We thought of him, with his eyes of ice and long
bent fingers, he, who sits within in the darkest corner
of the soul and tears our being to pieces, as old women
shred up bits of silk and wool.

    Bit by bit the long, hard, bent fingers had torn away,
until our whole self lay there like a heap of rags, and our
best feelings, our deepest thoughts, all that we had done
and said, had been searched, explored, taken to pieces,
gazed at by the icy eyes ; and the toothless mouth had
sneered and whispered—'Behold, it is rags, only rags.'

330

    . . L'éternel effort est le caractère de la moralité
moderne. Ce devenir douloureux a remplacé l'harmonie.

l'équilibre, la joie, c'est-à-dire l'être . . .   L'idéal n'est plus la beauté sereine de l'âme, c'est l'angoisse de Laocoon se débattant contre l'hydre du mal.   Le sort en est jeté.   Il n'y a plus d'hommes accomplis et heureux, il n'y a plus que des candidats du ciel, galériens sur la terre.

Nous ramons notre vie en attendant le port.

Molière a dit que le raisonnement bannissait la raison. Il est possible aussi que le perfectionnement dont nous sommes si fiers ne soit qu'une imperfection prétentieuse. Le devoir semble encore plus négatif que positif; il est le mal s'amoindrissant, mais il n'est pas le bien; il est le mécontentement généreux, mais non le bonheur; il est la poursuite incessante d'un but inaccessible, une noble folie, mais non pas la raison; il est la nostalgie de l'irréalisable, maladie touchante qui n'est pourtant pas la sagesse.

331

IF, dead, we cease to be; if total gloom
Swallow up life's brief flash . . .
O Man, thou vessel purposeless, unmeant! . . .
If rootless thus, thus substanceless thy state,
Go, weigh thy dreams, and be thy hopes, thy fears,
The counter-weights!—Thy laughter and thy tears
Mean but themselves, each fittest to create
And to repay each other!   Why rejoices
Thy heart with hollow joy for hollow good?
Why cowl thy face beneath the mourner's hood,
Why waste thy sighs, and thy lamenting voices,
Image of image, ghost of ghostly elf,
That such a thing as thou feel'st warm or cold?
Yet what and whence thy gain, if thou withhold

These costless shadows of thy shadowy self?
Be sad! be glad! be neither! seek, or shun!
Thou hast no reason why! Thou canst have none;
Thy being's being is contradiction.

332

   . . Like one that on a lonesome road
   Doth walk in fear and dread,
   And having once turn'd round, walks on,
   And turns no more his head;
   Because he knows a frightful fiend
   Doth close behind him tread . . .

333

MEN fear Death as Children fear to go in the
dark; And as that natural fear in Children is increased
with Tales, so is the other. Certainly the contemplation
of Death as the Wages of Sin, and passage to another
World, is Holy and Religious; but the fear of it, as
a tribute due unto Nature, is weak. Yet in Religious
Meditations there is sometimes mixture of vanity and
superstition . . .

The Stoics bestowed too much cost upon Death,
and by their great preparations made it appear more
fearful . . . It is as natural to die as to be born . . .

334

. . A freeman thinks of nothing less than of death.
His wisdom is a meditation not of death, but of life . . .

335

336

WHAT path of life may one hold? In the market-place are strifes and hard dealings, in the house cares; in the country labour enough, and at sea terror; and abroad, if thou hast aught, fear, and if thou art in poverty, vexation. Art married? thou wilt not be without anxieties; unmarried? thy life is yet lonelier. Children are troubles; a childless life is a crippled one. Youth is foolish, and grey hairs again feeble. In the end then the choice is of one of these two, either never to be born, or, as soon as born, to die.

HOLD every path of life. In the market-place are honours and prudent dealings, in the house rest; in the country the charm of nature, and at sea gain; and abroad, if thou hast aught, glory, and if thou art in poverty, thou alone knowest it. Art married? so will thine household be best; unmarried? thy life is yet lighter. Children are darlings; a childless life is an unanxious one: youth is strong, and grey hairs again reverend. The choice is not then of one of the two, either never to be born or to die; for all things are good in life.

337

Go then and eat thy bread in gladness, and drink with joy thy wine, for thy works please God. All times be thy clothes white, and oil from thy head fail not. Parfetly use life with the wife that thou lovest, all the days of the life of thine unsteadfastness that been given to thee under sun, in all the time of thy vanity;

for this is thy part in life, and in thy travail that thou travailest under sun.

338

Can it be doubted but that there are some who take more pleasure in enjoying pleasures than some other, and yet nevertheless are less troubled with the loss or leaving of them? . . . And it seemeth to me that most of the doctrines of the philosophers are more fearful and cautionary than the nature of things requireth. So have they increased the fear of death in offering to cure it. For when they would have a man's whole life to be but a discipline or preparation to die, they must needs make men think that it is a terrible enemy, against whom there is no end of preparing . . . So have they sought to make men's minds too uniform and harmonical, by not breaking them sufficiently to contrary motions: the reason whereof I suppose to be, because they themselves were men dedicated to a private, free, and unapplied course of life . . . Men ought so to procure serenity as they destroy not magnanimity.

339

CYRIACK, whose Grandsire on the Royal Bench
    Of Brittish *Themis*, with no mean applause
    Pronounc't and in his volumes taught our Lawes,
    Which others at their Barr so often wrench:
To day deep thoughts resolve with me to drench
    In mirth, that after no repenting drawes;
    Let *Euclid* rest and *Archimedes* pause,
    And what the *Swede* intend, and what the *French*.

To measure life, learn thou betimes, and know
  Toward solid good what leads the nearest way;
  For other things mild Heav'n a time ordains,
And disapproves that care, though wise in show,
  That with superfluous burden loads the day,
  And when God sends a cheerful hour, refrains.

340

THE study of the Classics . . . teaches us to believe
that there is something really great and excellent in the
world, surviving all the shocks of accident and fluctua-
tions of opinion, and raises us above that low and servile
fear, which bows only to present power and upstart
authority. . . We feel the presence of that power which
gives immortality to human thoughts and actions, and
catch the flame of enthusiasm from all nations and ages.

It is hard to find in minds otherwise formed, either
a real love of excellence, or a belief that any excellence
exists superior to their own. Everything is brought
down to the vulgar level of their own ideas and pursuits.
Persons without education certainly do not want either
acuteness or strength of mind in what concerns themselves, or in things immediately within their observation;
but they have no power of abstraction, no general standard of taste, or scale of opinion. They see their
objects always near, and never in the horizon. Hence
arises that egotism which has been remarked as the
characteristic of self-taught men, and which degenerates
into obstinate prejudice or petulant fickleness of opinion,
according to the natural sluggishness or activity of their
minds. For they either become blindly bigoted to the

first opinions they have struck out for themselves, and inaccessible to conviction; or else (the dupes of their own vanity and shrewdness) are everlasting converts to every crude suggestion that presents itself, and the last opinion is always the true one. Each successive discovery flashes upon them with equal light and evidence, and every new fact overturns their whole system. It is among this class of persons, whose ideas never extend beyond the feeling of the moment, that we find partizans, who are very honest men, with a total want of principle, and who unite the most hardened effrontery and intolerance of opinion, to endless inconsistency and self-contradiction.

341

LAWRENCE of vertuous Father vertuous Son,
　　Now that the Fields are dank, and ways are mire,
　　Where shall we sometimes meet, and by the fire
　　Help wast a sullen day; what may be won
From the hard Season gaining: time will run
　　On smoother, till *Favonius* re-inspire
　　The frozen earth; and cloth in fresh attire
　　The Lillie and Rose, that neither sow'd nor spun.
What neat repast shall feast us, light and choice,
　　Of Attick tast, with Wine, whence we may rise
　　To hear the Lute well toucht, or artfull voice
Warble immortal Notes and *Tuskan* Ayre?
　　He who of those delights can judge, and spare
　　To interpose them oft, is not unwise.

Book IV

❦

OFT by the marsh's quaggy edge
   I heard the wind-swept rushes fall;
Where through an overgrowth of sedge
   Rolled the slow mere funereal:
I heard the music of the leaves
   Unto the night-wind's fingering,
I saw the dropping forest-eaves
   Make in the mere their water-ring . . .

But day by day about the marge
   Of this slow-brooding dreaminess,
The shadow of the past lay large,
   And brooded low and lustreless;
Then vanished as I looked on it,
   Yet back returned with wider sweep,
And broad upon my soul would sit,
   Like a storm-cloud above the deep . . .

' I see (I cried) the waste of waves,
   That shifts from out the western tracts;
I see the sun that ever laves
   With liquid gold their cataracts;
And night by night I see the moon
   Career and thwart the waves of cloud;
I see great nature burgeon
   Through all her seasons, laughter-browed.

But what are these things unto me?
   They lack not me, they are full-planned:
I must have love in my degree,
   A human heart, a human hand.
For oh! 'tis better far to share,
   Tho' life all dark, all bitter be,
With human bosoms human care.'—
   I launched my boat upon the sea.

343

   TO find the Western path,
   Right through the Gates of Wrath
      I urge my way;
   Sweet Mercy leads me on
   With soft repentant moan:
      I see the break of day.

   The war of swords and spears,
   Melted by dewy tears,
      Exhales on high;
   The Sun is freed from fears,
   And with soft grateful tears
      Ascends the sky.

344

FURY

   In each human heart terror survives
The ravin it has gorged: the loftiest fear
All that they would disdain to think were true:
Hypocrisy and custom make their minds
The fanes of many a worship, now outworn.
They dare not devise good for man's estate,

And yet they know not that they do not dare.
The good want power, but to weep barren tears.
The powerful goodness want: worse need for them.
The wise want love; and those who love want wisdom;
And all best things are thus confused to ill.
Many are strong and rich, and would be just,
But live among their suffering fellow-men
As if none felt: they know not what they do.

PROMETHEUS

    Thy words are like a cloud of wingèd snakes;
And yet I pity those they torture not.

45

  . . And surely it is not a vain dream that man shall
come to find his joys only in acts of enlightenment and
of mercy, and not in cruel pleasures, as he doth now,
in gluttony, lust, pride, boasting and envious selfexalt-
ation.   I hold firmly that this is no dream but that the
time is at hand . . .   I believe that through Christ we
shall accomplish this great work . . . and all men will
say 'The stone which the builders rejected is become
the chief stone of the corner.' And of the mockers
themselves we may ask, If this faith of ours be a dream,
then how long is it to wait ere ye shall have finished
your edifice, and have ordered everything justly by the
intellect alone without Christ? . . . In truth they have
a greater faculty for dreaming than we have. They
think to order all wisely; but, having rejected Christ,
they will end by drenching the world with blood. For
blood crieth again for blood, and they that take the
sword shall perish by the sword.

346

LITTLE lamb, Who made thee?
Dost thou know who made thee,
Gave thee life, and bid thee feed
By the stream and o'er the mead;
Gave thee clothing of delight,
Softest clothing woolly bright;
Gave thee such a tender voice,
Making all the vales rejoice?
   Little lamb, Who made thee?
   Dost thou know who made thee?

Little lamb, I'll tell thee:
Little lamb, I'll tell thee:
He is callèd by thy name,
For he calls himself a Lamb.
He is meek and he is mild,
He became a little child.
I a child, and thou a lamb,
We are callèd by his name.
   Little lamb, God bless thee!
   Little lamb, God bless thee!

347

. . Serene will be our days and bright
And happy will our nature be,
When love is an unerring light,
And joy its own security. . .

348

. . My neighbour, or my servant, or my child, has
done me an injury, and it is just that he should suffer

an injury in return.   Such is the doctrine which Jesus
Christ summoned his whole resources of persuasion to
oppose.   'Love your enemy; bless those that curse
you': such, he says, is the practice of God, and such
must ye imitate if ye would be the children of God.

49

> A PITY beyond all telling
>   Is hid in the heart of love:
> The folk who are buying and selling;
>   The clouds on their journey above;
> The cold wet winds ever blowing;
>   And the shadowy hazel-grove
> Where mouse-gray waters are flowing,
>   Threaten the head that I love.

50

Like as it is with the several members of an organised
body, so is it with rational beings who exist separate;
the same principle rules, for they also are constituted for
a single co-operation.   And the perception of this will
more strongly strike thy mind, if thou say often to thyself, 'I am a member (melos) of the system of rational
beings.'   But if thou say, 'I am a part (meros)', though
thou change but one letter of the Greek, thou dost not
yet love men from thy heart.   Loving-kindness doth not
yet delight thee for its own sake: thou still doest it
barely as a thing of propriety, and not yet as doing good
to thyself.

351

. . Man, one harmonious soul of many a soul,
   Whose nature is its own divine control,
Where all things flow to all, as rivers to the sea ;
   Familiar acts are beautiful through love ;
   Labour, and pain, and grief, in life's green grove
Sportlike tame beasts, none knew how gentle they could be!

His will, with all mean passions, bad delights,
   And selfish cares, its trembling satellites.
A spirit ill to guide, but mighty to obey,
   Is as a tempest-wingèd ship, whose helm
   Love rules, through waves which dare not overwhelm,
Forcing life's wildest shores to own its sovereign sway.

All things confess his strength. Through the cold mass
   Of marble and of colour his dreams pass ;
Bright threads whence mothers weave the robes their
     children wear ;
   Language is a perpetual Orphic song,
   Which rules with Dædal harmony a throng
Of thoughts and forms, which else senseless and shape-
     less were . . .

352

. . Quand on veut respecter les hommes, il faut oublier
ce qu'ils sont et penser à l'idéal qu'ils portent caché en
eux, à l'homme juste et noble, intelligent et bon, inspiré
et créateur, loyal et vrai, fidèle et sûr, . . . à l'exemplaire
divin que nous appelons une âme.

353

   THE night has a thousand eyes,
     And the day but one ;
  Yet the light of the bright world dies
     With the dying sun.

Love of Creatures

The mind has a thousand eyes,
   And the heart but one;
Yet the light of a whole life dies,
   When love is done.

354

. . Love will teach us all things : but we must learn
how to win love; it is got with difficulty : it is a possession dearly bought with much labour and in long time;
for one must love not sometimes only, for a passing
moment, but always.   There is no man who doth not
sometimes love : even the wicked can do that.

And let not men's sin dishearten thee : love a man
even in his sin, for that love is a likeness of the divine
love, and is the summit of love on earth.   Love all God's
creation, both the whole and every grain of sand.   Love
every leaf, every ray of light.   Love the animals, love
the plants, love each separate thing.   If thou love each
thing thou wilt perceive the mystery of God in all; and
when once thou perceive this, thou wilt thenceforward
grow every day to a fuller understanding of it : until thou
come at last to love the whole world with a love that
will then be all-embracing and universal.

355

. O happy living things ! no tongue
Their beauty might declare :
A spring of love gush'd from my heart,
And I bless'd them unaware. . .

I

      .. 'High Prophetess,' said I, 'purge off,
Benign, if so it please thee, my mind's film.'

'None can usurp this height,' return'd that shade,
'But those to whom the miseries of the world
Are misery, and will not let them rest.
All else who find a haven in the world,
Where they may thoughtless sleep away their days,
If by a chance into this fane they come,
Rot on the pavement where thou rottedst half.'

'Are there not thousands in the world,' said I,
Encouraged by the sooth voice of the shade,
'Who love their fellows even to the death,
Who feel the giant agony of the world,
And more, like slaves to poor humanity,
Labour for mortal good?   I sure should see
Other men here, but I am here alone.'

'Those whom thou spakest of are no visionaries,'
Rejoin'd that voice; 'they are no dreamers weak;
They seek no wonder but the human face,
No music but a happy-noted voice:
They come not here, they have no thought to come;
And thou art here, for thou art less than they.
What benefit canst thou do, or all thy tribe,
To the great world?   Thou art a dreaming thing,
A fever of thyself: think of the earth;
What bliss, even in hope, is there for thee?
What haven? every creature hath its home,
Every sole man hath days of joy and pain,
Whether his labours be sublime or low—

Self-sacrifice

The pain alone, the joy alone, distinct :
Only the dreamer venoms all his days,
Bearing more woe than all his sins deserve '. . .

' . . If the wrong-doing of men fill thee with indignation and irresistible pain, so that thou desire even to take
vengeance on the wrong-doers, then above all things resist
that feeling. Go at once and seek suffering for thyself, as
though thou thyself wert guilty of the wrong-doing. Accept
that suffering, and endure it to the end, and so shall thine
heart be comforted, and thou wilt understand how thou
thyself art also guilty : for unto those evil-doers thou
mightest have let shine thy light, even like the one sinless
man ; and thou didst not. If thy light had shone forth,
it would have made clear the path for others, and the man
who sinned would perchance have been saved by thy light.
Or if it be that thou didst show thy light, and yet see'st
not that any are saved thereby ; nevertheless stand thou
firm, and doubt not the virtue of the heavenly light.
Believe that if they have not been saved now, they will
be saved hereafter : and if they should never be saved,
then their sons will be saved ; for thy light will not die
even when thou art dead. The just man passeth away,
but his light remaineth : and it is after the saviour's death
that men are mostly saved. Mankind will reject and
kill their prophets, but men love their martyrs and honour
those whom they have done to death. Thou, moreover,
art working for the whole, and for the future thou labour-
est. And look not for any outward reward, since, without that, thy reward on earth is already great : thine is

the spiritual joy which only the righteous man findeth. . .
Love all men and all things: seek this rapture and ecstasy.
Wet the earth with the tears of thy joy, and love those
tears.   Neither be ashamed of that ecstasy : Cherish it
highly, for it is the gift of God, a great gift ;   nor is it
granted to many, but only to the elect.

358

I REMEMBER a house where all were good
To me, God knows, deserving no such thing :
Comforting smell breathed at very entering,
Fetched fresh, as I suppose, off some sweet wood.
That cordial air made those kind people a hood
All over, as a bevy of eggs the mothering wing
Will, or mild nights the new morsels of spring :
Why, it seem'd of course ; seem'd of right it should.
    Lovely the woods, waters, meadows, combes, vales,
All the air things wear that make this house, this Wales :
Only the inmate does not correspond :
God, lover of souls, swaying considerate scales,
Complete thy creature dear O where it fails,
Being mighty a master, being a father and fond.

359

    True is it that we have seen better days,
And have with holy bell been knoll'd to church,
And sat at good men's feasts and wiped our eyes
Of drops that sacred pity hath engender'd ;
And therefore sit you down in gentleness
And take upon command what help we have,
That to your wanting may be minister'd.

Commiseration

360

. . I thought Love lived in the hot sunshine,
    But O, he lives in the moony light!
I thought to find Love in the heat of day,
    But sweet Love is the comforter of night.

Seek Love in the pity of others' woe,
    In the gentle relief of another's care,
In the darkness of night and the winter's snow,
    In the naked and outcast—seek Love there.

361

. . Poor naked wretches, wheresoe'er you are
That bide the pelting of this pitiless storm,
How shall your houseless heads and unfed sides,
Your loop'd and window'd raggedness, defend you
From seasons such as these? . . . Take physic, pomp;
Expose thyself to feel what wretches feel;
That thou may'st shake the superflux to them,
And show the heav'ns more just.

362

THERE was a roaring in the wind all night;
The rain came heavily and fell in floods;
But now the sun is rising calm and bright;
The birds are singing in the distant woods;
Over his own sweet voice the Stock-dove broods;
The Jay makes answer as the Magpie chatters;
And all the air is filled with pleasant noise of waters.

The Leechgatherer

All things that love the sun are out of doors;
The sky rejoices in the morning's birth;
The grass is bright with rain-drops;—on the moors
The hare is running races in her mirth;
And with her feet she from the plashy earth
Raises a mist; that, glittering in the sun,
Runs with her all the way, wherever she doth run.

I was a Traveller then upon the moor;
I saw the hare that raced about with joy;
I heard the woods and distant waters roar;
Or heard them not, as happy as a boy:
The pleasant season did my heart employ:
My old remembrances went from me wholly;
And all the ways of men, so vain and melancholy.

But, as it sometimes chanceth, from the might
Of joy in minds that can no further go,
As high as we have mounted in delight
In our dejection do we sink as low;
To me that morning did it happen so;
And fears and fancies thick upon me came;
Dim sadness—and blind thoughts, I knew not, nor could
    name.

I heard the sky-lark warbling in the sky;
And I bethought me of the playful hare:
Even such a happy Child of earth am I;
Even as these blissful creatures do I fare;
Far from the world I walk, and from all care;
But there may come another day to me—
Solitude, pain of heart, distress, and poverty.

My whole life I have lived in pleasant thought,
As if life's business were a summer mood;
As if all needful things would come unsought

The Leechgatherer

To genial faith, still rich in genial good;
But how can He expect that others should
Build for him, sow for him, and at his call
Love him, who for himself will take no heed at all?

I thought of Chatterton, the marvellous Boy,
The sleepless Soul that perished in his pride;
Of Him who walked in glory and in joy
Following his plough, along the mountain-side:
By our own spirits are we deified:
We Poets in our youth begin in gladness;
But thereof come in the end despondency and madness.

Now, whether it were by peculiar grace,
A leading from above, a something given,
Yet it befell that, in this lonely place,
When I with these untoward thoughts had striven,
Beside a pool bare to the eye of heaven
I saw a Man before me unawares:
The oldest man he seemed that ever wore grey hairs.

As a huge stone is sometimes seen to lie
Couched on the bald top of an eminence;
Wonder to all who do the same espy,
By what means it could thither come, and whence;
So that it seems a thing endued with sense:
Like a sea-beast crawled forth, that on a shelf
Of rock or sand reposeth, there to sun itself;

Such seemed this Man, not all alive nor dead,
Nor all asleep—in his extreme old age:
His body was bent double, feet and head
Coming together in life's pilgrimage;
As if some dire constraint of pain, or rage
Of sickness felt by him in times long past,
A more than human weight upon his frame had cast.

The Leechgatherer

Himself he propped, limbs, body, and pale face,
Upon a long grey staff of shaven wood :
And, still as I drew near with gentle pace,
Upon the margin of that moorish flood
Motionless as a cloud the old Man stood,
That heareth not the loud winds when they call ;
And moveth all together, if it move at all. . . .

.. He told, that to these waters he had come
To gather leeches, being old and poor :
Employment hazardous and wearisome !
And he had many hardships to endure :
From pond to pond he roamed, from moor to moor ;
Housing, with God's good help, by choice or chance ;
And in this way he gained an honest maintenance.

The old Man still stood talking by my side ;
But now his voice to me was like a stream
Scarce heard ; nor word from word could I divide ;
And the whole body of the Man did seem
Like one whom I had met with in a dream ;
Or like a man from some far region sent,
To give me human strength, by apt admonishment.

My former thoughts returned : the fear that kills ;
And hope that is unwilling to be fed ;
Cold, pain, and labour, and all fleshly ills ;
And mighty Poets in their misery dead. . . .

            . . . . the lonely place,
The old Man's shape, and speech—all troubled me :
In my mind's eye I seemed to see him pace
About the weary moors continually,
Wandering about alone and silently.
While I these thoughts within myself pursued,
He, having made a pause, the same discourse renew'd.

And soon with this he other matter blended,
Cheerfully uttered, with demeanour kind,
But stately in the main ; and when he ended,
I could have laughed myself to scorn to find
In that decrepit Man so firm a mind.
' God,' said I, ' be my help and stay secure :
I 'll think of the Leech-gatherer on the lonely moor ! '

363

OLD MEG she was a gipsy,
   And liv'd upon the moors :
Her bed it was the brown heath turf,
   And her house was out of doors.
Her apples were swart blackberries,
   Her currants, pods o' broom ;
Her wine was dew of the wild white rose,
   Her book a church-yard tomb.

Her brothers were the craggy hills,
   Her sisters larchen trees ;
Alone with her great family
   She liv'd as she did please.
No breakfast had she many a morn,
   No dinner many a noon,
And, 'stead of supper, she would stare
   Full hard against the moon.

But every morn, of woodbine fresh
   She made her garlanding,
And, every night, the dark glen yew
   She wove, and she would sing.
And with her fingers old and brown
   She plaited mats of rushes,

And gave them to the cottagers
    She met among the bushes.

Old Meg was brave as Margaret Queen,
    And tall as Amazon ;
An old red blanket cloak she wore,
    A chip-hat had she on :
God rest her aged bones somewhere !
    She died full long agone !

364

LE semoir, la charrue, un joug, des socs luisants,
La herse, l'aiguillon et la faulx acérée
Qui fauchait en un jour les épis d'une airée,
Et la fourche qui tend la gerbe aux paysans ;

Ces outils familiers, aujourd'hui trop pesants,
Le vieux Parmis les voue à l'immortelle Rhée
Par qui le germe éclôt sous la terre sacrée.
Pour lui, sa tâche est faite : il a quatre-vingts ans.

Près d'un siècle, au soleil, sans en être plus riche,
Il a poussé le coutre au travers de la friche ;
Ayant vécu sans joie, il vieillit sans remords.

Mais il est las d'avoir tant peiné sur la glèbe
Et songe que peut-être il faudra, chez les morts,
Labourer des champs d'ombre arrosés par l'Érèbe.

365

A QUATRE heures du matin l'été
    le sommeil d'amour dure encore
    sous les bosquets l'aube évapore
        l'odeur du soir fêté

Labourers

Or là-bas dans l'immense chantier
vers le soleil des Hespérides
en bras de chemise les charpentiers
    déjà s'agitent

Dans leur désert de mousse tranquilles
ils préparent les lambris précieux
où la richesse de la ville
    rira sous de faux cieux

Ah ! pour ces ouvriers charmants
sujets d'un roi de Babylone
Vénus ! laisse un peu les amants
    dont l'âme est en couronne

  O Reine des Bergers
porte aux travailleurs l'eau de vie
pour que leurs forces soient en paix
en attendant le bain dans la mer à midi.

366

. . Love had he found in huts where poor men lie;
His daily teachers had been woods and rills,
The silence that is in the starry sky,
The sleep that is among the lonely hills.

In him the savage virtue of the Race,
Revenge, and all ferocious thoughts were dead:
Nor did he change ; but kept in lofty place
The wisdom which adversity had bred.

367

. . Les vrais neureux sont bons, comme les bons, visités
par l'épreuve, deviennent meilleurs. Ceux qui n'ont pas

souffert sont légers, mais qui n'a pas de bonheur n'en
sait guère donner. On ne donne que du sien . . . La
vie seule ranime la vie. Ce que nous devons aux autres,
ce n'est pas notre soif et notre faim, mais notre pain et
notre gourde.

368

> . . Farewell, farewell! but this I tell
> To thee, thou Wedding-guest,
> He prayeth well who loveth well
> Both man and bird and beast.
>
> He prayeth best who loveth best
> All things both great and small;
> For the dear God who loveth us,
> He made and loveth all. . .

369

> BUT tell me, child, your choice; what shall I buy
> You?— Father, what you buy me I like best.—
> With the sweetest air that said, still plied and pressed,
> He swung to his first poised purport of reply.
>
> What the soul is! which, like carriers let fly—
> Doff darkness, homing nature knows the rest—
> To its own fine function, wild and self-instressed,
> Falls light as ten years long taught what and why.
>
> Mannerly-hearted! more than handsome face—
> Beauty's bearing or Muse of mounting vein,
> All, in this case, bathed in high hallowing grace—
>
> Of heaven what boon to buy you, boy, or gain
> Not granted? Only—O, on that path you pace
> Run all your race, O brace sturdier that young strain!

370

TOUJOURS ce souvenir m'attendrit et me touche,
Quand lui-même, appliquant la flûte sur ma bouche,
Riant et m'asseyant sur lui, près de son cœur,
M'appelait son rival et déjà son vainqueur.
Il façonnait ma lèvre inhabile et peu sûre
A souffler une haleine harmonieuse et pure ;
Et ses savantes mains prenaient mes jeunes doigts,
Les levaient, les baissaient, recommençaient vingt fois,
Leur enseignant ainsi, quoique faibles encore,
A fermer tour à tour les trous du buis sonore.

371

THERE is a shrine whose golden gate
    Was opened by the Hand of God ;
It stands serene, inviolate,
    Though millions have its pavement trod ;
As fresh, as when the first sunrise
Awoke the lark in Paradise.

'Tis compassed with the dust and toil
    Of common days, yet should there fall
A single speck, a single soil
    Upon the whiteness of its wall,
The angels' tears in tender rain
Would make the temple theirs again.

Without, the world is tired and old,
    But, once within the enchanted door,
The mists of time are backward rolled,
    And creeds and ages are no more ;
But all the human-hearted meet
In one communion vast and sweet.

I enter—all is simply fair,
    Nor incense-clouds, nor carven throne;
But in the fragrant morning air
    A gentle lady sits alone;
My mother—ah! whom should I see
Within, save ever only thee?

372

There is a spirit, which I feel, that delights to do no
evil nor to revenge any wrong, but delights to endure
all things, in hope to enjoy its own in the end. Its
hope is to outlive all wrath and contention, and to weary
out all exaltation and cruelty, or whatever is of a nature
contrary to itself. It sees to the end of all temptations:
As it bears no evil in itself, so it conceives none in
thoughts to any other: If it be betrayed, it bears it;
for its ground and spring is the mercies and forgiveness
of God. Its crown is meekness, its life is everlasting
love unfeigned, and it takes its kingdom with entreaty
and not with contention, and keeps it by lowliness of
mind. In God alone it can rejoice, though none else
regard it or can own its life. It is conceived in sorrow
and brought forth without any to pity it; nor doth it
murmur at grief and oppression. It never rejoiceth but
through sufferings; for with the world's joy it is murdered.
I found it alone, being forsaken: I have fellowship
therein with them who lived in dens and desolate places
in the earth; who through death obtained their resurrection and eternal holy life.

Saints in Heaven

SING me the men ere this
Who, to the gate that is
A cloven pearl uprapt,
The big white bars between
With dying eyes have seen
The sea of jasper, lapt
About with crystal sheen ;

And all the far pleasance
Where linkèd Angels dance,
With scarlet wings that fall
Magnifical, or spread
Most sweetly over-head,
In fashion musical,
Of cadenced lutes instead.

Sing me the town they saw
Withouten fleck or flaw,
Aflame, more fine than glass
Of fair Abbayes the boast,
More glad than wax of cost
Doth make at Candlemas
The Lifting of the Host :

Where many Knights and Dames,
With new and wondrous names,
One great Laudatè Psalm
Go singing down the street ;—
Tis peace upon their feet,
In hand 'tis pilgrim palm
Of Goddes Land so sweet :—

Where Mother Mary walks
In silver lily stalks,
Star-tirèd, moon-bedight ;
Where Cecily is seen,

Saints in Heaven

With Dorothy in green,
And Magdalen all white,
The maidens of the Queen.

Sing on—the Steps untrod,
The Temple that is God,
Where incense doth ascend,
Where mount the cries and tears
Of all the dolorous years,
With moan that ladies send
Of durance and sore fears :—

And Him who sitteth there,
The Christ of purple hair,
And great eyes deep with ruth,
Who is of all things fair
That shall be, or that were,
The sum, and very truth.
Then add a little prayer,

That since all these be so,
Our Liege, who doth us know,
Would fend from Sathanas,
And bring us, of His grace,
To that His joyous place :
So we the Doom may pass,
And see Him in the Face.

374

. . They came out on a lovely pleasance, that dream'd of oasis,
Fortunat isle, the abode o' the blest, their fair Happy Woodland.
Here is an ampler sky, those meads ar' azur'd by a gentler
Sun than th' Earth, an' a new starworld their darkness adorneth.
    Some were matching afoot their speed on a grassy arena,
In playful combat some wrestling upon the yellow sand,

The Just in Elysium

Part in a dance-rhythm or poetry's fine phantasy engage;
While full-toga'd anear their high-priest musical Orpheus
Bade his prime sev'n tones in varied harmony discourse,
Now with finger, anon sounding with an ivory plectrum.
And here Æneas met Teucer's fortunate offspring,
High-spirited heroes, fair-favor'd sons o' the morning,
Assarac and Ilos, and Dardan founder of Ilium:
Their radiant chariots he espied rank't empty afar off,
Their spears planted afield, their horses wandering at large,
Grazing around:—as on earth their joy had been, whether armour
Or chariot had charm'd them, or if 'twere good manage and care
Of the gallant warhorse, the delight liv'd here unabated:
Lo! then others, that about the meadow sat feasting in idless,
And chanting for joy a familiar pæan of old earth,
By fragrant laurel o'ercanopied, where 'twixt enamel'd banks
Bountiful Eridanus glides throu' their bosky retirement.
Here were men who bled for honour, their country defending;
Priests, whose lives wer' a flame of chastity on God's altar;
Holy poets, content to await their crown of Apollo;
Discoverers, whose labour had aided life or ennobled;
Or who fair memories had left through kindly deserving.
On their brow a fillet pearl-white distinguisheth all these:
Whom the Sibyl, for they drew round, in question accosted,
And most Musæus, who tower'd noble among them,
Center of all that sea of bright faces looking upward.
'Tell, happy souls, and thou poet and high mystic illustrious,
Where dwelleth Anchises? what home hath he? for 'tis in his quest
We hither have made journey across Hell's watery marches.'
    Thereto with brief parley rejoin'd that mystic of old-time.
'In no certain abode we remain: by turn the forest glade
Haunt we, lilied stream-bank, sunny mead; and o'er valley and rock
At will rove we: but if ye aright your purpose arede me,

Mount ye the hill : myself will prove how easy the pathway.'
Speaking he led : and come to the upland, sheweth a fair plain
Gleaming aneath ; and they, with grateful adieu, the descent made.
　　Now lord Anchises was down i' the green valley musing,
Where the spirits confin'd that await mortal resurrection
While diligently he mark'd, his thought had turn'd to his own kin,
Whose numbers he reckon'd, an' of all their progeny foretold
Their fate and fortune, their ripen'd temper an' action.
He then, when he espied Æneas t'ward him approaching
O'er the meadow, both hands uprais'd and ran to receive him,
Tears in his eyes, while thus his voice in high passion outbrake.
'Ah, thou'rt come, thou'rt come ! at length thy dearly belov'd grace
Conquering all hath won thee the way. 'Tis allow'd to behold thee,
O my son,—yea again the familiar raptur' of our speech.
Nay, I look't for 't thus, counting patiently the moments,
And ever expected ; nor did fond fancy betray me.
From what lands, my son, from what life-dangering ocean
Art thou arrived ? full mighty perils thy path hav' opposèd :
And how nearly the dark Libyan thy destiny oerthrew !'
Then he, ' Thy spirit, O my sire, 'twas thy spirit often
Sadly appearing aroused me to seek thy far habitation.
My fleet moors i' the blue Tyrrhene : all with me goeth well.
Grant me to touch thy hand as of old, and thy body embrace.'
Speaking, awhile in tears his feeling mutinied, and when
For the longing contact of mortal affection, he out-held
His strong arms, the figure sustain'd them not : 'twas as empty
E'en as a windworn cloud, or a phantom of irrelevant sleep.
　　On the level bosom of this vale more thickly the tall trees
Grow, an' aneath quivering poplars and whispering alders
Lethe's dreamy river throu' peaceful scenery windeth.
Whereby now flitted in vast swarms many people of all lands,
As when in early summer honey-bees on a flowery pasture

Lethe

Pill the blossoms, hurrying to an' fro,—innumerous are they,
Revisiting the ravish'd lily cups, while all the meadow hums.

Æneas was turn'd to the sight, and marvelling inquired,
'Say, sir, what the river that there i' the vale-bottom I see?
And who they that thickly along its bank have assembled?'

Then Lord Anchises, 'The spirits for whom a second life
And body are destin'd ar' arriving thirsty to Lethe,
And here drink th' unmindful draught from wells of oblivion.
My heart greatly desired of this very thing to acquaint thee,
Yea, and show thee the men to be born, our glory her'after,
So to gladden thine heart where now thy voyaging endeth.'
'Must it then be believed, my sire, that a soul which attaineth
Elysium will again submit to her old body-burden?
Is this well? what hap can awake such dire longing in them?'
'I will tell thee, O son, nor keep thy wonder awaiting,'
Answereth Anchises, and all expoundeth in order.
'Know first that the heavens, & th' Earth, & space fluid or void,
Night's pallid orb, day's Sun, and all his starry coævals,
Are by one spirit inly quickened, and, mingling in each part,
Mind informs the matter, nature's complexity ruling.
Thence the living creatures, man, brute, & ev'ry feather'd fowl,
And what breedeth in Ocean aneath her surface of argent:
Their seed knoweth a fiery vigour, 'tis of airy divine birth,
In so far as unimpeded by an alien evil,
Nor dull'd by the body's framework condemn'd to corruption.
Hence the desires and vain tremblings that assail them, unable
Darkly prison'd to arise to celestial exaltation;
Nor when death summoneth them anon earth-life to relinquish,
Can they in all discard their stain, nor wholly away with
Mortality's plaguespots. It must be that, O, many wild graffs
Deeply at heart engrain'd have rooted strangely upon them
Wherefore must suffering purge them, yea, Justice atone them

With penalties heavy as their guilt : some purify exposed
Hung to the viewless winds, or others long watery searchings,
Low i' the deep, wash clean ; some bathe in fiery renewal :
Each cometh unto his own retribution,—if after in ample
Elysium we attain, but a few, to the fair Happy Woodland,
Yet slow time still worketh on us to remove the defilement,
Till it hath eaten away the acquir'd dross, leaving again free
That first fiery vigour, the celestial virtue of our life.
All whom here thou seest, hav' accomplished purification :
Unto the stream of Lethe a god their company calleth,
That, forgetful of old failure pain & disappointment,
They may again into earthly bodies with glad courage enter.'

 * * * * * * *

Twin be the gates o' the house of sleep : as fable opineth
One is of horn, and thence for a true dream outlet is easy :
Fair the other, shining perfected of ivory carven ;
But false are the visions that thereby find passage upward.
Soon then as Anchises had spok'n, he led the Sibyl forth
And his son, and both dismisst from th' ivory portal.

375

 . . Farr off from these a slow and silent stream,
Lethe the River of Oblivion roules
Her watrie Labyrinth, whereof who drinks,
Forthwith his former state and being forgets,
Forgets both joy and grief, pleasure and pain.
Beyond this flood a frozen Continent
Lies dark and wilde, beat with perpetual storms
Of Whirlwind and dire Hail, which on firm land
Thaws not, but gathers heap, and ruin seems
Of ancient pile ; all else deep snow and ice,

Hell

A gulf profound as that *Serbonian* Bog
Betwixt *Damiata* and mount *Casius* old,
Where Armies whole have sunk: the parching Air
Burns frore, and cold performs th' effect of Fire.
Thither by harpy-footed Furies hail'd,
At certain revolutions all the damn'd
Are brought: and feel by turns the bitter change
Of fierce extreams, extreams by change more fierce,
From Beds of raging Fire to starve in Ice
Thir soft Ethereal warmth, and there to pine
Immovable, infixt, and frozen round,
Periods of time, thence hurried back to fire.
They ferry over this *Lethean* Sound
Both to and fro, thir sorrow to augment,
And wish and struggle, as they pass, to reach
The tempting stream, with one small drop to loose
In sweet forgetfulness all pain and woe,
All in one moment, and so neer the brink;
But fate withstands, and to oppose th' attempt
Medusa with *Gorgonian* terror guards
The Ford, and of it self the water flies
All taste of living wight, as once it fled
The lip of *Tantalus*.   Thus roving on
In confus'd march forlorn, th' adventrous Bands
With shuddring horror pale, and eyes agast
View'd first thir lamentable lot, and found
No rest: through many a dark and drearie Vaile
They pass'd, and many a Region dolorous,
O're many a Frozen, many a Fierie Alpe,
Rocks, Caves, Lakes, Fens, Bogs, Dens, and shades of
  death,
A Universe of death, which God by curse
Created evil, for evil only good,
Where all life dies, death lives, and nature breeds,
Perverse, all monstrous, all prodigious things,

Abominable, inutterable, and worse
Then Fables yet have feign'd, or fear conceiv'd,
Gorgons and *Hydra's*, and *Chimera's* dire.

376

WHEN the Son of man shall come in his glory, and all his holy angels with him; then shall he sit upon the throne of his glory.

And before him shall be gathered all nacions, and he shall sever them won from another, as a shepherd putteth asunder the sheep from the goats. And he shall set the sheep on his right hand, and the goats on his left.

Then shall the king say to them on his right hand— Come ye blessed children of my father, inherit the kingdom prepared for you from the foundation of the world:

For I was anhungred, and ye gave me meat; I thirsted and ye gave me drink; I was harbourless, and ye lodged me;

I was naked, and ye clothed me; I was sick and ye visited me; I was in prison, and ye came unto me.

Then shall the just answer him, saying,—Master, when saw we thee anhungred, and fed thee; or athirst, and gave thee drink?

When saw we thee harbourless, and lodged thee; or naked, and clothed thee? or when saw we thee sick, or in prison, and came unto thee?

And the king shall answer and say unto them,—Verily I say unto you, in as much as ye have done it unto won of the leest of these my brethren, ye have done it unto me.

Then shall the king say unto them that shalbe on the left hand,—Depart from me, ye cursed, into everlasting fire, which is prepared for the devil and his angels:

For I was anhungred, and ye gave me no meat; I thirsted, and ye gave me no drink; I was harbourless, and ye lodged me not; I was naked, and ye clothed me not; I was sick and in prison, and ye visited me not.

Then shall they also answer him, saying,—Master, when saw we thee anhungred or athirst or harbourless or naked or sick or in prison, and have not ministred unto thee?

Then shall he answer them, and say,—Verily, I say unto you, in as much as ye did it not to won of the leest of these, ye did it not to me.

And these shall go into everlasting punishment; and the righteous into life eternal.

77

. . The moral of the whole story, Simmias, is this: that we should do all that we can to partake of Virtue and Wisdom in this life. Fair is the prize, and the hope great. Not that I insist upon all the particulars of my tale,—no sensible man would; but that it or something like it is true concerning our souls and their mansions after death,—since we are agreed that the soul is immortal—this, it seems to me, is a proper opinion and enough to justify some venture of imagination in a believer. For the venture is noble: and it is right to relate such things, and fortify oneself as with enchantments. It was for this reason that I told the myth at so great length.

Socrates is speaking

Wherefore a man should be of good cheer about his soul, if in this life he has despised all bodily pleasures and ornaments as alien to her, and to the perfecting of the life that he has chosen. He will have zealously

applied himself to Understanding, and having adorned
his soul not with any foreign ornament but with her own
proper jewels, Temperance, Justice, Courage, Nobility
and Truth, he awaits thus prepared his journey to Hades...
But a little while and you, Simmias and Cebes, and the
rest of my friends will be departing: Me already, as
they say on the stage, fate is calling: and in a few minutes
I must go to the bath; for I think I had better bathe
before drinking the poison, and not give the women the
trouble of washing my body after I am dead.

378

. . Mortals that would follow me,
Love Virtue; she alone is free:
She can teach ye how to climb
Higher than the sphery chime:
Or, if Virtue feeble were,
Heav'n itself would stoop to her.

379

pres =
press, the
crowd.
For glos-
sary etc.
see index

FLEE fro the pres, and dwelle with sothfastnessë,
Suffyce unto thy good, though it be smal;
For hord hath hate, and climbing tikelnessë,
Pres hath envye, and welë blent overal;
Savour no more than thee bihovë shal;
    Reule thyself, that other folk canst redë;
And trouthë shal delivere, it is no dredë.

Tempest thee not al croked to redressë,
In trust of hir that turneth as a bal:

Fortitude

Gret restë stant in litel besinessë;
And eek be ware to sporn ageyn an al;
Stryve not, as doth the crokkë with the wal.
   Daunte thyself, that dauntest otheres dedë;
And trouthë shal delivere, it is no dredë.

That thee is sent, receyve in buxumnessë,
The wrastling for this worlde axeth a fal.
Her is non hoom, her nis but wildernessë:
Forth, pilgrim, forth!   Forth, beste, out of thy stal!
Know thy contree, look up, thank God of al;
   Weyve thy lust, and lat thy gost thee ledë:
And trouthë shal delivere, it is no dredë.

Explicit Le bon counseill de G. Chaucer.

379 (*bis*)

O that I were an Orange-tree,
         That busy plant!
Then should I ever laden be,
         And never want
Some fruit for him that dressed me.

380

HUMILITY and patience in adversity more please me,
      my son,
   than much comfort and devotion in prosperity.
And why should a little thing spoken against thee make
      thee sad?
   had it been greater, thou shouldst not have been dis-
      turbed.
But now let it pass: 'tis nothing strange; it hath happed
      before;
   and if thou live longer, it will happen again.

Thou art manly enough while there is nought to oppose
thee :
   thou canst give good counsel, and hast encouraged
      others with words :
But when suddenly the trouble cometh to thine own door,
   thou lackest to thyself both in courage and counsel.
Consider thy great weakness, which thou discoverest
   often in trifling concerns :
   and yet it is all for thy good, when these or such like
      things befal thee.
Put the matter as well as thou canst out of thy mind ;
   and if the tribulation hath touched thee, let it not cast
      thee down nor entangle thee.
Bear it patiently, if gladly thou canst not :
   or even if thou resent this saying and feel indignation,
      yet govern thyself ;
   nor suffer an unchastened word to escape thee, whereby
      the little ones may stumble.
The storm that hath arisen will quickly subside :
   and thy hidden pain will be soothed by returning grace.
I still Am saith the Lord, ready to aid thee and console
   thee more than ever,
   if thou but trust me, and beseech me with all thy heart.
Be more tranquil in mind, and brace thyself to better
   fortitude ;
   All is not lost, even though again and again thou feel
      thyself broken or well-nigh spent.

381

. . Our law surely would say that it is best to keep as
tranquil as possible in misfortune, and not to be vexed or
resentful : for we cannot see what good or evil there is in
such things, and impatience does not in any way help us

forwards ; also because nothing in human affairs deserves serious anxiety, and grief stands in the way to hinder the self-succour that our duty immediately requires of us.

382

IL est dangereux de se laisser aller à la volupté des larmes ; elle ôte le courage et même la volonté de guérir.

383

WHEN I consider how my light is spent
E'er half my days, in this dark world and wide,
And that one Talent which is death to hide
Lodg'd with me useless, though my Soul more bent
To serve therewith my Maker and present
My true account, least he returning chide,—
Doth God exact day-labour, light deny'd ?
I fondly ask : But patience, to prevent
    That murmur, soon replies, God doth not need
Either man's work or his own gifts : who best
Bear his mild yoke, they serve him best: his State
Is Kingly :   Thousands at his bidding speed
And post o'er Land and Ocean without rest :
They also serve who only stand and wait.

384

. . Il n'y a qu'une chose nécessaire, . . . l'immolation de la volonté propre, le sacrifice filial de ses désirs.   Le mal est de vouloir son moi, c'est-à-dire sa vanité, son orgueil, sa sensualité, sa santé même.   Le bien est de vouloir son sort, d'accepter et d'épouser sa destinée, de vouloir ce que Dieu commande . . .

385

ELECTED Silence, sing to me
And beat upon my whorlèd ear,
Pipe me to pastures still and be
The music that I care to hear.

Shape nothing, lips; be lovely-dumb:
It is the shut, the curfew sent
From there where all surrenders come
Which only makes you eloquent. . .

386

GIVE me my scallop-shell of quiet,
My staff of faith to walk upon,
My scrip of joy, immortal diet,
My bottle of salvation,
My gown of glory, hope's true gage;
And thus I'll take my pilgrimage.

Blood must be my body's balmer;
No other balm will there be given;
Whilst my soul, like quiet palmer,
Travelleth towards the land of heaven;
    Over the silver mountains,
    Where spring the nectar fountains:
        There will I kiss
        The bowl of bliss,
And drink mine everlasting fill
Upon every milken hill.
My soul will be a-dry before:
But, after, it will thirst no more.

Selfrenunciation

I ASKED for Peace—
　My sins arose,
　And bound me close,
I could not find release.

I asked for Truth—
　My doubts came in,
　And with their din
They wearied all my youth.

I asked for Love—
　My lovers failed,
　And griefs assailed
Around, beneath, above.

I asked for Thee—
　And thou didst come
　To take me home
Within Thy Heart to be.

. . Tous les sens, toutes les forces de l'âme et de l'esprit, toutes les ressources extérieures sont autant d'échappées ouvertes sur la divinité : autant de manières de déguster et d'adorer Dieu. Il faut savoir se détacher de tout ce qu'on peut perdre, ne s'attacher absolument qu'à l'éternel et à l'absolu et savourer le reste comme un prêt, un usufruit . . . Adorer, comprendre, recevoir, sentir, donner, agir : voilà ta loi, ton devoir, ton bonheur, ton ciel. Advienne que pourra, même la mort. Mets-toi d'accord avec toi-même, vis en présence de Dieu, en

communion avec lui et laisse guider ton existence aux
puissances générales contre lesquelles tu ne peux rien.—
Si la mort te laisse du temps, tant mieux. Si elle t'emporte, tant mieux encore. Si elle te tue à demi, tant
mieux toujours, elle te ferme la carrière du succès pour
t'ouvrir celle de l'héroïsme, de la résignation et de la
grandeur morale.

389

. . Nekhlyudov sat down on the steps of the porch,
and inhaling the strong scent of the young birch-leaves
which filled the warm air, gazed long at the garden as it
gradually darkened in the failing light. He listened to
the thud of the mill-wheel, and to the nightingales, and
some other bird that whistled monotonously in a bush
close by the steps . . . [Presently] in the east, behind
the coach-house, flamed the glow of the rising moon :
summer lightning ever more brightly began to illumine
the rank-flowering neglected garden, and the dilapidated
house, and distant thunder could be heard, where in the
west a black cloud was towering upwards overspreading
the sky.

The moon, but just past her full, emerged from behind
the coach-house and glistening on the iron roof of the
tumble-down house threw black shadows across the
courtyard.

Nekhlyudov remembered how at Kuzminskoye he had
meditated on his life and tried to solve the questions,
what he ought to do, and how he ought to do it ; and
he remembered how he had become perplexed in these
questions and had been unable to decide them, so many

were the considerations involved in each. He now put
to himself the same questions, and was astonished how
simple it all was. It was simple because he now took
no thought of what would happen to himself:—that no
longer even interested him,—he was thinking only of
what he ought to do. And strangely enough, while he
was not considering his own needs, he knew without
any doubt what he ought to do for others . .

The black cloud had moved on till it stood right
above him: lightning lit up the whole courtyard and
the thunder sounded directly overhead. The birds had
all ceased singing, the leaves began to rustle, and the
first flaws of the storm-wind reached the steps where he
sat . . . Nekhlyudov went into the house. ' Yes, yes,'
he thought, ' The work which is carried out by our life,
the whole work, the whole meaning of this work is dark
to me, and cannot be made intelligible . . . Why should my
friend die, and I be left alive ? . . Why was Katyusha
born ? . . Why did this war come about ? Of what
use was my subsequent dissolute life ? To understand
all this, to understand the whole work of the Master is
not in my power ; but to do his will, written in my conscience, that is in my power, and that I know without
a doubt. And when I do this, then undoubtedly I am
at peace.'

390

HOW soon hath Time the suttle theef of youth,
    Stoln on his wing my three and twentith yeer !
    My hasting dayes flie on with full career,
    But my late spring no bud or blossom shew'th.

Perhaps my semblance might deceive the truth,
      That I to manhood am arriv'd so near,
      And inward ripenes doth much less appear,
      That som more timely-happy spirits indu'th.
Yet be it less or more, or soon or slow,
      It shall be still in strictest measure eev'n,
      To that same lot, however mean, or high,
Toward which Time leads me, and the will of Heav'n;
      All is, if I have grace to use it so,
      As ever in my great Taskmasters eye.

391

. . Tu ne me chercherais pas si tu ne me possédais.
Ne t'inquiète donc pas.

392

            YE that do your Master's will,
            Meek in heart be meeker still:
            Day by day your sins confess,
            Ye that walk in righteousness:
            Gracious souls in grace abound,
            Seek the Lord, whom ye have found.

            He that comforts all that mourn
            Shall to joy your sorrow turn:
            Joy to know your sins forgiven,
            Joy to keep the way of heaven,
            Joy to win his welcome grace,
            Joy to see Him face to face.

393

      Good and evill we know in the field of this World
grow up together almost inseparably; and the knowledge

of good is so involv'd and interwoven with the knowledge of evill, and in so many cunning resemblances hardly
to be discern'd, that those confused seeds which were
impos'd on Psyche as an incessant labour to cull out and
sort asunder were not more intermixt.   It was from out
the rinde of one apple tasted, that the knowledge of good
and evill as two twins cleaving together leapt forth into
the World. And perhaps this is that doom which Adam
fell into of knowing good and evill, that is to say of knowing good by evill.   As therefore the state of man now is,
what wisdom can there be to choose, what continence to
forbear, without the knowledge of evill ?   He that can
apprehend and consider vice with all her baits and seem-
ing pleasures, and yet abstain, and yet distinguish, and yet
prefer that which is truly better, he is the true warfaring
Christian. I cannot praise a fugitive and cloister'd virtue,
unexercis'd and unbreath'd, that never sallies out and sees
her adversary, but slinks out of the race, where that
immortal garland is to be run for, not without dust and
heat.

394

IF thou wast still, O stream,
   Thou would'st be frozen now :
And 'neath an icy shield
   Thy current warm would flow.

But wild thou art and rough ;
   And so the bitter breeze,
That chafes thy shuddering waves,
   May never bid thee freeze.

K

395

. . O ye gifted ones, follow your calling, for however
various your talents may be, ye can have but one calling ;
. . . follow resolutely the one straight path before you,
it is that of your good angel ; let neither obstacles nor
temptations induce you to leave it ; bound along if you
can ; if not, on hands and knees follow it, perish in it,
if needful ; but ye need not fear that ; no one ever yet
died in the true path of his calling before he had attained
the pinnacle. Turn into other paths, and for a momentary
advantage or gratification ye have sold your inheritance,
your immortality.

396

. . To whom the Angel. ' Son of Heav'n and Earth,
Attend : That thou art happie, owe to God ;
That thou continu'st such, owe to thy self.' . .

397

HE is the true Saint, who can reveal the form of the
        formless to the vision of these eyes :
Who teacheth the simple way of attaining Him,
        that is other than rites and ceremonies :
Who requireth thee not to close the doors,
        to hold the breath, and renounce the world :
Who maketh thee perceive the supreme Spirit
        wherever the mind resteth :
Who teacheth thee to be still amidst all thine activities :
Who, ever immersed in bliss, having no fear,
        keepeth the spirit of union thro'out all enjoyments . . .

DU point de vue du bonheur, la question de la vie est insoluble, car ce sont nos plus hautes aspirations qui nous empêchent d'être heureux. Du point de vue du devoir, même difficulté, car le devoir accompli donne la paix, non le bonheur. C'est l'amour divin, le saint amour, la possession de Dieu par la foi qui résout la difficulté ; car si le sacrifice est devenu lui-même une joie, joie permanente, croissante et indéfectible, alors l'âme a un aliment suffisant et indéfini.

399

I LAUGH when I hear that the fish in the water is
    thirsty.
Perceivest thou not how the god is in thine own house,
    that thou wanderest from forest to forest so listlessly ?
In thy home is the Truth. Go where thou wilt, to
    Benares or to Mathura ;
    if thy soul is a stranger to thee, the whole world is
    unhomely.

400

. . Le problème serait d'accomplir sa tâche quotidienne sous la coupole de la contemplation, d'agir en présence de Dieu, d'être religieusement dans son petit rôle. On redonne ainsi au détail, au passager, au temporaire, à l'insignifiant de la beauté et de la noblesse. On dignifie, on sanctifie la plus mesquine des occupations. On a ainsi le sentiment de payer son tribut à l'œuvre universelle, à la volonté éternelle. On se réconcilie avec la vie et l'on cesse de craindre la mort. On est dans l'ordre et dans la paix.

401

TOUTE la gloire, que je pretens de ma vie, c'eſt de l'avoir veſcue tranquille : Tranquille, non ſelon Metrodorus, ou Arceſilas, ou Ariſtippus, mais ſelon moy. Puiſque la Philoſophie n'a ſceu trouver aucune voye pour la tranquillité, qui fuſt bonne en commun, que chaſcun la cherche en ſon particulier. A qui doivent Céſar & Alexandre cette grandeur infinie de leur renommée, qu'à la fortune ? . . . Au travers de tant & ſi extremes dangers il ne me ſouvient point avoir leu que Céſar ait eſté jamais bleſſé. Mille ſont morts de moindres perils, que le moindre de ceux qu'il franchit. Infinies belles actions ſe doivent perdre ſans teſmoignage, avant qu'il en vienne une à profit. On n'eſt pas tousjours ſur le haut d'une breſche, ou à la teſte d'une armée, à la veue de ſon General, comme ſur un eſchaffaut. On eſt ſurpris entre la haye & le foſſé : il faut tenter fortune contre un poullailler : il faut dénicher quatre chetifs harquebuſiers d'une grange : il faut ſeul s'eſcarter de la troupe & entreprendre ſeul, ſelon la neceſſité qui s'offre. Et ſi on prend garde, on trouvera, à mon advis, qu'il advient par experience, que les moins eſclattantes occaſions ſont les plus dangereuſes : & qu'aux guerres, qui ſe ſont paſſées de noſtre temps, il s'eſt perdu plus de gens de bien, aux occaſions legeres & peu importantes, & à la conteſtation de quelque bicoque, qu'és lieux dignes & honorables.

Qui tient ſa mort pour mal employée, ſi ce n'eſt en

occafion fignalée; au lieu d'illuftrer fa mort, il obfcurcit volontiers fa vie: laiffant efchapper cependant plufieurs juftes occafions de se hazarder. Et toutes les juftes font illuftres affez: fa confcience les trompettant fuffifamment à chafcun. *Gloria noftra eft, testimonium confcientiae noftrae.* Qui n'eft homme de bien que parce qu'on le fçaura, & parce qu'on l'en eftimera mieux, aprés l'avoir fceu, qui ne veut bien faire qu'en condition que fa vertu vienne à la cognoiffance des hommes, celuy-là n'eft pas perfonne de qui on puiffe tirer beaucoup de fervice....

Il faut aller à la guerre pour fon debvoir, & en attendre cette recompenfe, qui ne peut faillir à toutes belles actions pour occultes qu'elles foyent, non pas mefmes aux vertueufes penfées: c'eft le contentement qu'une confcience bien reiglée reçoit en foy, de bien faire. Il faut eftre vaillant pour foy-mefmes, & pour l'advantage que c'eft d'avoir fon courage logé en une affiette ferme & affeurée, contre les affauts de la fortune . . .

402

. . There is one way for thee; but one; inform
Thyself of it; pursue it; one way each
Soul hath by which the infinite in reach
Lyeth before him; seek and ye shall find;
. . . . O joy, joy, joy to fill
The day with leagues! go thy way, all things say,
Thou hast thy way to go, thou hast thy day
To live; thou hast thy need of thee to make
In the heart of others; do thy thing; yea, slake
The world's great thirst for yet another man!
And be thou sure of this; no other can
Do for thee that appointed thee of God. . .

403

> Wha does the utmost that he can
> Will whyles do mair.

404

. . It is therefore our business carefully to cultivate in our minds, to rear to the most perfect vigour and maturity, every sort of generous and honest feeling that belongs to our nature. To bring the dispositions that are lovely in private life into the service and conduct of the commonwealth; so to be patriots as not to forget we are gentlemen. To cultivate friendships, and to incur enmities. To have both strong, but both selected: in the one, to be placable; in the other, immoveable. To model our principles to our duties and our situation. To be fully persuaded that all virtue which is impracticable is spurious; and rather to run the risk of falling into faults in a course which leads us to act with effect and energy, than to loiter out our days without blame, and without use. Public life is a situation of power and energy; he trespasses against his duty who sleeps upon his watch, as well as he that goes over to the enemy. . .

405

Pericles is
speaking

. . We have a form of government not fetched by imitation from the laws of our neighbouring states (nay we are rather a pattern to others than they to us), which, because in the administration it hath respect not to the few but to the multitude, is called a democracy. Wherein there is not only an equality amongst all men in point of law for their private controversies, but in election to public offices we consider neither class nor rank, but each man is preferred according to his virtue or to the esteem in which he is held for some special excellence: nor is any one put back even through poverty, because of the obscurity of his person, so long as he can do good service to the commonwealth. Moreover this liberty which we enjoy in the administration of the state, we use also one with another in our daily course of life, neither quarrelling with our neighbour for following his own humour, nor casting on him censorious looks, which, tho' they be no punishment, yet they grieve. So that conversing among ourselves without private offence, we stand chiefly in fear to transgress against the public, and are obedient to those that are for the time in office, and to the laws, and principally to such laws as are written for protection against injury, and those which being un-written, bring undeniable shame to the transgressors.

We have also found out many ways whereby to recreate our minds from labour, both by public institu-tion of games and sacrifices for all seasons of the year, and also in the comfort and elegancy of our homes, by the daily delight whereof we expel sadness. We have this further, that, owing to the greatness of our city, all things from all parts of the earth are imported hither, whereby we no less familiarly enjoy the commodities of other nations than our own. Then in the practice of war, we excel our enemies in this : we leave our city open to all men, nor is it ever seen that by the banishing of strangers we deny them the learning or sight of anything, from the knowledge of which an enemy might reap advantage : for we trust not to secret preparation and deceit, but on our own courage in the action. They in their discipline hunt after valour presently from their youth with laborious exercise, and yet we that live remissly undertake as great dangers as they. . .

Such is the city for which these men, since they disdained to be robbed of it, valiantly fighting have died. And it is fit that every man of you that is left, should be like-minded, to undergo any travail for the same.

I have therefore spoken so much concerning the city in general, as well to show you that the stakes between us and our enemies, who have nothing comparable to it, are not equal : as also to establish on a firm foundation the eulogy of those of whom I will now speak,—the greater part of their praises being hereby delivered . . . There was none of these who preferring the further enjoyment of his wealth was thereby grown cowardly . . . They fled from shame, but with their bodies they stood out the battle ; and so, in a moment big with fate it was from their glory, rather than from their fear that they passed away. Such were these men, worthy of their country : and for you that remain, you may pray for a safer fortune ; but you ought to be no less venturously minded against the foe : not weighing the profit . . . but contemplating the power of Athens, in her constant activity ; and thereby becoming enamoured of her. And when she shall appear great to you, consider then that her glories were purchased by valiant men, and by men that learned their duty ; by men that were sensible of dishonour when they came to act ; by such men as, tho' they failed in their attempt, yet would not be wanting to the city with their virtue, but made unto it a most honourable contribution. And having each one given his body to the commonwealth they receive in stead thereof a most remarkable sepulchre, not that wherein they are buried so much as that other wherein their glory is laid up, on all occasions both of word and deed, to be remembered evermore; for TO FAMOUS MEN ALL THE EARTH IS A SEPULCHRE: and their virtues shall be testified not only by the inscription on stone at home but in all lands wheresoever in the unwritten record of the mind, which far beyond any monument will remain with all men everlastingly. Be zealous therefore to emulate them, and judging that happiness is freedom, and freedom is valour, be forward to encounter the dangers of war.

406

. . L'Angleterre est à présent le pays le plus libre qui soit au monde, je n'en excepte aucune république . . .   1729

407

. . It has long been a grave question whether any government not too strong for the liberties of its people, can be strong enough to maintain its existence in great emergencies. . .

408

. . Fourscore and seven years ago our fathers brought forth upon this continent a new nation, conceived in LIBERTY, and dedicated to the proposition that all men are created equal.

Now we are engaged in a great civil war, testing whether that nation, or any nation so conceived and so dedicated, can long endure. We are met on a great battlefield of that war. We have come to dedicate a

Lincoln is speaking 1863

portion of that field as a final resting-place for those who here gave their lives that that nation might live. It is altogether fitting and proper that we should do this.

But in a larger sense we cannot dedicate, we cannot consecrate, we cannot hallow this ground. The brave men, living and dead, who struggled here, have consecrated it far above our power to add or detract. The world will little note, nor long remember, what we say here, but it can never forget what they did here. It is for us, the living, rather, to be dedicated here to the unfinished work which they who fought here have thus far so nobly advanced. It is rather for us to be here dedicated to the great task remaining before us; that from these honoured dead we take increased devotion to that cause for which they gave the last full measure of devotion; that we here highly resolve that these dead shall not have died in vain; that this nation, under God, shall have a new-birth of Freedom; and that government of the people, by the people, and for the people, shall not perish from the earth.

409

Burke is
speaking
1775

.. My hold of the Colonies is in the close affection which grows from common names, from kindred blood, from similar privileges, and equal protection. These are ties which, though light as air, are as strong as links of iron. Let the Colonists always keep the idea of their civil rights associated with your Government;—they will cling and grapple to you; and no force under heaven will be of power to tear them from their allegiance... As long as you have the wisdom to keep the sovereign authority of this country as the sanctuary of liberty, the sacred temple consecrated to our common faith, wherever the chosen race and sons of England worship freedom, they will turn their faces towards you. The more they multiply, the more friends you will have; the more ardently they love liberty, the more perfect will be their obedience. Slavery they can have anywhere. It is a weed that grows in every soil. They may have it from Spain, they may have it from Prussia. But until you become lost to all feeling of your true interest and your natural dignity, freedom they can have from none but you. This is the commodity of price of which you have the monopoly. . . It is the spirit of the English Constitution, which, infused through the mighty mass, pervades, feeds, unites, invigorates, vivifies every part of the empire, even down to the minutest member. . .

All this, I know well enough, will sound wild and chimerical to the profane herd of those vulgar and mechanical politicians, who have no place among us; a sort of people who think that nothing exists but what is gross and material; and who therefore, far from being qualified to be directors of the great movement of empire, are not fit to turn a wheel in the machine. But to men truly initiated and rightly taught, these ruling and master principles, which in the opinion of such men as I have mentioned, have no substantial existence, are in truth everything, and all in all. Magnanimity in politicks is not seldom the truest wisdom; and a great empire and little minds go ill together. If we are conscious of our station and glow with zeal to fill our places as becomes our situation and ourselves, we ought to . . . elevate our minds to the greatness of that trust to which the order

of Providence has called us. By adverting to the dignity
of this high calling, our ancestors have turned a savage
wilderness into a glorious empire; and have made the
most extensive, and the only honourable conquests, not
by destroying, but by promoting the wealth, the number,
the happiness, of the human race.

410

Milton is
speaking
1643

. . And lest som should perswade ye, Lords and
Commons, that these arguments of lerned men . . . are
meer flourishes, and not reall, I could recount what I
have seen and heard in other Countries, where this kind
of inquisition tyrannizes; when I have sat among their
lerned men,—for that honor I had,—and bin counted
happy to be born in such a place of *Philosophic* freedom,
as they suppos'd England was, while themselvs did
nothing but bemoan the servil condition into which lern-
ing amongst them was brought; that this was it which
had dampt the glory of Italian wits; that nothing had
bin there writt'n now these many years but flattery
and fustian. There it was that I found and visited the
famous *Galileo* grown old, a pris'ner to the Inquisition,
for thinking in Astronomy otherwise than the Franciscan
and Dominican licencers thought. And though I knew
that England then was groaning loudest under the Pre-
latical yoak, neverthelesse I tooke it as a pledge of future
happines, that other Nations were so perswaded of her
liberty. Yet was it beyond my hope that those Worthies
were then breathing in her air, who should be her leaders
to such a deliverance, as shall never be forgott'n by any
revolution of time that this world hath to finish. . .

411

AND did those feet in ancient time
Walk upon England's mountains green?
And was the holy Lamb of God
On England's pleasant pastures seen?

And did the Countenance Divine
Shine forth upon our clouded hills?
And was Jerusalem builded here
Among these dark Satanic mills?

Bring me my Bow of burning gold!
Bring me my Arrows of desire!
Bring me my Spear!   O clouds, unfold!
Bring me my Chariot of fire!

I will not cease from Mental Fight,
Nor shall my Sword sleep in my hand,
Till we have built Jerusalem
In England's green and pleasant land.

412

BREATHES there the man, with soul so dead,
Who never to himself hath said,
    'This is my own, my native land!'
Whose heart hath ne'er within him burned,
As home his footsteps he hath turned,
    From wandering on a foreign strand?

    O Caledonia! stern and wild,
Meet nurse for a poetic child!
Land of brown heath and shaggy wood,
Land of the mountain and the flood,
Land of my sires! what mortal hand
Can e'er untie the filial band,
That knits me to thy rugged strand! . . .

Heroism

413

Ay, tear his body limb from limb,
　Bring cord, or axe, or flame:
He only knows, that not through him
　Shall England come to shame.

414

　OH HOW comely it is and how reviving
To the Spirits of just men long opprest!
When God into the hands of thir deliverer
Puts invincible might
To quell the mighty of the Earth, th' oppressour,
The brute and boist'rous force of violent men
Hardy and industrious to support
Tyrannic power, but raging to pursue
The righteous and all such as honour Truth;
He all thir Ammunition
And feats of War defeats
With plain Heroic magnitude of mind
And celestial vigour arm'd,
Thir Armories and Magazins contemns,
Renders them useless, while
With winged expedition
Swift as the lightning glance he executes
His errand on the wicked, who surpris'd
Lose thir defence distracted and amaz'd.
　But patience is more oft the exercise
Of Saints, the trial of thir fortitude,
Making them each his own Deliverer,
And Victor over all
That tyrannie or fortune can inflict. . .

418

USE me, England,
in thine hour of need,
　Let thy ruling
rule me now in deed.

　Sons and brothers
take for armoury,
　All love's jewels
crushed, thy warpath be!

　Thou hast given
joyous life and free,
　Life whose joy now
anguisheth for thee.

　Give then, England,
if my life thou need,
　Gift yet fairer,
Death, thy life to feed.

419

THEY truly live who yield their lives fighting against
the foe in the fierce battle amid the flash of swords and
the whirling of the spear :

The men of ancient race that were foremost in the
fight wielding their swords ; who stood in the mellay as
some mountain-top rises above the flood : What wonder
if their glory liveth when all dissemblers have passed
away !

420

WHO is the happy Warrior? Who is he
That every man in arms should wish to be?

The Happy Warrior

—It is the generous Spirit, who, when brought
Among the tasks of real life, hath wrought
Upon the plan that pleased his boyish thought:
Whose high endeavours are an inward light
That makes the path before him always bright:
Who, with a natural instinct to discern
What knowledge can perform, is diligent to learn;
Abides by this resolve, and stops not there,
But makes his moral being his prime care;
Who, doomed to go in company with Pain,
And Fear, and Bloodshed, miserable train!
Turns his necessity to glorious gain;
In face of these doth exercise a power
Which is our human nature's highest dower;
Controls them and subdues, transmutes, bereaves
Of their bad influence, and their good receives:
By objects, which might force the soul to abate
Her feeling, rendered more compassionate;
Is placable—because occasions rise
So often that demand such sacrifice;
More skilful in self-knowledge, even more pure,
As tempted more; more able to endure,
As more exposed to suffering and distress;
Thence, also, more alive to tenderness.
—'Tis he whose law is reason; who depends
Upon that law as on the best of friends;
Whence, in a state where men are tempted still
To evil for a guard against worse ill,
And what in quality or act is best
Doth seldom on a right foundation rest,
He labours good on good to fix, and owes
To virtue every triumph that he knows:
—Who, if he rise to station of command,
Rises by open means; and there will stand
On honourable terms, or else retire,

And in himself possess his own desire;
Who comprehends his trust, and to the same
Keeps faithful with a singleness of aim;
And therefore does not stoop, nor lie in wait
For wealth, or honours, or for worldly state;
Whom they must follow; on whose head must fall,
Like showers of manna, if they come at all:
Whose powers shed round him in the common strife,
Or mild concerns of ordinary life,
A constant influence, a peculiar grace;
But who, if he be called upon to face
Some awful moment to which Heaven has joined
Great issues, good or bad for human kind,
Is happy as a Lover; and attired
With sudden brightness, like a Man inspired;
And, through the heat of conflict, keeps the law
In calmness made, and sees what he foresaw;
Or if an unexpected call succeed,
Come when it will, is equal to the need:
—He who, though thus endued as with a sense
And faculty for storm and turbulence,
Is yet a Soul whose master-bias leans
To homefelt pleasures and to gentle scenes;
Sweet images! which, wheresoe'er he be,
Are at his heart; and such fidelity
It is his darling passion to approve;
More brave for this, that he hath much to love:—
'Tis, finally, the Man, who, lifted high,
Conspicuous object in a Nation's eye,
Or left unthought-of in obscurity,—
Who, with a toward or untoward lot,
Prosperous or adverse, to his wish or not—
Plays, in the many games of life, that one
Where what he most doth value must be won:
Whom neither shape of danger can dismay,

Nor thought of tender happiness betray;
Who, not content that former worth stand fast,
Looks forward, persevering to the last,
From well to better, daily self-surpast:
Who, whether praise of him must walk the earth
For ever, and to noble deeds give birth,
Or he must fall, to sleep without his fame,
And leave a dead unprofitable name—
Finds comfort in himself and in his cause;
And, while the mortal mist is gathering, draws
His breath in confidence of Heaven's applause:
This is the happy Warrior; this is He
That every Man in arms should wish to be.

421

. . With these words Hermes sped away for lofty Olympus;
And Priam all fearlessly from off his chariot alighted,
Ordering Idæus to remain in the entry to keep watch
Over the beasts: th' old king meanwhile strode doughtily onwards,
Where Achiles was then most wont to be, and sitting indoors
Found he him: all his men sat apart; for his only attendance
His squire Automedon and Alkimos, in battle upgrown,
Mov'd busilie to' an' fro serving, for late he had eaten
And the supper-table disfurnish'd yet stood anigh him.
And Priam entering unperceiv'd till he well was among them,
Clasp't his knees and seiz'd his hands all humbly to kiss them,
Those dread murderous hands, which his sons so many had slain.
    As when a man whom spite of fate hath curs'd in his own land
For homicide, that he flee-eth abroad and seeketh asylum
With some lord; and they that see him are fill'd with amazement,
Ev'n so now Achiles was amazed as he saw Priam enter,
And the men all wer amazed, and look'd upon each other in turn.
    But Priam, as Hermes had bade, bow'd down to beseech him.

'O God-like Achiles, thy father call to remembrance;
How he is halting as I, i' the dark'ning doorway of old age,
And desolately liveth, while all they that dwell about him
Vex him, nor hath he one from their violence to defend him :
But yet an' heareth he aught of thee, thy well-being in life,
Then he rejoiceth an' all his days are glad with a good hope
Soon to behold thee again, his son safe home fro' the warfare.
But most hapless am I, for I had sons numerous and brave
In wide Troy :—where be they now ? scarce is one o' them left.
They were fifty, the day ye arrived hither out of Achaia,
Nineteen royally born princes from one mother only,
While the others women of my house had borne me ; of all these
Truly the greater part hath Arês in grim battle unstrung :
But hé, who was alone the city's lov'd guardian and stay,
Few days since thou slew'st him, alas, his country defending,
Hector ; for whose sake am I come to the ships of Achaia
His body dear to redeem, offering thee a ransom abundant.
O God-like Achiles, have fear o' the gods, pity him too,
Thy sire also remember, having yet more pity on mé,
Who now stoop me beneath what dread deed mortal ever dared,
Raising the hand that slew his son, pitiably to kiss it.'

Then did Achilles yearn for thought of his ancient father,
And from th' old king's seizure his own hand gently disengaged.
And each brooded apart ; Priam o'er victorious Hector
Groan'd, low fal'n to the ground unnerved at feet of Achilles,
Who sat mourning awhile his sire, then turn'd to bewailing
Patroclus, while loudly the house with their sobbing outrang.

But when Achilles now had soothed his soul in affection,
And all his bosom had disburden'd of passion extreme,
Swiftly from off his seat he arose, and old Priam upraised,
In pity and reverence for his age and silvery blanch'd head ;
And making full answer address'd him in airy-wingèd words.

'Unhappy man ! what mighty sorrows must thy spirit endure !

Nay, how durst thou come thus alone to the ships of Achaia
Into the sight of him who thy sons so many and good
Spoil'd and sent to the grave?   Verilie thy heart is of iron.
But come, sit-thee beside me upon my couch; let us alwise
Now put away our griefs, sore tho' we be plagued with affliction.
Truly there is no gain in distressful lamentation,
Since the eternal gods hav assign'd to us unhappy mortals
Hardship enough, while théy enjoy bliss idly without end.

   Two jars, say they, await God's hand at th' entry of his courts,
Stored ready with free gifts, of good things one, one of evil.
If mingling from both heav'ns-thunderer equally dispense,
Then will a man's fortune be chequer'd with both sorrow and joy;
But t'whom Zeus giveth only of ill, that man is an outcast;
Hunger houndeth him on disconsolate over the brave earth,
Unrespected alike whether of mortals or immortals.
So my sire Peleus was dower'd with favour abounding,
And from birth and cradle honour'd, all men living outshone
In wealth and happiness, king o'er his Myrmidon armies:
And tho' he was but a man, Zeus made him a fair goddess espouse.
But yet an' ev'n to him was an ill thrown in, that he hath not
Sons born into his house to retain its empery;—one son
Only he gat, one doom'd to a fate unkindly, nor ev'n he
Comforts the' old man at home, since exiled far from him I bide
Here at Troy, thy sons' destruction compassing, and thine.

   Thou, sir, too we hav heard enjoy'dst good fortune aforetime,
From Makar in rocky Lesbos away to the boundary eastward
Of Phrygia's highlands, and north to the briny Hellespont,
Thou, sir, didst all men for wealth and progeny excel:
But when once th' high gods let loose this mischief anigh thee,
Thy city was compass'd with nought but fierce battle and blood.
Bear up, allow thy temper awhile some respite of anguish:
Thou wilt not benefit thy dear son vainly bewailing,
Nor restore him alive till thou taste further affliction.' . . .

422

. . Chief Poet ! and ye clouds of Albion,
   Begetters of our deep eternal theme,
When I am through the old oak forest gone,
   Let me not wander in a barren dream ;
But when I am consumèd with the Fire,
Give me new Phœnix-wings to fly at my desire.

423

. . O man ! hold thee on in courage of soul
   Through the stormy shades of thy worldly way,
And the billows of cloud that around thee roll
   Shall sleep in the light of a wondrous day,
Where hell and heaven shall leave thee free
To the universe of destiny.

Who telleth a tale of unspeaking death ?
   Who lifteth the veil of what is to come ?
Who painteth the shadows that are beneath
   The wide-winding caves of the peopled tomb ?
Or uniteth the hopes of what shall be
With the fears and the love for that which we see ?

424

I KNOW not what my secret is,
   I know but it is mine,
I know to dwell with it were bliss,
   To die for it divine.
I cannot yield it in a kiss,
   Nor breathe it in a sigh ;
Enough that I have lived for this,
   For this, my love, I die.

I confess that I do not see why the very existence of an invisible world may not in part depend
on the personal response which any one of us may
make to the religious appeal. God himself, in short,
may draw vital strength and increase of very being from
our fidelity. For my own part, I do not know what the
sweat and blood and tragedy of this life mean, if they
mean anything short of this. If this life be not a real
fight, in which something is eternally gained for the
universe by success, it is no better than a game of private
theatricals from which one may withdraw at will. But
it *feels* like a real fight,—as if there were something
really wild in the universe which we, with all our idealities
and faithfulnesses, are needed to redeem ; and first of all
to redeem our own hearts from atheisms and fears. For
such a half-wild half-saved universe our nature is adapted.
The deepest thing in our nature is this dumb region
of the heart in which we dwell alone with our willing-
nesses and our unwillingnesses, our faiths and our fears.
As through the cracks and crannies of caverns those
waters exude from the earth's bosom which then form
the fountain-heads of springs, so in these crepuscular
depths of personality the sources of all our outer deeds
and decisions take their rise. Here is our deepest organ
of communication with the nature of things ; and compared with these concrete movements of our soul all
abstract statements and scientific arguments—the veto,
for example, which the strict positivist pronounces upon
our faith—sound to us like mere chatterings of the
teeth. . .

These then are my last words to you: Be not afraid
of life.   Believe that life *is* worth living, and your belief
will help create the fact.   The 'scientific' proof that
you are right may not be clear before the day of judgment
(or some stage of being which that expression may serve
to symbolize) is reached.   But the faithful fighters of
this hour, or the beings that then and there will represent
them, may turn to the faint-hearted, who here decline
to go on, with words like those with which Henry IV
greeted the tardy Crillon after a great battle had been
gained: 'Hang yourself, brave Crillon! We fought at
Arques, and you were not there!'

426

ENGLAND! awake! awake! awake!
Jerusalem thy sister calls:
Why wilt thou sleep the sleep of death,
And close her from thy ancient walls?

Thy hills and valleys felt her feet
Gently upon their bosoms move:
Thy gates beheld sweet Zion's ways;
Then was a time of joy and love.

And now the time returns again:
Our souls exult, and London's towers
Receive the Lamb of God to dwell
In England's green and pleasant bowers.

427

THE naked earth is warm with Spring,
    And with green grass and bursting trees
Leans to the sun's gaze glorying,
    And quivers in the sunny breeze;

Into Battle

And life is Colour and Warmth and Light,
   And a striving evermore for these;
And he is dead who will not fight,
   And who dies fighting has increase.

The fighting man shall from the sun
   Take warmth, and life from the glowing earth;
Speed with the light-foot winds to run,
   And with the trees to newer birth;
And find, when fighting shall be done,
   Great rest, and fullness after dearth.

All the bright company of Heaven
   Hold him in their high comradeship,
The Dog-star, and the Sisters Seven,
   Orion's Belt and sworded hip.

The woodland trees that stand together,
   They stand to him each one a friend;
They gently speak in the windy weather;
   They guide to valley and ridge's end.

The kestrel hovering by day,
   And the little owls that call by night,
Bid him be swift and keen as they,
   As keen of ear, as swift of sight.

The blackbird sings to him, 'Brother, brother,
   If this be the last song you shall sing
Sing well, for you may not sing another;
   Brother, sing.'

In dreary doubtful waiting hours,
   Before the brazen frenzy starts,
The horses show him nobler powers;—
   O patient eyes, courageous hearts!

Joy of Battle

And when the burning moment breaks,
  And all things else are out of mind,
And only Joy of Battle takes
  Him by the throat and makes him blind,

Through joy and blindness he shall know,
  Not caring much to know, that still
Nor lead nor steel shall reach him, so
  That it be not the Destined Will.

The thundering line of battle stands,
  And in the air Death moans and sings;
But Day shall clasp him with strong hands,
  And Night shall fold him in soft wings.

428

. . Herein lives wisdom, beauty, and increase;
  Without this, folly, age, and cold decay. . .

429

NOW, God be thank'd Who has match'd us with His hour,
  And caught our youth, and waken'd us from sleeping,
With hand made sure, clear eye, and sharpen'd power,
  To turn, as swimmers into cleanness leaping,
Glad from a world grown old and cold and weary,
  Leave the sick hearts that honour could not move,
And half-men, and their dirty songs and dreary,
  And all the little emptiness of love!

Oh! we who have known shame, we have found release there,
  Where there's no ill, no grief, but sleep has mending,
  Nought broken save this body, lost but breath;
Nothing to shake the laughing heart's long peace there
  But only agony, and that has ending;
  And the worst friend and enemy is but Death.

Life in Death

ASIA

Oh, mother! wherefore speak the name of death?
Cease they to love, and move, and breathe, and speak,
Who die?

THE EARTH

It would avail not to reply:
Thou art immortal, and this tongue is known
But to the uncommunicating dead.
Death is the veil which those who live call life:
They sleep, and it is lifted: and meanwhile
In mild variety the seasons mild
With rainbow-skirted showers, and odorous winds,
And long blue meteors cleansing the dull night,
And the life-kindling shafts of the keen sun's
All-piercing bow, and the dew-mingled rain
Of the calm moonbeams, a soft influence mild,
Shall clothe the forests and the fields, ay, even
The crag-built deserts of the barren deep,
With ever-living leaves, and fruits, and flowers. . .

IF I should die, think only this of me:
That there's some corner of a foreign field
That is for ever England.   There shall be
In that rich earth a richer dust conceal'd;
A dust whom England bore, shaped, made aware,
Gave, once, her flowers to love, her ways to roam;
A body of England's, breathing English air,
Washed by the rivers, blest by suns of home.

And think, this heart, all evil shed away,
A pulse in the eternal mind, no less
Gives somewhere back the thoughts by England given,

Her sights and sounds ; dreams happy as her day ;
And laughter, learnt of friends ; and gentleness
In hearts at peace, under an English heaven.

432

UNDER the wide and starry sky,
Dig the grave and let me lie.
Glad did I live and gladly die,
    And I laid me down with a will.

This be the verse you grave for me :
Here he lies where he longed to be;
Home is the sailor, home from sea,
    And the hunter home from the hill.

433

HOW sleep the brave, who sink to rest,
By all their country's wishes blest !
When Spring, with dewy fingers cold,
Returns to deck their hallow'd mould,
She there shall dress a sweeter sod
Than Fancy's feet have ever trod.

By fairy hands their knell is rung,
By forms unseen their dirge is sung ;
There Honour comes, a pilgrim gray,
To bless the turf that wraps their clay,
And Freedom shall awhile repair
To dwell, a weeping hermit, there !

434

NOT a drum was heard, not a funeral note,
    As his corpse to the rampart we hurried ;
Not a soldier discharged his farewell shot
    O'er the grave where our hero we buried.

Honour's Dirge

We buried him darkly at dead of night,
  The sods with our bayonets turning;
By the struggling moonbeam's misty light
  And the lantern dimly burning.

No useless coffin enclosed his breast,
  Not in sheet nor in shroud we wound him;
But he lay like a warrior taking his rest
  With his martial cloak around him.

Few and short were the prayers we said,
  And we spoke not a word of sorrow;
But we steadfastly gazed on the face that was dead,
  And we bitterly thought of the morrow.

We thought, as we hollow'd his narrow bed
  And smoothed down his lonely pillow,
That the foe and the stranger would tread o'er his head,
  And we far away on the billow!

Lightly they'll talk of the spirit that's gone
  And o'er his cold ashes upbraid him,—
But little he'll reck, if they let him sleep on
  In the grave where a Briton has laid him.

But half of our heavy task was done
  When the clock struck the hour for retiring:
And we heard the distant and random gun
  That the foe was sullenly firing.

Slowly and sadly we laid him down,
  From the field of his fame fresh and gory;
We carved not a line, and we raised not a stone,
  But we left him alone with his glory.

435

. . Their praise is hymn'd by loftier harps than mine:
Yet one I would select from that proud throng,
Partly because they blend me with his line,
And partly that I did his sire some wrong,
And partly that bright names will hallow song;
And his was of the bravest, and when shower'd
The death-bolts deadliest the thinn'd files along,
Even where the thickest of war's tempest lower'd,
They reach'd no nobler breast than thine, young gallant
    Howard. . .

436

YET once more, O ye Laurels, and once more
Ye Myrtles brown, with Ivy never-sear,
I com to pluck your Berries harsh and crude,
And with forc'd fingers rude,
Shatter your leaves before the mellowing year.
Bitter constraint, and sad occasion dear,
Compels me to disturb your season due:
For *Lycidas* is dead, dead ere his prime
Young *Lycidas*, and hath not left his peer:
Who would not sing for *Lycidas*? he knew
Himself to sing, and build the lofty rhyme.
He must not flote upon his watry bier
Unwept, and welter to the parching wind,
Without the meed of som melodious tear. . .

    For we were nurst upon the self-same hill,
Fed the same flock, by fountain, shade, and rill.
Together both, ere the high Lawns appear'd
Under the opening eye-lids of the morn,
We drove a field, and both together heard
What time the Gray-fly winds her sultry horn,

Heaven's Praise

Batt'ning our flocks with the fresh dews of night,
Oft till the Star that rose, at Ev'ning, bright
Toward Heav'ns descent had slop'd his westering wheel...

But O the heavy change, now thou art gon,
Now thou art gon, and never must return!
Thee Shepherd, thee the Woods, and desert Caves,
With wilde Thyme and the gadding Vine o'ergrown,
And all their echoes mourn.
The Willows, and the Hazle Copses green,
Shall now no more be seen,
Fanning their joyous Leaves to thy soft layes.
As killing as the Canker to the Rose,
Or Taint-worm to the weanling Herds that graze,
Or Frost to Flowers, that their gay wardrop wear,
When first the White thorn blows;
Such, *Lycidas*, thy loss to Shepherds ear...

Alas! What boots it with uncessant care
To tend the homely slighted Shepherds trade,
And strictly meditate the thankles Muse,
Were it not better don as others use,
To sport with *Amaryllis* in the shade,
Or with the tangles of *Neæra's* hair?
Fame is the spur that the clear spirit doth raise
(That last infirmity of Noble mind)
To scorn delights, and live laborious dayes;
But the fair Guerdon when we hope to find,
And think to burst out into sudden blaze,
Comes the blind *Fury* with th'abhorred shears,
And slits the thin spun life. But not the praise,
Phœbus repli'd, and touch'd my trembling ears;
Fame is no plant that grows on mortal soil,
Nor in the glistering foil
Set off to th'world, nor in broad rumour lies,
But lives and spreds aloft by those pure eyes,

The Rose of Martyrdom

And perfet witnes of all judging *Jove*;
As he pronounces lastly on each deed,
Of so much fame in Heav'n expect thy meed. . .

Weep no more, woful Shepherds weep no more,
For *Lycidas* your sorrow is not dead,
Sunk though he be beneath the watry floar,
So sinks the day-star in the Ocean bed,
And yet anon repairs his drooping head,
And tricks his beams, and with new spangled Ore,
Flames in the forehead of the morning sky:
So *Lycidas* sunk low, but mounted high,
Through the dear might of him that walk'd the waves
Where other groves, and other streams along,
With *Nectar* pure his oozy Lock's he laves,
And hears the unexpressive nuptiall Song,
In the blest Kingdoms meek of joy and love.
There entertain him all the Saints above,
In solemn troops, and sweet Societies
That sing, and singing in their glory move,
And wipe the tears for ever from his eyes. . .

437

. . And some are there unscathed of flame or sword
Yet on their brows the seal of suffering,
And in their hands the rose of martyrdom, . .
A fount of wonder in their pensive eyes,
Sprung from the thought that pain is consummate—
'To him that overcometh'—half forgotten
The victory, so long the battle was,
Begun when manhood was a thing to be:
Not as they send the boyish sailor out,
A father's lingering hand amid his hair,
A mother's kisses warm upon his cheek,

And in his heart the unspoken consciousness
That though upon his grave no gentle fingers
Shall set the crocus, yet in the old home
There shall be aye a murmur of the sea,
A fair remembrance and a tender pride.
Not so for these the dawn of battle rose. . .

438

HE had understanding of righteousness, and discernèd
great and marvellous wonders : and he prevailèd with
the Most High, and is numberèd among the saintly
company.

439

. . Nothing is here for tears, nothing to wail
Or knock the breast, no weakness, no contempt,
Dispraise, or blame, nothing but well and fair,
And what may quiet us in a death so noble. . .

440

The setting sun, and music at the close.

441

. . Peace, peace ! he is not dead, he doth not sleep—
He hath awakened from the dream of life—
'Tis we, who lost in stormy visions, keep
With phantoms an unprofitable strife,
And in mad trance, strike with our spirit's knife
Invulnerable nothings.—*We* decay
Like corpses in a charnel ; fear and grief
Convulse us and consume us day by day,
And cold hopes swarm like worms within our living clay.

L

Salvation

He has outsoared the shadow of our night;
Envy and calumny and hate and pain,
And that unrest which men miscall delight,
Can touch him not and torture not again;
From the contagion of the world's slow stain
He is secure, and now can never mourn
A heart grown cold, a head grown gray in vain;
Nor, when the spirit's self has ceased to burn,
With sparkless ashes load an unlamented urn. . .

He is made one with Nature: there is heard
His voice in all her music, from the moan
Of thunder to the song of night's sweet bird;
He is a presence to be felt and known
In darkness and in light, from herb and stone,
Spreading itself where'er that Power may move
Which has withdrawn his being to its own;
Which wields the world with never-wearied love,
Sustains it from beneath, and kindles it above.

He is a portion of the loveliness
Which once he made more lovely: he doth bear
His part, while the one Spirit's plastic stress
Sweeps through the dull dense world, compelling there
All new successions to the forms they wear;
Torturing th' unwilling dross that checks its flight
To its own likeness, as each mass may bear;
And bursting in its beauty and its might
From trees and beasts and men into the Heaven's light.

The splendours of the firmament of time
May be eclipsed, but are extinguished not;
Like stars to their appointed height they climb,
And death is a low mist which cannot blot
The brightness it may veil. When lofty thought
Lifts a young heart above its mortal lair,

The Fight against Evil

415

GIRD on thy sword and join in the fight!
   Fight, O my brother, so long as life lasteth!
Strike off the enemy's head and there make an end of
   him quickly:
   Then come, bow thyself in the King's Assembly.
A brave man leaveth not the battle;
   He who flieth from it is no true warrior.
In the field of this body a great war is toward
   Against Passion Anger Pride and Greed.
It is for the kingdom of Truth of Contentment and of
   Purity that this battle is raging:
   And the sword that ringeth most loudly is the sword
   of His Name. . .

416

  . . A power from the unknown God,
A Promethean conqueror, came;
Like a triumphal path he trod
   The thorns of death and shame.
   A mortal shape to him
   Was like the vapour dim
Which the orient planet animates with light. . .

417

ARM yourselves, and be ye men of valour, and be in
readiness for the conflict: for it is better for us to perish
in battle than to look upon the outrage of our nation and
our altars. As the will of God is in heaven, even so
let Him do.

Immortality

> And love and life contend in it, for what
> Shall be its earthly doom, the dead live there
> And move like winds of light on dark and stormy air...

> The One remains, the many change and pass;
> Heaven's light forever shines, Earth's shadows fly;
> Life, like a dome of many-coloured glass,
> Stains the white radiance of Eternity,
> Until Death tramples it to fragments.—Die,
> If thou wouldst be with that which thou dost seek!
> Follow where all is fled!—...

442

> .. Salute the sacred dead,
> Who went and who return not.—Say not so!..
> We rather seem the dead, that stayed behind.
> Blow, trumpets, all your exultations blow!
> For never shall their aureoled presence lack..
> They come transfigured back,
> Secure from change in their high-hearted ways,
> Beautiful evermore, and with the rays
> Of morn on their white shields of Expectation.

443

> .. And many more whose names on Earth are dark,
> But whose transmitted effluence cannot die
> So long as fire outlives the parent spark,
> Rose, robed in dazzling immortality...

444

> WHAT happy bonds together unite you, ye living and
> dead,
> Your fadeless love-bloom, your manifold memories!

445

IN the heavenly kingdom the souls of the Saints are rejoicing, who follow'd the footsteps of CHRIST their Master: and since for love of Him they freely poured forth their life-blood, therefore with CHRIST they reign for ever and ever.

446

WHEN blessed Vincent was put to the torture, with eager countenance, and strengthened by the presence of God, he cried: This it is which I have alway desired, and for which in all my prayers I have made request.

447

SERVANT of God, well done, well hast thou fought
The better fight, who single hast maintaind
Against revolted multitudes the Cause
Of Truth, in word mightier then they in Armes;
And for the testimonie of Truth hast born
Universal reproach, far worse to beare
Then violence: for this was all thy care
To stand approv'd in sight of God, though Worlds
Judg'd thee perverse . . .

448

Speak! thy strong words may never pass away . . .

Love, from its awful throne of patien: power
In the wise heart, from the last giddy hour
    Of dread endurance, from the slippery, steep,
And narrow verge of crag-like agony, springs
And folds over the world its healing wings.

The True Light

Gentleness, Virtue, Wisdom, and Endurance,
These are the seals of that most firm assurance
   Which bars the pit over Destruction's strength;
And if, with infirm hand, Eternity,
Mother of many acts and hours, should free
   The serpent that would clasp her with his length;
These are the spells by which to reassume
An empire o'er the disentangled doom.

To suffer woes which Hope thinks infinite;
To forgive wrongs darker than death or night;
   To defy Power, which seems omnipotent;
To love, and bear; to hope till Hope creates
From its own wreck the thing it contemplates;
   Neither to change, nor falter, nor repent;
This, like thy glory, Titan, is to be
Good, great and joyous, beautiful and free;
This is alone Life, Joy, Empire, and Victory.

449

HOLY is the true light, and passing wonderful, lending radiance to them that endured in the heat of the conflict: from CHRIST they inherit a home of unfading splendour, wherein they rejoice with gladness evermore.

❀ FINIS ❀

PREFACE TO THE INDEX

IF the reader will put the book-marker between those pages of the Index which correspond with the pages of the text where he is reading, he will readily find the information that he wants.

How to use the Index.

It is true that very often one cannot fully understand a passage unless one knows who wrote it; on the other hand it is an idle and pernicious habit to ask for information on any question before bringing one's own judgment to bear upon it: and this book may even have a secondary usefulness in providing material for the exercise of literary judgment, in those who have any taste for the practice.

It was a part of the original scheme to quote nothing from the Bible, for several reasons—chiefly because it is so well-known that a reader might resent having such familiar quotations offered to him, and might pass them over unread; and again because this familiarity implies deep-rooted associations, which would be likely to distort the context. When the idea of total exclusion was relinquished, the objection of familiarity was met by not always using the familiar version. Convenient opportunities have been taken for representing Wyclif and Tyndale; and in some other places the compiler has (with the help of his more learned friends) attempted to bring the authorised version nearer to the Hebrew, where it seemed that its beauty might thereby be increased without damage to the style or the rhythm.

The Bible.

There are but twenty pages of French in all this anthology, and one-fifteenth is so small a proportion that the English reader cannot complain that he has been cheated in his bargain. French is the foreign language best known in Britain, and the easiest for us to read, if not to speak: and it is to be wished that our international entente and happy alliance in the cause of honour and humanity may lead to a nearer and more general acquaintance with our neighbours' beautiful literature. Since both their prose and their poetry (in its earlier and latest schools) excel in those

The French pieces.

Preface to the Index

qualities which our authors most lack, it is well to put ourselves side by side for comparison. There is no literature from which our writers could learn more, and to encourage the study of it is a first duty of any one who can further it. This book gains great beauty from the grace and excellence of the French items.

Original
Translations.

Those passages translated by the compiler are marked with an asterisk * in the Index; but his originality is of different amount in the several translations. While in all cases he is wholly responsible for the rendering, he has sometimes merely corrected another's version to suit his own taste. Such obligations are described in the notes to each piece.

Personal.

As the compiler was guided by his own moods, it is evident that he might be considered as under a perpetual temptation to quote from himself. He has put in but one of his own original poems (No. 49), and this is in a classic metre, as are a few other half-original verse-translations by him: his chief motive for introducing these was the variety of their form. If it be thought that in the choice of some other pieces he has been influenced by personal feeling, his reply is that he did not wish to put his honest likings aside.

Errors.

As for errors due to inaccuracy or ignorance, he hopes that they are not so many as to lessen the delight of reading, or cause him to be suspected of negligence: But he knows that they are likely to be so numerous that he is afraid to make more than a general acknowledgment of the assistance which many friends have readily given him, lest they should be involved in the discredit of his blunders. The special notice of collaboration given in the Index does not make those helpers in any way responsible for his mistakes.

N.B. Abbreviations, &c., in Index.—O.B.E.V. or O.B.V. = Oxford Bk. of English Verse.—Palgrave = P.'s Golden Treasury, 1861.—References, &c., given under first quotation from an author are not repeated: the first entry can be found by reference to List of Authors.

INDEX

INDEX

INDEX

INDEX

terest. There is no doubt about the meaning, but translation is difficult and the text is corrupt in two places : these are marked by daggers †, between which I give probably true paraphrases of what A. said or wrote. The words in italics offer the logical equivalent of a part of the argument, the detail of which is to us obscurely remote and logically negligible. I have attempted to give as readable an English version as possible. Dante, who got at Aristotle through the Latin and Thos. Aquinas, thus versifies the doctrine :

> Ed io rispondo : Credo in uno Dio
> Solo ed eterno, che tutto 'l ciel muove,
> Non moto, con amore e con disio.

Par. xxiv. t. 44 (*moto* = *mosso*), and see Cant. xxvi. I consulted W. D. Ross's valuable translation, Oxford, 1908, but worked on a MS. rendering by my friend Mr. Thos. Case, President of C.C.C., who has supervised my translation.*

40. PLATO. 'Phaedo', 96. [See 16.] The bracketed words are added to ease a modern reader's objections to Socrates' irony, which raises difficulties. However it be understood, one should remember that a Greek could well imagine the body to frame wishes opposed to the rational resolutions of the soul. Aristotle accuses Anaxagoras of confounding νοῦς with ψυχή.*

41. From 'The Proverbs of Solomon ', ch. viii. Date altogether uncertain. This from Auth. and Rev. Versions : but I am responsible for ver. 28.

42. S. JOHN. Opening of Gospel. 'In the beginning was the Word.' In the original Greek this name for the second Person of the Trinity is LOGOS, a masculine word, which, like our old English word *Discourse*, had two significations, namely *Reason* and *Speech*. It is thus found in Aristotle, and passed from him to the Stoics and thence to Philo : and its adoption by theologians was no doubt encouraged by its double signification, which allowed it to cover much ground ; for, indicating both Mind and the expression of Mind, it served to convey the idea of Mind expressing God in the world, and acting thus as a Mediator between God and man. A contemporary rival term was SOFIA, that is *Wisdom*, a feminine noun, which is seen in the preceding quotation [and see Augustine in 32]. This theological *Logos* came to be represented in Latin sometimes by *Sermo*, but eventually by *Verbum*, a neuter noun, which

INDEX

our translators rendered literally by THE WORD. In the Vulgate the passage is continued by a neuter pronoun, and Tyndale followed, translating 'all thynges were made by it'. The gender of *Logos* must have aided its adoption. In the Italian gospel THE WORD is feminine.

Translation of *Logos* being impossible, it is apparent that there is an advantage in the orthodox THE WORD, because that term has no applicable meaning, and cannot therefore be mistaken for a definition : the disadvantage of mistrans-iating *Logos* by *Mind* is that in suggesting meaning it may cause misunderstanding. But it does suggest the main underlying meaning and sets a plain man on the right track of ideas, which is essential to the context in this book. It removes a veil from the fundamental truth of the theological terms, and that truth is of the greatest value to common thought.

Theologians worked the metaphor of human speech in the creative Fiat of Genesis to connect *Logos* through *Verbum* with the creation of the world. And this is helped by S. John's Gospel beginning with the same words as Genesis.

43. KABIR. Bk. I. 104. [See 17.]

44. PSALM cxxxix. One of the later psalms. My text is an attempt to bring our magnificent Prayer-book version (from Coverdale's Bible of 1535) nearer to the original, where that seemed desirable. Ver. 12, *The stirrings of my heart* in the Hebrew is *my kidneys*, 'regarded by the Hebrews as the springs of feeling' (Driver's glossary). If so, then the English equivalent is the *heart* : and since the heart-beat is the first palpable sign of vertebrate life, this makes a beauty where our church version somewhat needs it.

45. SHELLEY. From *Mont Blanc*. This poem is difficult and obscure. Briefly, the 'dizzy ravine of the Arve' is com-pared with the mind of man, wherethrough, as a river, the Power or the Universe of things flows. The human mind is 'full of that unresting sound', and the smaller streams that swell the torrent are likened to the spontaneous thoughts of the mind. Later (*Some say that dreams*) it is questioned whether there be not something great and exterior to the human mind, as M. Blanc is to the Arve ravine (cp. Prom. ii. 3) ; and M. Blanc is used to typify that Power. With this explanation my selection gives all that I need, and

may perhaps be more easily intelligible than the whole poem. *But for such faith* seems to mean *If only for*. I have repunctuated *Ghosts of all things that are*.

46. From same book as 18. No. xxi.

47. JELLALUDIN. The greatest Sufi poet of Islam. Born at Balkh 1207. He wrote in Persian. [See 19.]

48. PLOTINUS. Enn. IV. 4, § 7.*

49. R. B. *Johannes Milton Senex*. From Oxford edition of Poems, p. 443. This shows the Latin scazon in English verse.

50. RIVAROL. Died æt. 44 at Berlin. 1801. My quotations from Rivarol are taken from Sainte-Beuve's Memoir. 'Lundis', V.

51. PLATO. 'Laws', 888. This was a favourite passage with my old friend Robt. Wm. Raper, V.P. of Trin. Coll., Oxford; who died while the book was making : I took it at his suggestion.*

52. TOLSTOI. From 'War and Peace', Vol. ii, ch. xii. All the Russian pieces in this book were Englished by me from literal translations made for me by my friend Mr. Nevill Forbes.*

53. GERARD HOPKINS. The first stanza of *The wreck of the Deutschland*. 1876. Unpublished.

54. AUGUSTINE. Confessions, x. 6.*

55. JELLALUDIN. [See 47.]

56. GEO. HERBERT. *Love.* The last poem in 'The Temple'.

57. KABIR. II. 120. [See 17.]

58. GEO. HERBERT. From *Matins*. No. 34.

59. JELLALUDIN. [See 47.]

60. GEO. HERBERT. From *Easter*. No. 12.

61. SHELLEY. From *Prince Athanase*. Frag. 3.

62. EPICTETUS. 'Discourses', I. xvi. Ed. Long.

63. GEO. HERBERT. From the second part of *Christmas*. No. 56.

64. AUGUSTINE. Conf. i. 1 init.*

65. Psalm viii. An early psalm. In ver. 5 the familiar mistranslation of *Elohim* by *Angels* increases the difficulty of satisfying the reader.

BOOK II.

66. KABIR. Bk. II. 103. [See 17.]

67. KEATS. The opening lines of 'Endymion'.

68. SHELLEY. 'Prometheus', iii. 3. The great beauty of this passage suffers from the involved grammar, which deepens its obscurities. I have made my own punctuation and added some capitals. For the original text and corrections in this impression see note after Errata at end of Index.—Note that in *as the mind* (line 7) *as* means *when* not *like as*.

69. PLOTINUS. Enn. vi. 9, § 4. This is a paraphrase.*

70. SPINOZA. Eth. Schol. ad fin.

71. KEATS. From Letters. Sept. 22 and Oct. 1818.

72. DIXON. 'Lyrical Poems'. Daniel. 1887. *To Fancy.* One stanza omitted.

73. SHELLEY. 'Prometheus', i. 1.

74. SHELLEY. *Witch of Atlas*, xxxiv.

75. SHAKESPEARE. Song in 'Hen. VIII', iii. 1.

76. MILTON. *Arcades*, line 68.

77. SHELLEY. First stanzas of unfinished poem called *Music.*

78. MILTON. *L'Allegro*, l. 135.

79. MILTON. Stanzas viii, ix, and xii from *Hymn on the Morning of Christ's Nativity.*

80. SHAKESPEARE. The opening lines of 'Twelfth-Night'. *South* is Pope's happy conjecture for *sound.*

81. SHELLEY. From *Epipsychidion*, line 520.

82. Sir PH. SIDNEY. 'Apology for Poetry'. 1595. Spelling modernized.

83. WORDSWORTH. From pref. to 2nd edit. of 'Lyrical Ballads'.

84. BACON. 'Advancement of Learning'. 1605. II. 4, § 2. Spelling modernized. The omission of the conjunction that I have inserted was probably intended to couple *magnanimity* with *morality.* The Latin is 'Non solum ad delectationem sed etiam ad animi magnitudinem et ad mores conferat.' But for this sense we require the conjunction.

85. D. M. DOLBEN. From *Core.* 'Poems'. 1911.

86. SHELLEY. 'A Defence of Poetry', written at Pisa. 1821. Forman's edition. 1880.

INDEX

INDEX

INDEX

In the last stanza *mountainless* means 'void of ambition', and *unechoing* means 'awakening no spiritual echoes'. This is some of Darley's meaning as I understand him.

127. KEATS. From *Sleep and Poetry*. 1817. Keats tells how the luxury of Poetry, in which he was indulging, was broken by a vision, that revealed to him the true meaning of Poetry. He foresees that it must lead him to a life of action. He narrates the vision with this intention.

128. KEATS. From the letters. Feb. 18, 1819.

129. AMIEL. Vol. i, p. 108. [See 99.]

130. MILTON. P. L. iii. 26.

131. DARLEY. From 'Nepenthe'. I. 411.

132. PLATO. 'Phaedrus', 249.*

133. WORDSWORTH. From the *Ode on Intimations of Immortality from Recollections of early Childhood*. The end is quoted No. 202.

134. EMILY BRONTE. This poem is thus given in 'The Complete Poems of Emily Brontë', Hodder and Stoughton, 1910, p. 92, where it is printed with wrong punctuation and without a division between the two parts. In the 'Brontë Poems' [see 121] the second part is judged not to belong to the first. I failed in my enquiries for external evidence: but am unwilling to discard so beautiful a sequel: for, as I had read it, the second half poetically supplies the stimulus needed to arouse the child's divination: and shows the reaction on herself, when its full meaning dawns on her consciousness.

135. WORDSWORTH. 1802. Palgrave prints *is on* for *broods o'er*.

136. CH. FONTAINE. 1515–1585. From 'Les Poëtes Français'. Paris. 1861. Vol. i, p. 631.

137. WORDSWORTH. From *Lines composed a few miles above Tintern Abbey*, &c. 1798.

138. THOREAU. From 'Walden, or Life in the Woods'. 1854.

139. SHAKESPEARE. From Sonnet XXI.

140. VLADIMIR SOLOVEV, d. 1900 (?). Given me by Mr. Nevill Forbes.*

141. SHAKESPEARE. Sonnet XXXI.

142. SHAKESPEARE. Sonnet CVI.

INDEX

INDEX

BOOK III

INDEX

offence to restore, next before the Epitaph, the beautiful
stanza which he ultimately rejected as too parenthetical.
The omitted stanzas (10, 11, 18, 20, 22, 23) have a strongly
marked character, and tend to overload the poem with the
particular quality that critics have misliked in it. Note.
If chance some kindred spirit shall enquire is not of
the best English, and *Large was his bounty* is a conceit,
which, though a large one. is of questionable propriety in
the Epitaph.

INDEX

from Act. III. sc. 1, when she hears that Philip has bar-
gained away his support of Arthur's claim for a marriage
alliance with John. The second section is from Scene 4,
after Arthur had been taken prisoner by K. John: who
had already given orders for his murder.

INDEX

INDEX

INDEX

INDEX

INDEX

INDEX

warning of Socrates (in 377) that the myth of his own telling should not be taken too literally. The English is a line-for-line paraphrase of the Latin, in the original metre. From Poems, R. B., p. 460.*

375. MILTON, P. L. ii. 582. In line 2 from end of quotation—I think that Milton would have approved Bentley's emendation here. B. says that as *Fear* is personified so *Fable* should be, and would read *Than Fable yet hath feigned*. If the passage is a reminiscence of Bruno, then the plural *fables* would be accounted for, since Bruno has

Quos esse magis non posse putamus
Quam vatum figmenta, Orcum, Rhadamantia regna,
Gorgona, Centaurum, Scyllam, Geriona [sic], Chimaeram.
De innumerabilibus immenso etc. vii. 8.

376. S. MATTHEW, xxv. 31. I have taken this incomparable vision or myth from Tyndale's translation, 1526, to show how much our Bible owes to him: but I have kept the following words from the Authorised Version. *Glory, throne of his glory, foundation, unto* in one place for *to*: and *punishment* for *pain*. I have also omitted *ye* once and *hand* once. I have modernised Tyndale's spelling for convenience, but have kept *won* (one) to show how old that pronunciation was: and have left other old spellings alongside of it to keep it company, lest it should seem a misprint. I followed Dr. Bosworth's reprint.

377. PLATO. 'Phaedo', 114. Socrates, just before his execution, has been narrating a myth concerning the condition of souls in the next world, and this is his comment on it.

378. MILTON. End of 'Comus'. Spelling modernised.

379. CHAUCER, *Truth*. The MSS. of this poem vary much. One of the best preserves a fourth stanza, thus

Envoy.

Therfore, thou vache, leve thyn old wrecchedness
Unto the worlde; leve now to be thral;
Crye him mercy, that of his hy goodnesse
Made thee of noght, and in especial
Draw unto him, and pray in general
For thee, and eek for other, hevenlich mede;
And trouthe shal delivere, it is no drede.

This *Vache*, or cow, puzzled every one until Miss Edith Rickert (in 'Modern Philology', 1913) showed that Sir Philip la Vache, K.G., was probably a friend of Chaucer,

INDEX

whence it seems that the poem was sent to him with the *Envoy*, but was circulated without it, as of general application; and this agrees with the artistic inferiority of the *Envoy*.

I have ventured to make my own text from the MSS. Finding that the 6th line of the 2nd stanza has overwhelming authority for its 'nine' syllables, and that the most poetic reading of III, 6 is also a 'nine-syllable' line, and that the Lansdowne MS. gives a 'nine-syllable' line in I. 6 (which I preferred also on other grounds), I was led to conclude that it was part of the construction of the original poem to have a 'nine-syllable' line in this place in each stanza: and so I have printed it. It is very effective; and if it was originally thus, the 'emendations' would be accounted for. Thus one of the best MSS. [Add. B. M. 10, 340], the one that gives the *Envoy*, reads *Rewle weel thyself*.

There are difficulties for the modern reader.—l. 2. If Skeat's choice, which I adopt, be right, it means 'Do not despise and neglect your talent, though it be but one.' *Suffice thin owene thing* has good authority; but among sixteen imperatives to change the subject of one of them is awkward: therefore *suffice unto* is preferable.—l. 4. *Blent* = blindeth, as *stant* in II. 3 is also 3rd sing. pres. *Welë blent overal* means 'Prosperity blinds a man completely.' *overal* is read as a disyllable: Chaucer said *ov'rall* as we say o'erall.—II. 1. *Tempest* (= disturb) is a rare verb.—4. *Sporn against an al* (awl) is to 'kick against the pricks', and in the next line *crokkë* is the proverbial earthenware pitcher. These seem the unworthiest lines in the poem.—III. 6. Skeat adopts *Hold the hye wey, and lat thy gost thee lede*; which has much authority; but his explanation that hye wey = high road makes nonsense of it: and he is right in saying that it means this in Chaucer. The reading *Weyve thy lust* is also supported by a passage in Chaucer's 'Boethius', which has, *Weyve thou Joy, dryf fro thee drede . . . that is to seyn, lat none of thise passions overcomen thee or blende thee.*

I have marked with the double dot the final E's that are pronounced syllabically. My friend Dr. Henry Bradley, who showed me Miss Rickert's paper, is my authority for this, and other M. E. scholarship: though I do not know that he approves of my results.

INDEX

INDEX

Thucydides, when he passes from mere narration and engages in reflection or argument or rhetoric, becomes uncomfortably conscious of grammar and seems often in great difficulties. This quality, due perhaps to his not being a native Greek, is wholly bad; and yet he will again and again win a powerful beauty from it; as a man struggling desperately through a raging torrent may show movements of more forceful grace than one who is walking unimpeded. Such a manner is inimitable in modern English without affectation: But it happens that Hobbes in his old age translated Thucydides (helped probably by a French version?) and his masterful diction, encountering obstacles, dealt with them so as to produce a not dissimilar effect. For that reason I took his translation, and, where I altered it in order to give a more faithful interpretation, I attempted to maintain his strenuous style. If the result has any merit it is due to him; but I have made too many changes to be able to leave his name to it.*

NOTE TO FOURTH IMPRESSION

ERRATA

The following corrections were made in the 2nd impression; lesser errors and broken letters are not noticed:

216. l. 2, *wind* for *winds*.

227. l. 10, *chastré* for *chartré*.

362. l. 2 of last stanza, *demeanour* for *deameanour*.

Index 12. iii for ii.

66. moved to its place in Bk. ii.

404. *Discontents* for *Disturbances*.

424. l. 2, *and* for *et*.

List of Authors, *Wotton* for *Wootton*.

In this impression the following are corrected:

68, in ll. 2 and 3 original punctuation restored, see note below.

157, lines 5 and 6, *soul, Though* for *soul; Thro'*.

251, in l. 9, *might* for *night*.

267. l. 13, *fuit* for *fuie*, as corrected in later edits. *Merc. de France*.

389. *Nekhlyudov* for *Nekhlyudor*, which was wrongly corrected by printer in 2nd impression.

Index, 68. This note is altered in accordance with change in the text.

165. § 4 for § 3.

249. The second section is from Pascal and not from Amiel, and it escaped attribution in indexes.

NOTES

42. In 'Christian Mysticism' by Wm. Ralph Inge (Methuen, 1899) there is a discussion in Lecture II, p. 46, on the metaphysical ideas implied by St. John's mystical identification of the LOGOS with Jesus of Nazareth, to which I would have referred the reader, if I had known of it.

NOTE TO FOURTH IMPRESSION

68. In all previous impressions this passage of Shelley was printed with the second and third lines thus:

> Of the low voice of Love, almost unheard,
> And dove-eyed Pity's murmured pain; and Music,

In this impression I return to the original text, having been convinced by critics that I did wrong to alter it. They approve of my other changes in punctuation, etc. As readers may wish to compare the whole passage, as it stands in Mrs. Shelley's first reprint, I give it below, including the four preceding lines, which supply the verb that completes the sentence (though it is not necessary to the understanding of the passage), and also, one line at the end, which carries on to the full stop:

> And hither come, sped on the charmed winds,   40
> Which meet from all the points of heaven, as bees
> From every flower aërial Enna feeds,
> At their known island-homes in Himera,
> The echoes of the human world, which tell
> Of the low voice of love, almost unheard,
> And dove-eyed pity's murmured pain, and music,
> Itself the echo of the heart, and all
> That tempers or improves man's life, now free;
> And lovely apparitions, dim at first,
> Then radiant, as the mind, arising bright   50
> From the embrace of beauty, whence the forms
> Of which these are the phantoms, casts on them
> The gathered rays which are reality,
> Shall visit us, the progeny immortal
> Of Painting, Sculpture, and rapt Poesy,
> And arts, though unimagined, yet to be.
> The wandering voices and the shadows these
> Of all that man becomes, the mediators
> Of that best worship, love, by him and us
> Given and returned; swift shapes and sounds, which grow   60
> More fair and soft as man grows wise and kind,
> And veil by veil, evil and error fall:
> Such virtue has the cave and place around.

It is believed that Mrs. Shelley in editing this text (Moxon, 1839) worked with the table of errata which Shelley had sent to his publisher for the correction of his first edition (1820). But the only changes made by her in this passage are, line 42, the diæresis over *aerial*, 55. *rapt* for *wrapt*, 56. *though* for *tho'*, and 59. comma after *worship*.

NOTE TO FOURTH IMPRESSION

In the Bodleian Library there is a fair copy of the Prometheus in Shelley's own hand: the punctuation in this is deficient and of no assistance. Dr. Henry Bradley, who kindly allows me to quote from his letter, wrote thus to me, 'I read the passage something like this; the liberated spirit of man throughout the world awakes to countless activities of blessing. The "echoes" of all its voices—of the whisper of love, of the murmurs of pity, of music, of the utterance of " all that tempers or improves man's life "—and the " apparitions " of all its visible creations, shall visit us here . . . Music is thought of as one of the voices conveying humanizing and ennobling influences; and then the thought is interposed that this voice, the echo of which is heard, is itself an echo of the heart.'—[This is of course from Shakespeare: *It gives a very echo to the seat where love is throned.*] 'That is, its value is not only in its beneficial influence, but in its revelation of the unexhausted wealth from which it issues.'

The word *music*, therefore, should not have a capital initial, since it ranges not with love and pity, but with their vocal utterances : and Dr. Bradley objects to giving capitals to love and pity, because that tends to personify them more than is intended: an objection which does not forbid the capitals to Painting, Sculpture, and Poesy ; nor the capitals which I have given to Love and Beauty below, where they serve another purpose.

This is a long note, but my mistake made it necessary, and the passage deserves it. Its detail would be imperfect without two other remarks : First, that in Shelley's MS., referred to above, the word *hither* in line 40 is written *thither*. *Hither* is defensible, and may have been a correction, but it is very possibly an uncorrected misprint. The second remark is on the strange epithet *dove-eyed* in line 46. Dr. Bradley says that he thinks this word was invented by one Elijah Fenton. It is no doubt traceable to the Song of Solomon, *Oculi tui columbarum,* which our revisers now translate ' Thine eyes are as doves behind thy veil ' (iv. 2 ; cp. v. 12) : that is, they are like doves, not like doves' eyes. The unfortunate word can only be defended as meaning 'eyes that express the tenderness of the Dove ', which the dove's eyes do not.

N.B. The references to Marcus Aurelius in the Index are to the older Greek texts, and do not correspond with Gataker's revision, to which the references would be

173. iv. 23 (for 15)	289. xi. 18 (for 16)
181. vii. 59 (for 34)	350. vii. 13 (for 9)

LIST OF AUTHORS

List of Authors

The Title-page was designed by Mr. Emery Walker. The drawing is from Michelangelo's Fresco of the Creation of Adam in the Sistine Chapel.